LSD WORLDPEACE

JOE ROBERTS

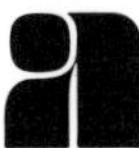

1

Some families seem to live forever. Parents, grandparents, great-grandparents sit smiling on stiff floral couches at yearly reunions, the fruits of their labor milling around with red plastic cups and beer bottles, children with sticky faces screaming across lawns. They make big pots of spaghetti and cut up loaf after loaf of bread. They give speeches. To Grandma's ninetieth, to good health, to good luck. They call on the weekends, they send out newsletters. But in some families, like ours, death looms around like a distant relative. Death, death, a shadow lying listless in a corner, holding his plastic cup, waiting for a swing of moods and circumstances to join the party again. Uninvited and often untimely, but inevitable.

When death lives at your doorstep, you learn to regard it in a different way. If you are open to it, you can transform the idea of death. Remove it from its religious and societal implications. If you are open to it, death becomes no longer a finite and regimented experience. It is an illusion. It is transcendence. In the midst of life we are in death. "You are already dead." And so, in families like this, if one adopts the right attitude, we will miss and we will cry and we will mourn and we will cry, but, ultimately, we will explore. Explore the divisions between the tangible and the perceived, explore that act of breaking through to other planes of reality, other realms of existence. Dreams. Drugs. Manipulation of childhood objects and activities, our connections to the people who've moved past our everyday reality. We will represent them in our actions, their lives pulsing through ours.

It was our grandfather who taught us to make art. A spry, skinny, Hungarian American war veteran, he lived on McDonald's coffee and stiff bananas. The jokester. The trickster. In a Native American legend he would be the coyote, all sly grins and twinkling eyes. His face looked like it had been carved out of wood. A moustache to twirl and a full head of silver hair hidden beneath his black cap. Or was it navy? And those stiff, stiff pants and threadbare shirts. Strong hands and a soft heart. Stephen Joseph Vasy.

Stephen had lived many lives, but the one he lived with us was the loving family man, the born-again artist. Taking up residency in a local university's art department and print shop, he reinvented himself as a multi-media master. Time spent with Grandpa was a lesson in creativity and introspection. To teach art is to encourage the exploration of the self. So we thought about what we were interested in, what was important to us, and we scratched line drawings of dogs into copper etching plates and smudged acid across lithograph stones. Each visit from Grandpa presented a new tool, a bouquet of supplies. Bricks of clay and stacks of watercolor paper, boxes of pastels and charcoal and pots of paint, and tucked in between, warm apple pies from his last trip to Mickey D's.

But the real supplies we were encouraged to use didn't come from the store or the leftover stock he lifted from school cabinets. No, he was a found-objects enthusiast. Any garbage can was ripe for the picking, and dumpsters were treasure troves of sculptural accessories. We combed the shores of Lake Michigan, searching for aptly shaped chunks of driftwood and sea glass, tied them together with bits of colored wire and painted faces and fingers on them. We spent afternoons scanning sidewalks for candy and cigarette wrappers, slicing them into strips and

mushing them, glue-dipped, on chunks of mason board.
A barcode became a moustache, a grassy field bloomed
Newport green.

Among a handful of grandchildren, Joe was the only boy.
A golden child, carrying Grandpa's middle name and his
carefully hidden favoritism. It was Joe that got to hop into
the dumpsters, Joe that received secret instructions in
shoplifting. And it is in Joe's work that we can best see this
influence of family, and this deeply veined exploration of
the afterlife, the sublime. Childhood caricatures mingle
with one another in cavernous hallways and catacombs,
float weightlessly in starry skies. Watches stop, time stops,
time circles around, and we are back at the beginning.
Back to what we share with the ones who are gone. Gone
but not gone.

Myla Dalbesio
New York, 2014

There's something in humankind's mad search for the Divine that has caused the creation of thousands of symbols, unfolding over millennia in narratives of fantasy, violence, and transformation. Artists and craftsmen have long used the circle, the triangle, the dot, and the line to create visual languages that capture life experiences of

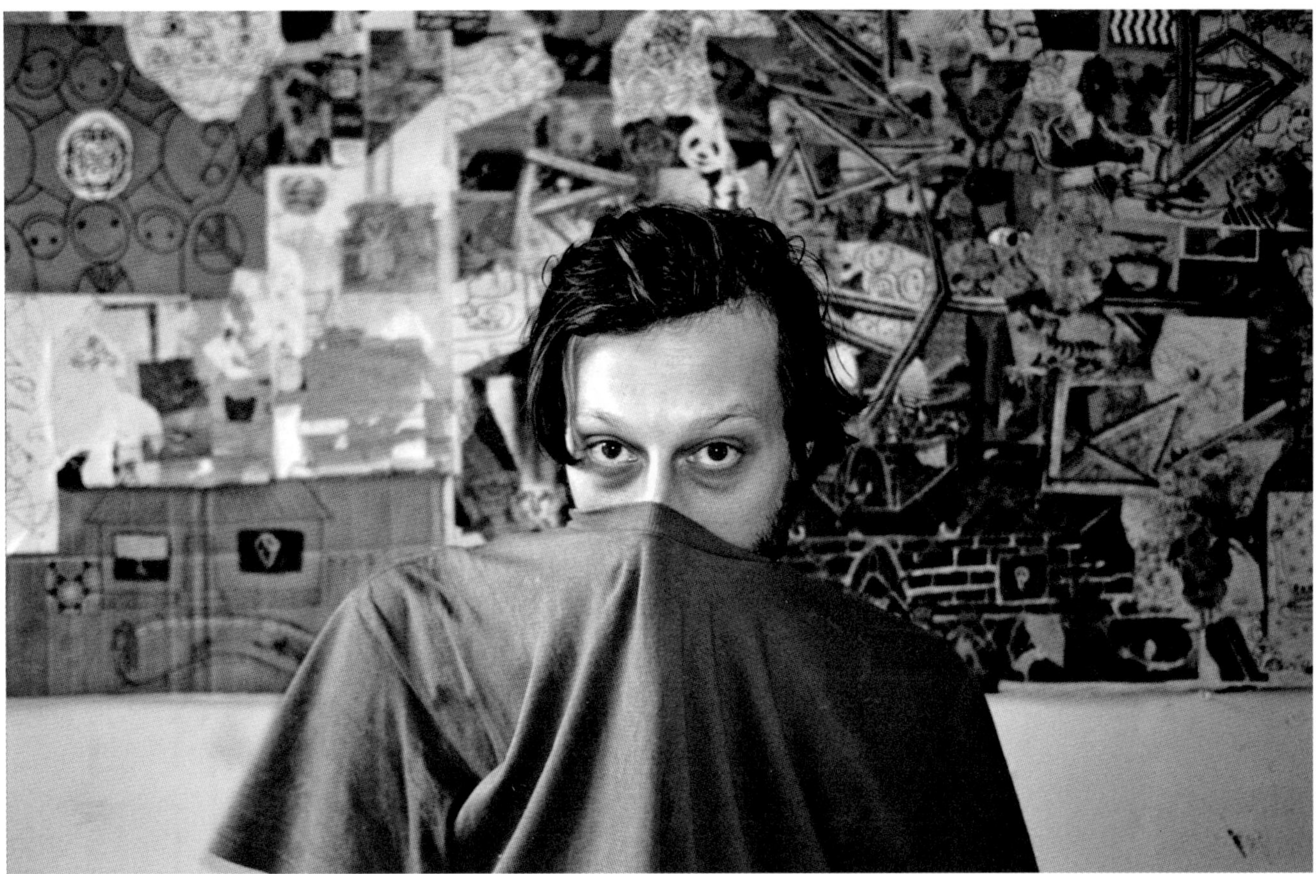

change and metamorphosis. One might think the oldest symbols would disappear as technology and science explain away the kinder uses for religion and mythology. On the contrary, popular culture has embraced them, as they are permanently embedded in our inherited memory and consciousness.

Since we gained the ability to create beyond necessity, all prototypical artists have undergone a kind of self-discovery/transformation. In his seminal work *The Hero with a Thousand Faces*, Joseph Campbell charted the paths taken by protagonists in works written, visualized, and sung, showing their simple similarity. This common route, the Monomyth, depicts a character being drawn into an adventure of the unknown, usually full of danger and mystery. Once there they must fight and overcome an evil hoarding entity. This process transforms them, and they may then return to the known world to share the knowledge gained on their journey. It is the ancient tale of the unending struggle to find one's identity. The idea of the Monomyth, or Hero's Journey, has roots in Jungian and Freudian psychoanalytic theory and is tied to the dissolving of the ego. This narrative can be seen in many of the world's mythological stories (Buddha, Osiris, Jesus), as well as more recent examples (such as the 1979 film *Alien* and the cartoon *Teenage Mutant Ninja Turtles*). The Monomyth can also be found in shamanistic cultures, in coming-of-age rituals in which people must take responsibility for their lives by going through ordeals of starvation or ingesting medicines to induce visions that often follow the arc of the Hero's Journey. Abstracting this principle, people often take the journey themselves by using psychedelics, practicing martial arts, or meditation, or making artwork.

It is in this last category that we find Joe Roberts. In his practice, Roberts has created a popular cryptic index that feeds off his quest for the Divine, using a process of osmosis and personal experience. How this came to be may not be as important as the actual combinations and origins of

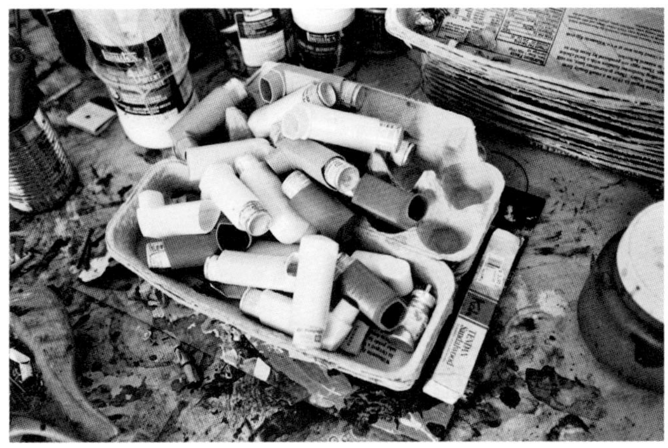

his imagery. Roberts's images are repeated over and over again, and thus share the economical line of comic book figures, logos, and toys. Lines and shapes, to be easily reproduced, must be simplified. This simplicity gives the work a humble quality and the directness of a note written to remind oneself of something. There is a shorthand involved that uses an encyclopedia of pop cultural symbols to transmit the idea of transformation. The current protagonists in Roberts's world of searching and transforming are the turtles from *Teenage Mutant Ninja Turtles* and Mickey Mouse as he appears in *The Sorcerer's Apprentice*, a chapter in the 1940 Disney film *Fantasia*.

The *Teenage Mutant Ninja Turtles* comic fits the mold of the Monomyth in that the monsters fought by the radioactively transformed turtles represent the greedy, capitalistic ego. In Monomyth stories a hero often fights a monster who is keeping riches, or a virgin hidden away in its cave, reflecting the ego and its covetous desire to protect its construction of self. *The Sorcerer's Apprentice*, known to Americans mostly through Disney but based on a poem by Goethe, tells the story of a young apprentice whose premature desire to experiment with his skills causes chaos, teaching him that only a master should use magic. The synthesis of these two themes of Roberts's suggests a parallel with his own personal search for the unknown, the shedding of the ego through experimentation with LSD, DMT, and psilocybin. Roberts is a Teenage Mutant hero, but he is also the Sorcerer's Apprentice when his experimentations with magic turn dark, leading him to an awareness that the tools of self-discovery must be used with respect. Joe Roberts's journey to the unknown is dotted with the protective guardians of childhood nostalgia. These come in the flavors of the films, comics, candies, logos, and branding of the eighties and early nineties, not to mention latent countercultural references from the sixties and seventies. This is the bulk of the content in his works, and it is these references that place him in his time period and in a group of people bent on breaking through the illusions to find themselves. Below is a list of objects and characters found in Roberts's work, along with some subjective associations.

Matthew Ronay
Long Island City, 2014

CHARACTERS

TMNT: With my friends I can separate from society, fight evil, and become disciplined in the art of mind control

Mickey Mouse as Wizard: Clumsy, not yet a master sorcerer, but dedicated to the quest to find the Divine

Wu Tang Clan: Martial Arts discipline and philosophical tribe

Aliens: Who is other? Is this the way I look in the mirror? Neil Blender, H.R. Giger, acid tab, the 1979 film *Alien*

Owl: White Father, God of Wisdom

Batman: Dark do-gooder, found his ego and annihilated it

Jason / Hockey Mask: From the 1980 film *Friday the 13th*, misogynistic misanthrope, Jung's Shadow Archetype

Scream Mask: Melting death hallucination, becoming familiar with the shadow side, insecurity, impermanence

Jungle: Henri Rousseau, harmony (where danger and beauty intertwine)

Grateful Dead: Drugs, counterculture

Ninja, Kung Fu: Physical mysticism; see *Skateboard*

Pumpkin: From the 1979 film *Halloween*, body impermanence

MEDICINES

Smiley Face LSD Blotter: "I always wear a smile / because anything but a smile / would make me have to explain / and they wouldn't understand anyway." Slight smile ideal for meditations, agent of change, mutagen

Weed: Door of perception is slightly ajar

Jungle Spice / Dune: Quest to experience the Eternal

Mushrooms: Hidden helpers, aliens, Terence McKenna

Pizza: Vehicle for shrooms, TMNT favorite food

Life Cereal: Mikey likes it

Butterfinger: Bart Simpson

Sprite, 7UP: Elixir

Cheetos: Chester the Cheetah, great Jaguar God

Skittles: Energy pills

Rice Krispies: Elf food

Pills: When discipline and plants fail

Kool-Aid: Jim Jones, *The Electric Kool-Aid Acid Test*

BOOKS (Information Food)

Be Here Now, Ram Das: Breathe

Dune, Frank Herbert: "I must not fear. Fear is the mind-killer. Fear is the little-death that brings total obliteration. I will face my fear. I will permit it to pass over me and through me. And when it has gone past I will turn the inner eye to see its path. Where the fear has gone there will be nothing. Only I will remain."

Food of the Gods, Terence McKenna: Map

Psilocybin: Magic Mushroom Grower's Guide: A Handbook for Psilocybin Enthusiasts, O. T. Oss and O. N. Oeric, Terence McKenna Foreword: Agents of Evolution

Finnegans Wake, James Joyce: Hero's Journey

The Soft Machine, William S. Burroughs: Um . . .

Phillip K. Dick: Sci-fi god

WEAPONS/TOOLS

Rubik's Cube: Broken/put back together ego

Skateboard: Physical/mystical journey portal

Bong: Portal

Nintendo GameBoy: Labyrinth, PTSD calmer

Crossbow: Conan, Dungeons & Dragons

Uzi: Eighties gun of choice

Clock: Social contract, 11:11, 4:20

Air Jordans: Hermes, god of transitions and boundaries

Butterfly Knife: Hidden dangers

Nunchaku: Phallic dangers

Throwing Star: Universe danger

Ouija Board: Other side connection, tool for the unconscious

Volcano Vaporizer: Inside must come out under pressure

Crystals/Geodes: Nature's hidden spectacle, hiddenness in general, refined growth locus

SYMBOLS

Yin and Yang: Comes in waves, coping mechanism, contrary forces working together

Rose Window: Terence McKenna, divine geometry

Spiral: Repetition that is never quite the same

Eye: Everythingness

Rainbow: Ego's sacred illusion, beautiful only from outside, not to be mistaken for a prism

Prism: Making visible all moods and all in between

Peace Sign: Zen compassion and disillusionment in one

Tree: Tree of Life, Food of the Gods

UFO: Seedpods, unknowns

Eyes Peeking Out From Darkness: Hide-and-seek, the first game

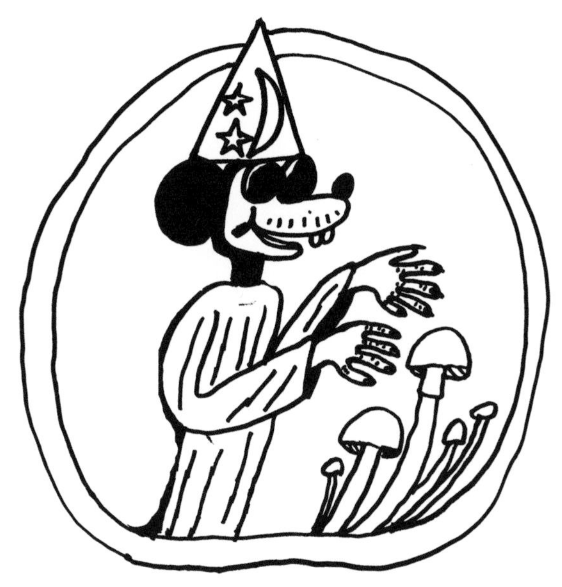

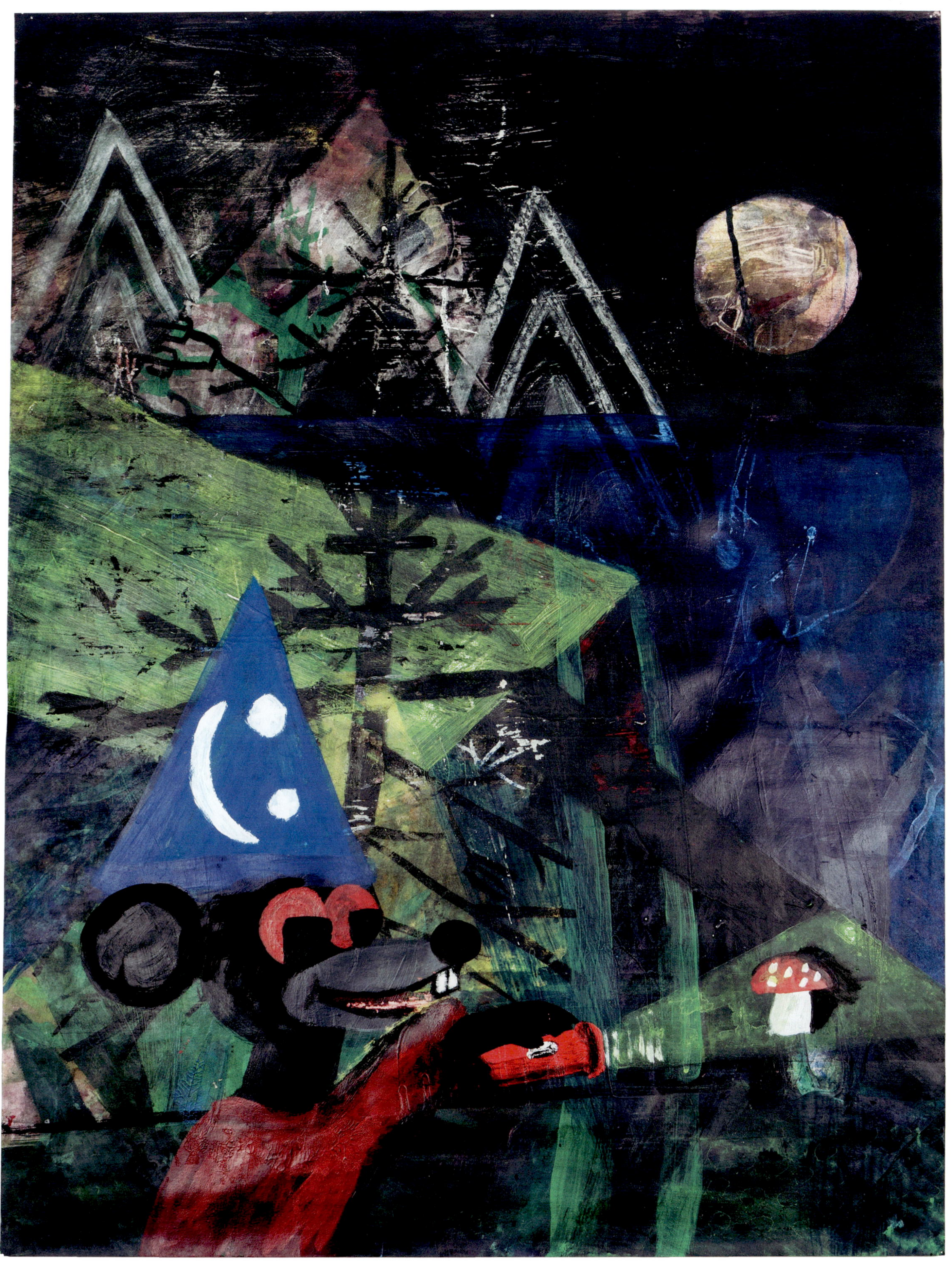

The Flesh of God, 2014

13

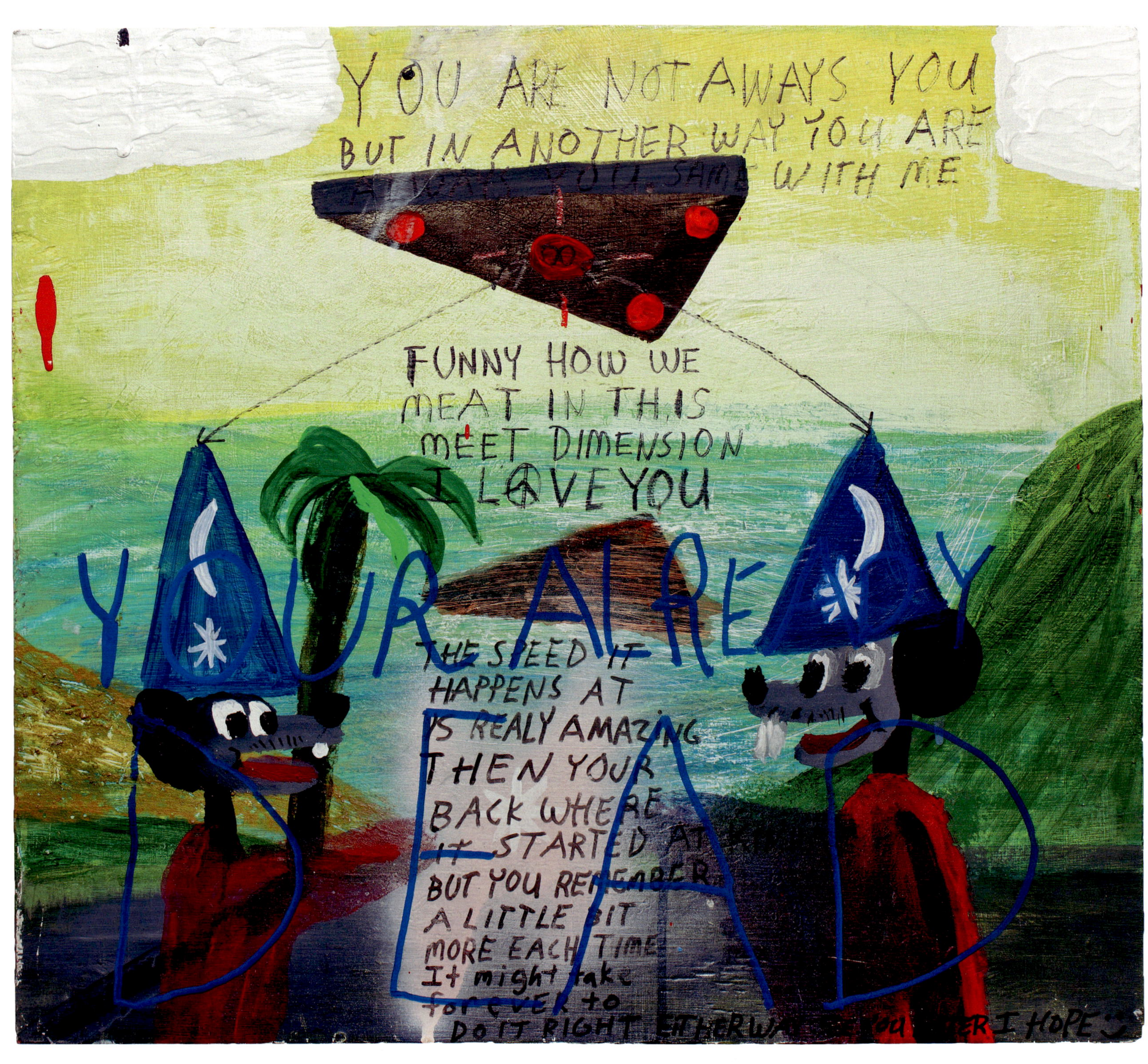

It's Whatever You Take from It, 2013

14

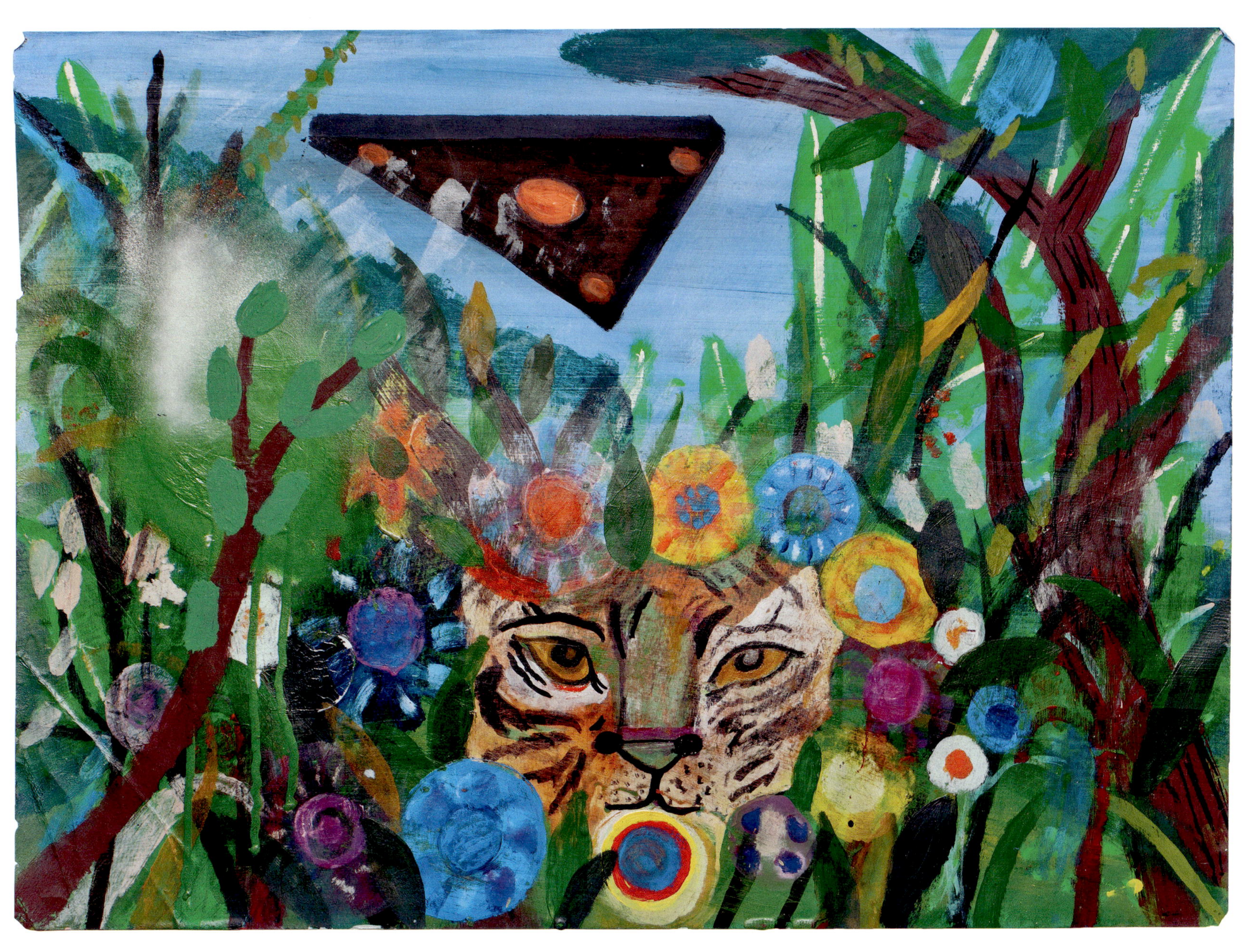

Jungle, 2012

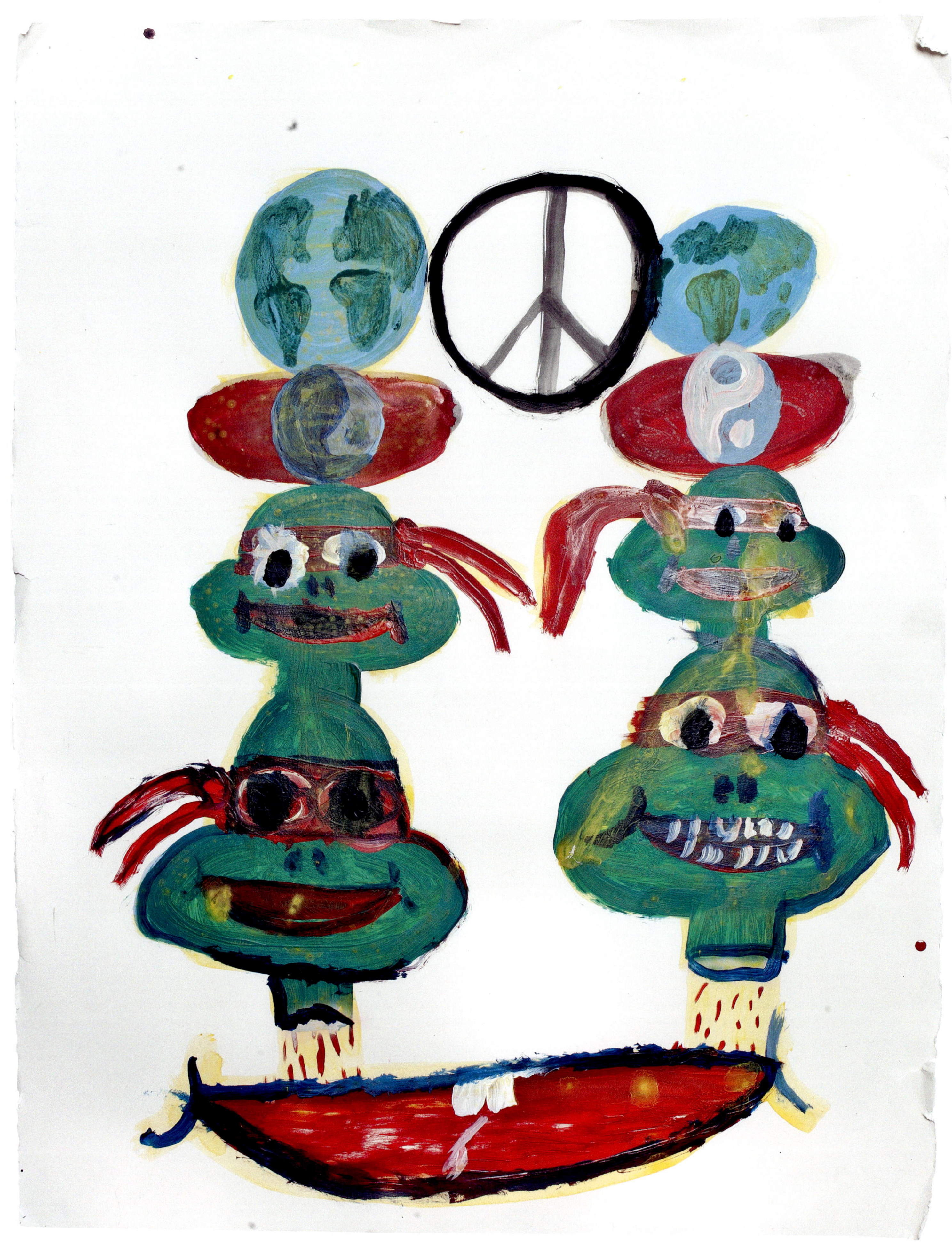

Code of Peace, 2012

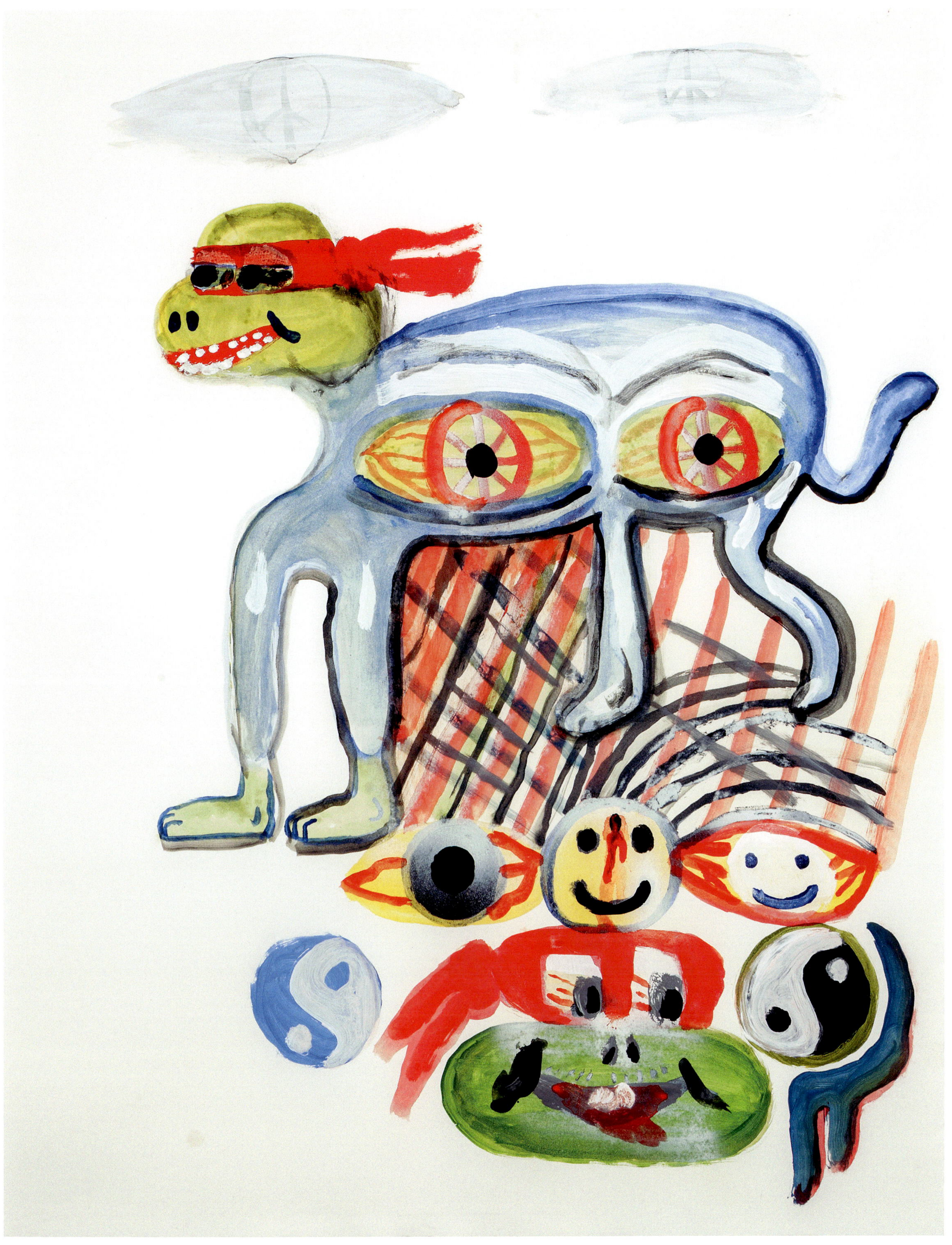

Face, 2012

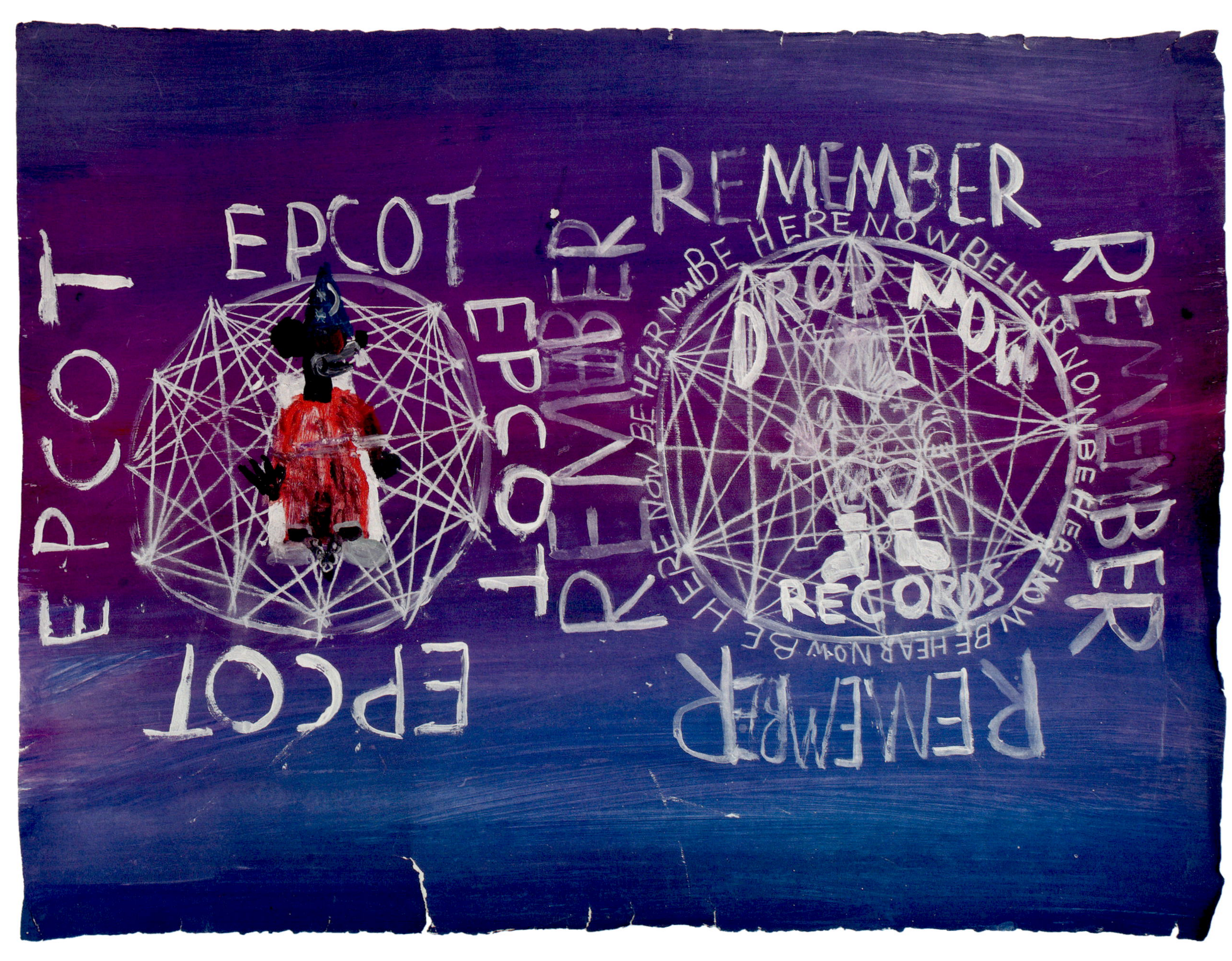

Remember, 2014

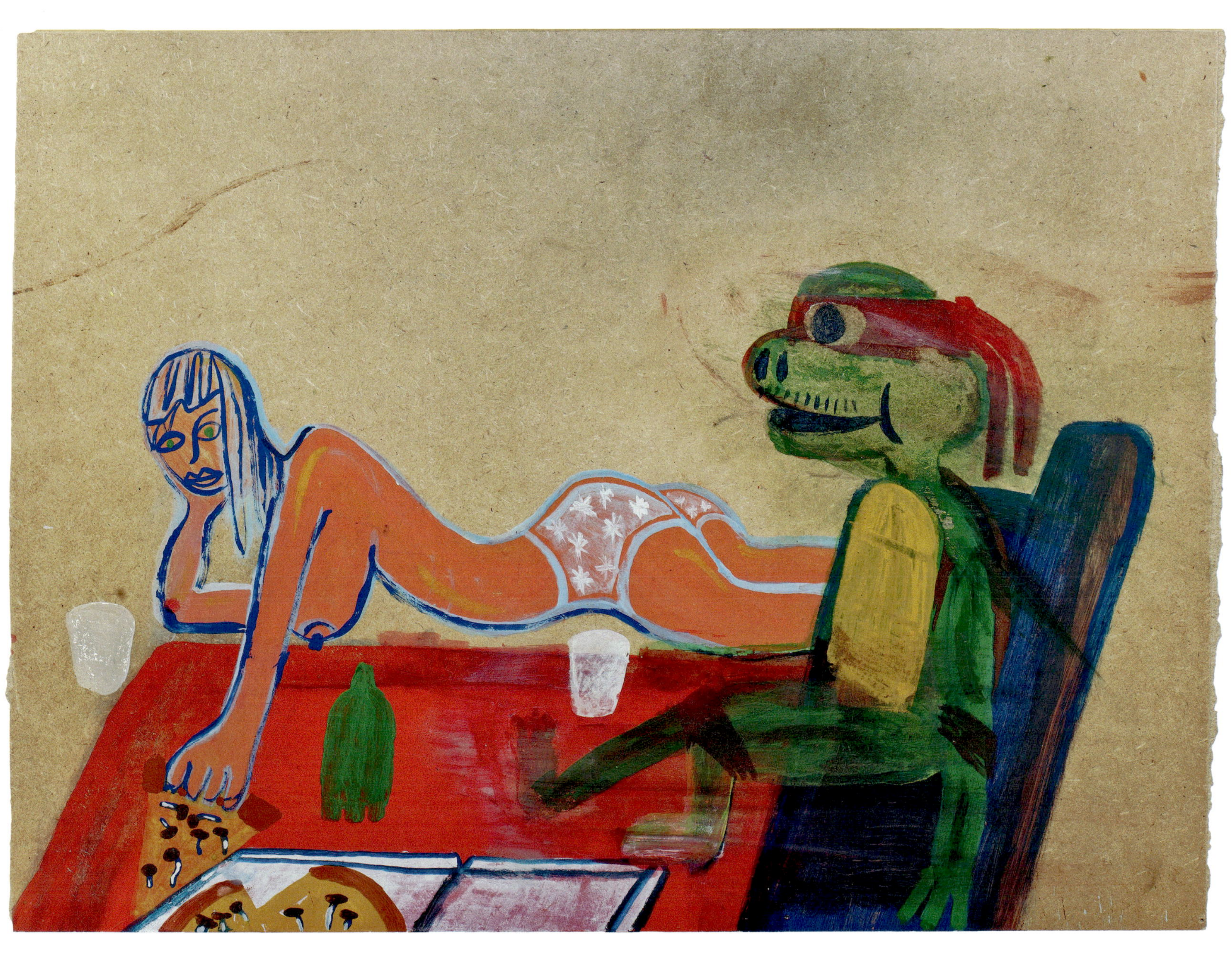

Friday Night, 2014

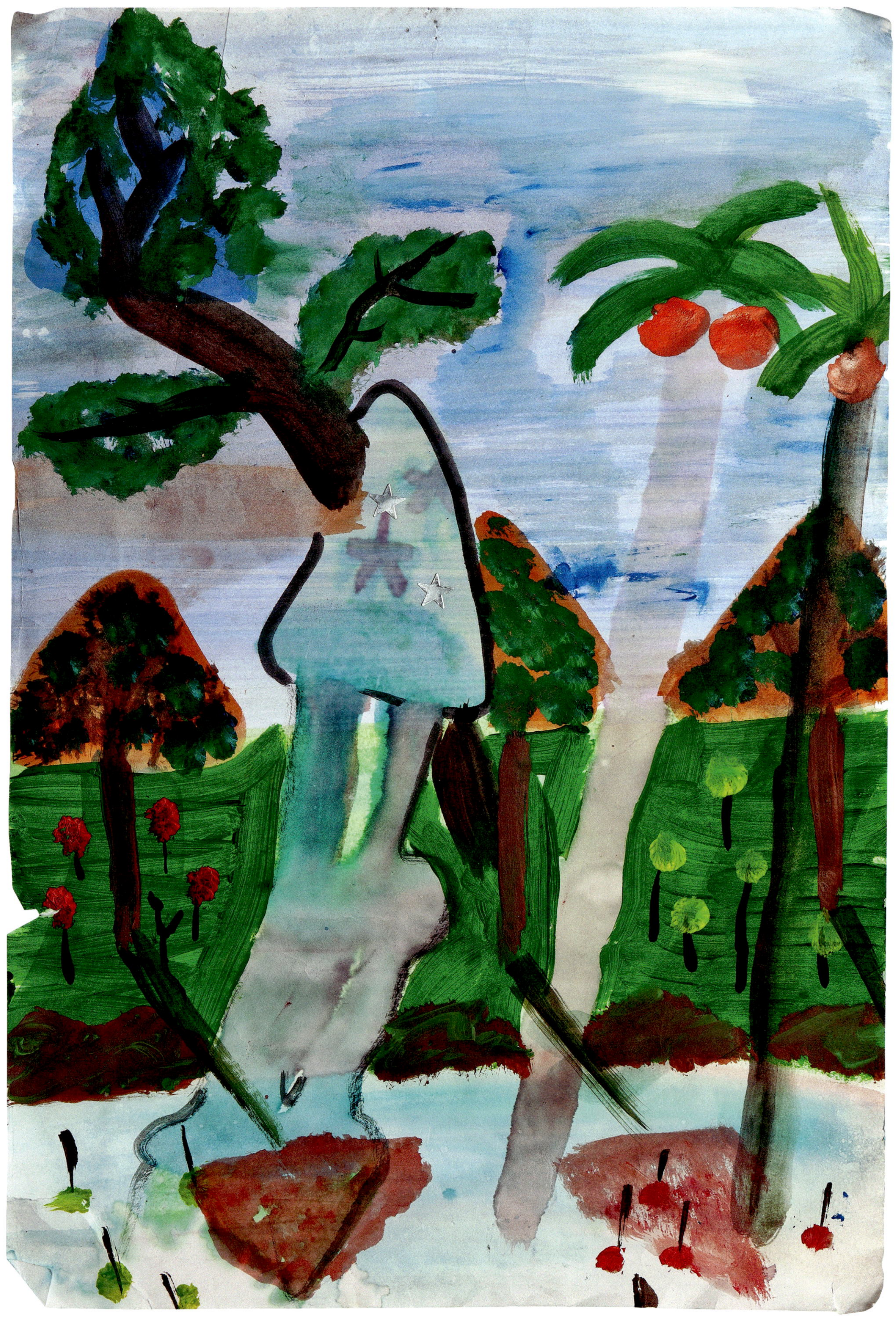

Tropics, 2012

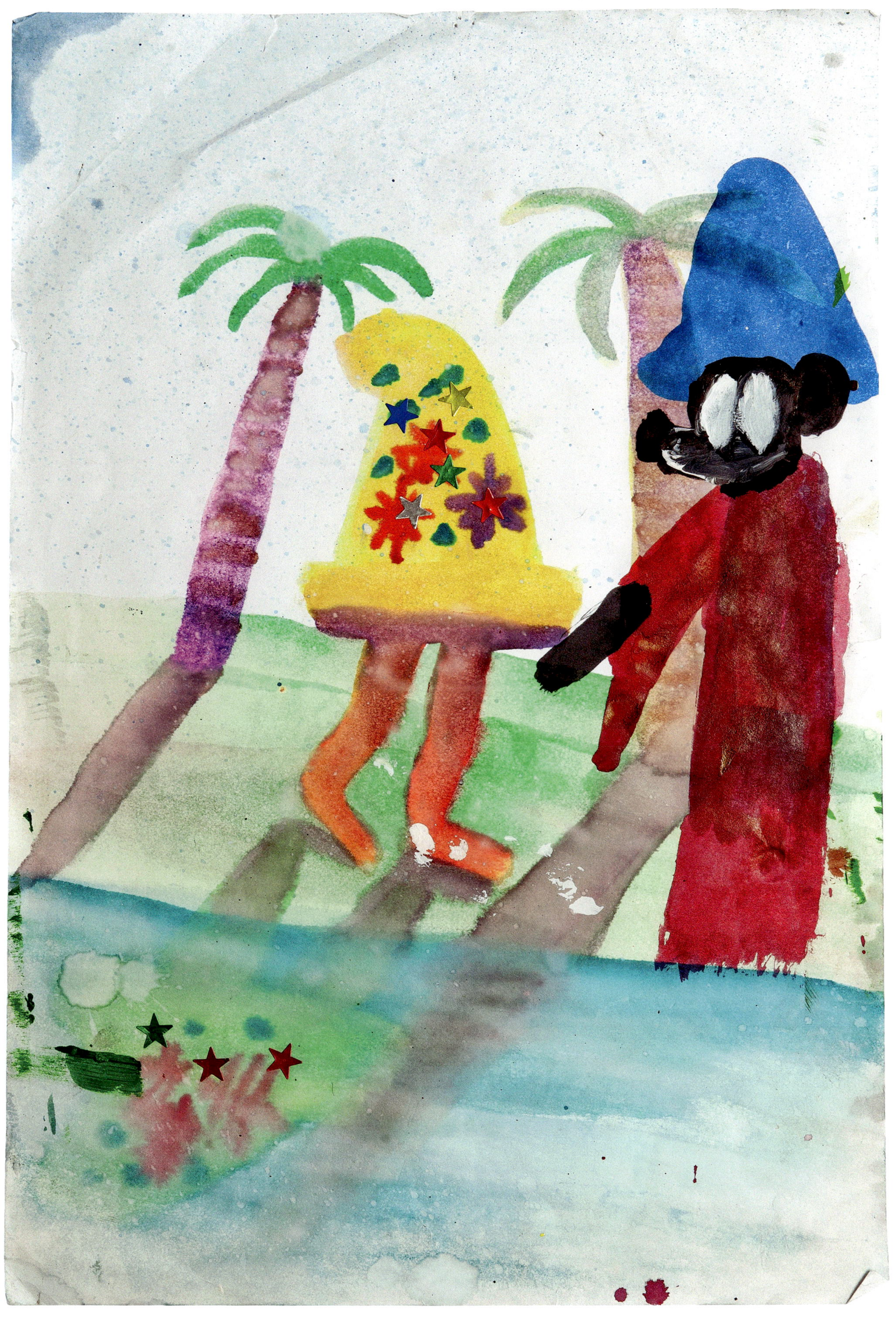

False Profits, 2012

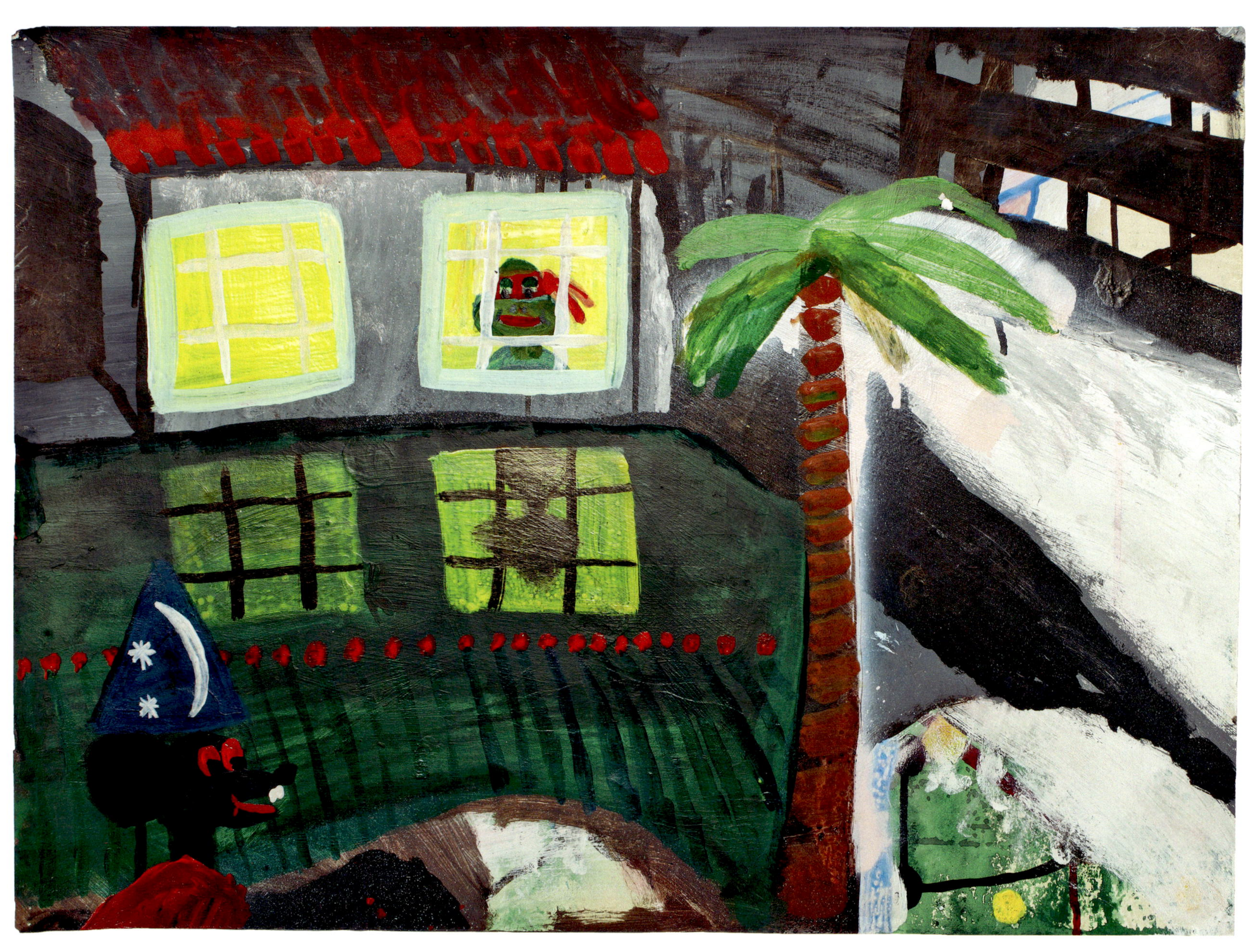

Nightwatch, 2013

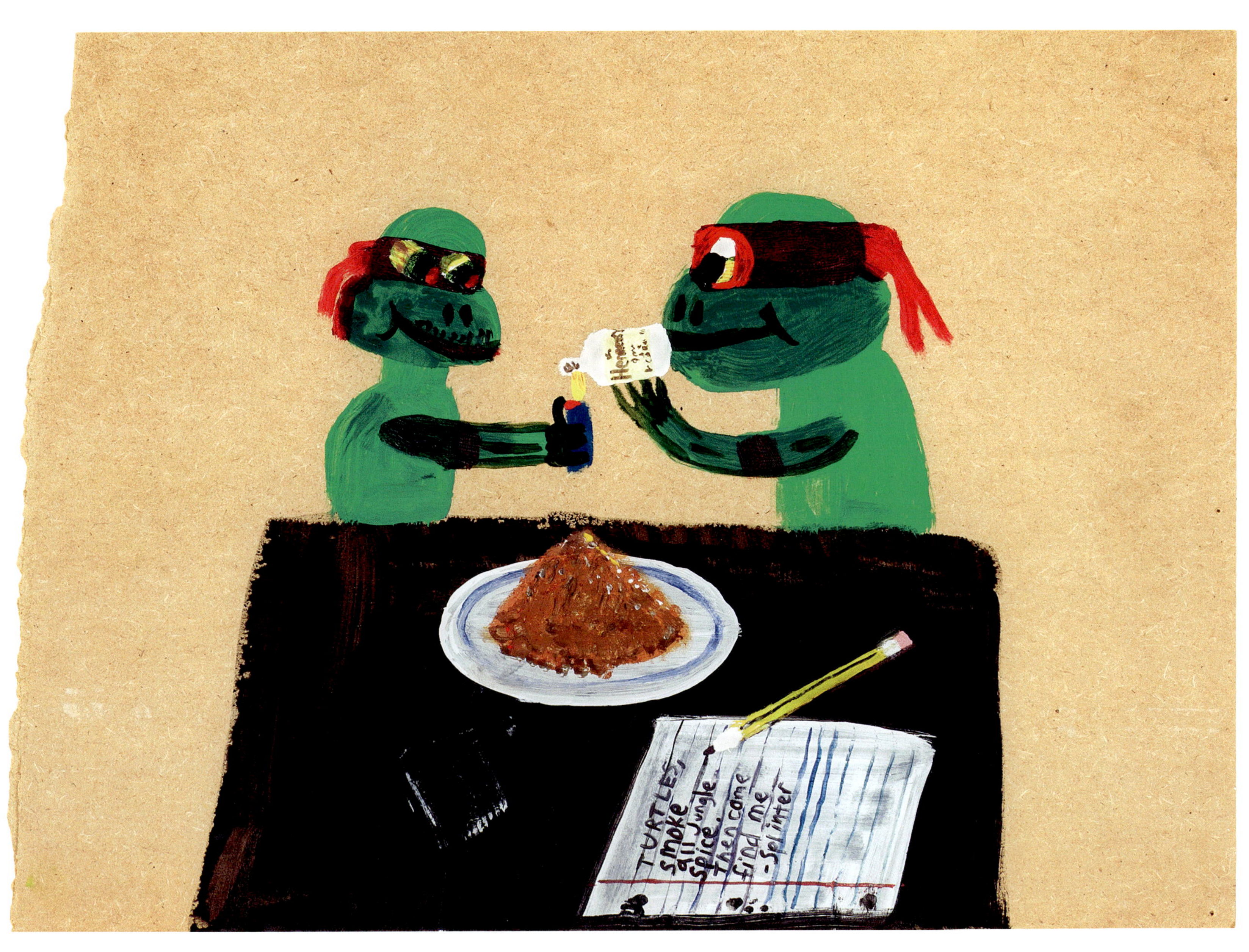

Jungle Spice, 2013

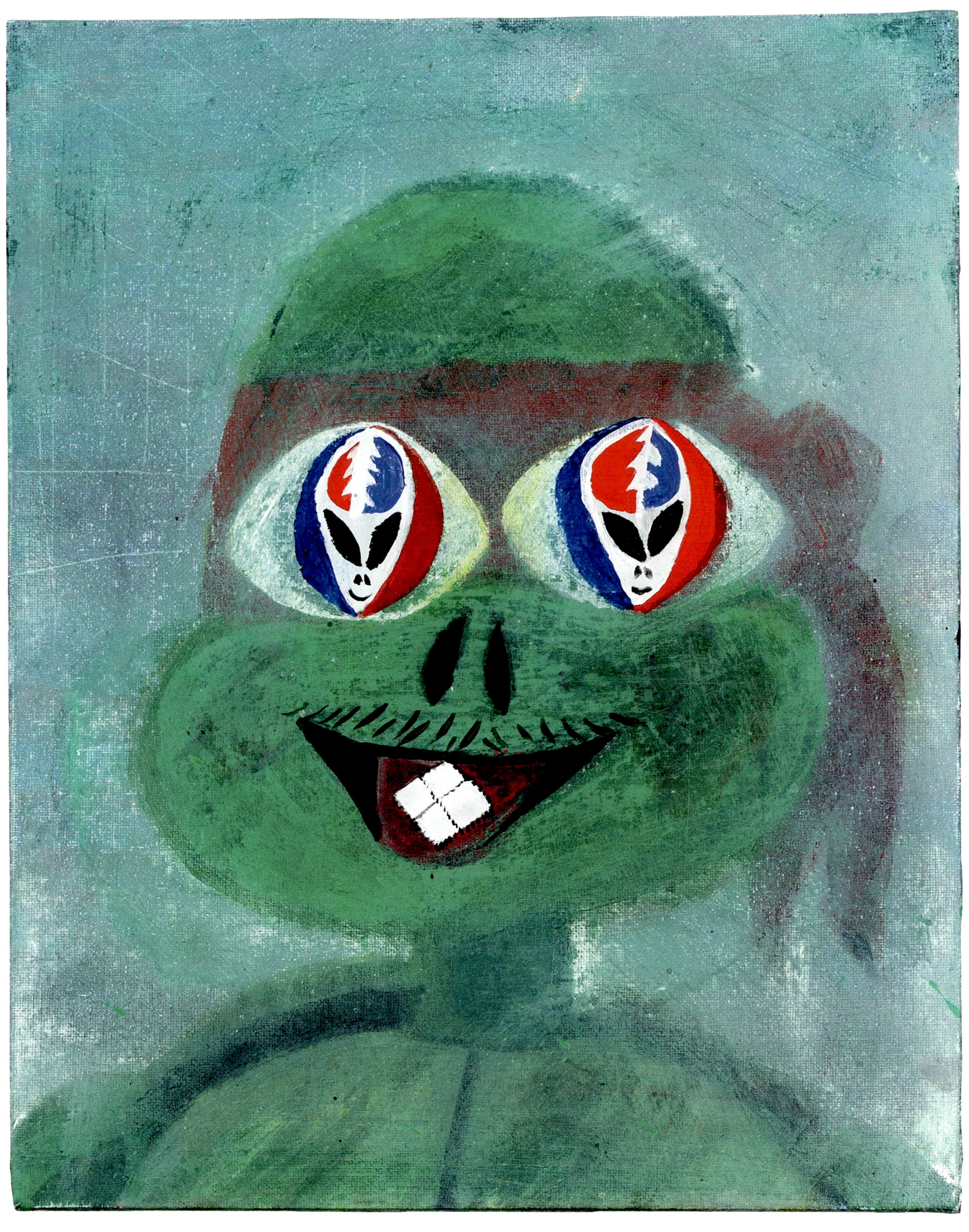

Raph's Trip, 2011

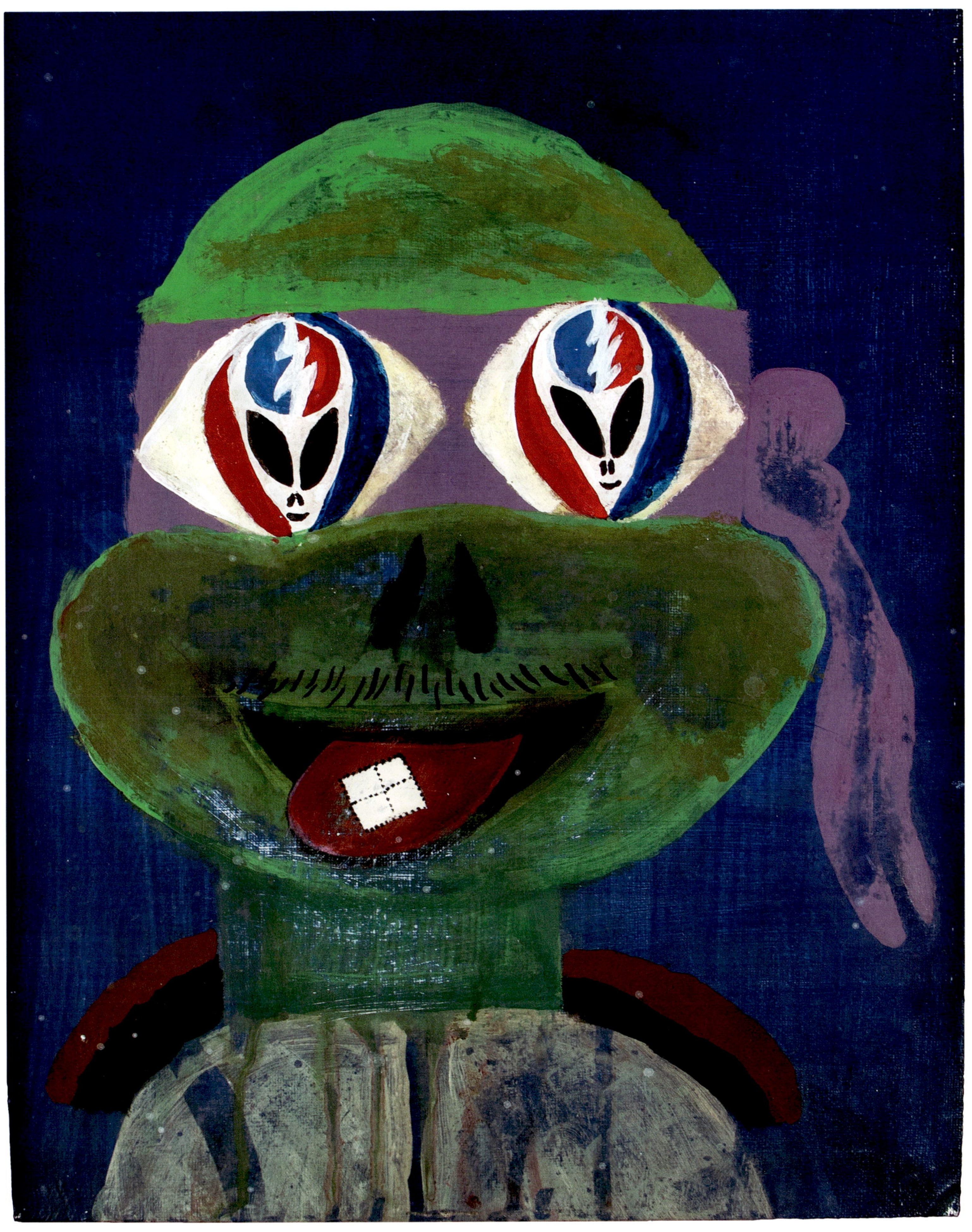

Donatello's Trip, 2011

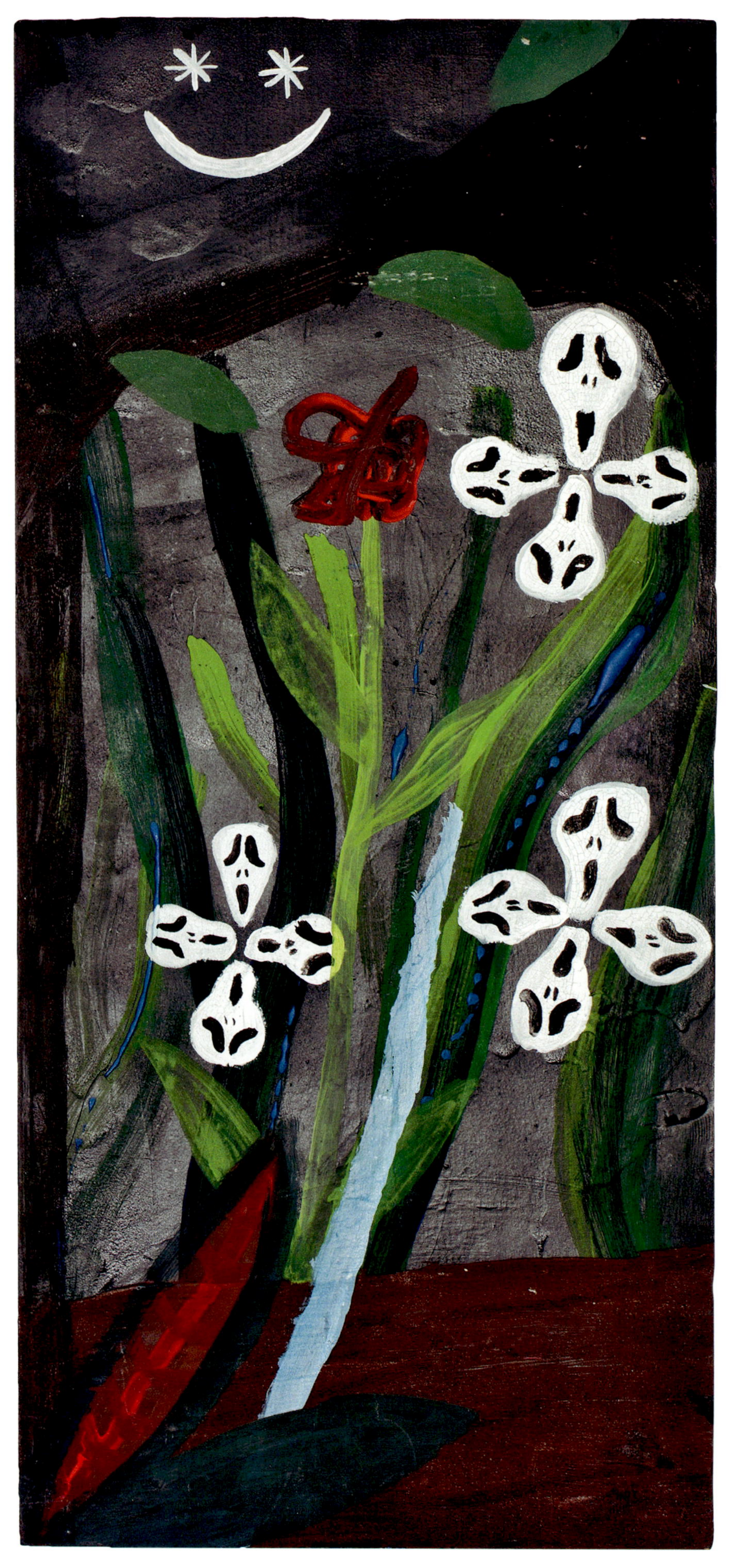

Flowers and Cat, 2013

26

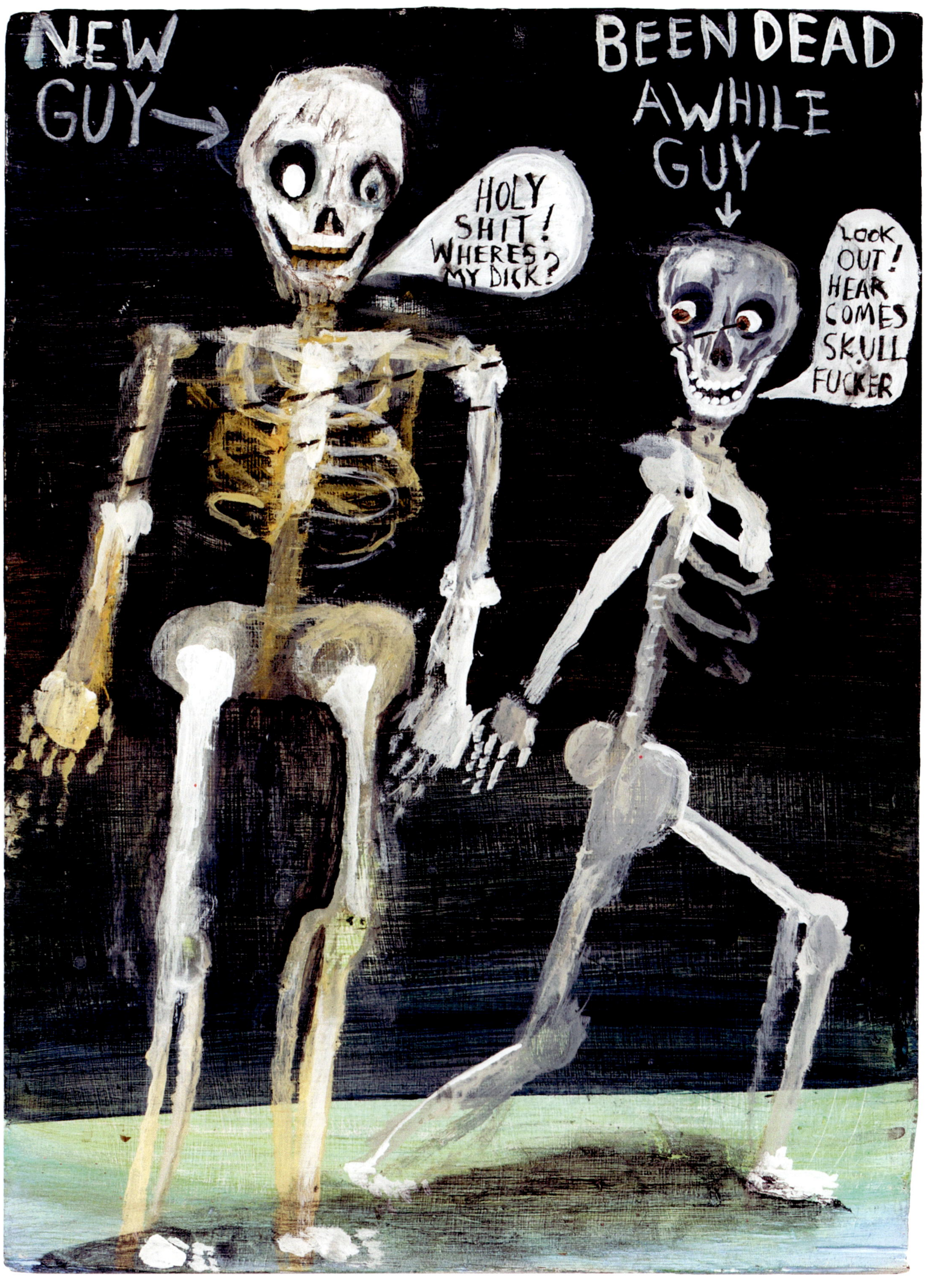

New Guy in the Land of the Dead, 2009

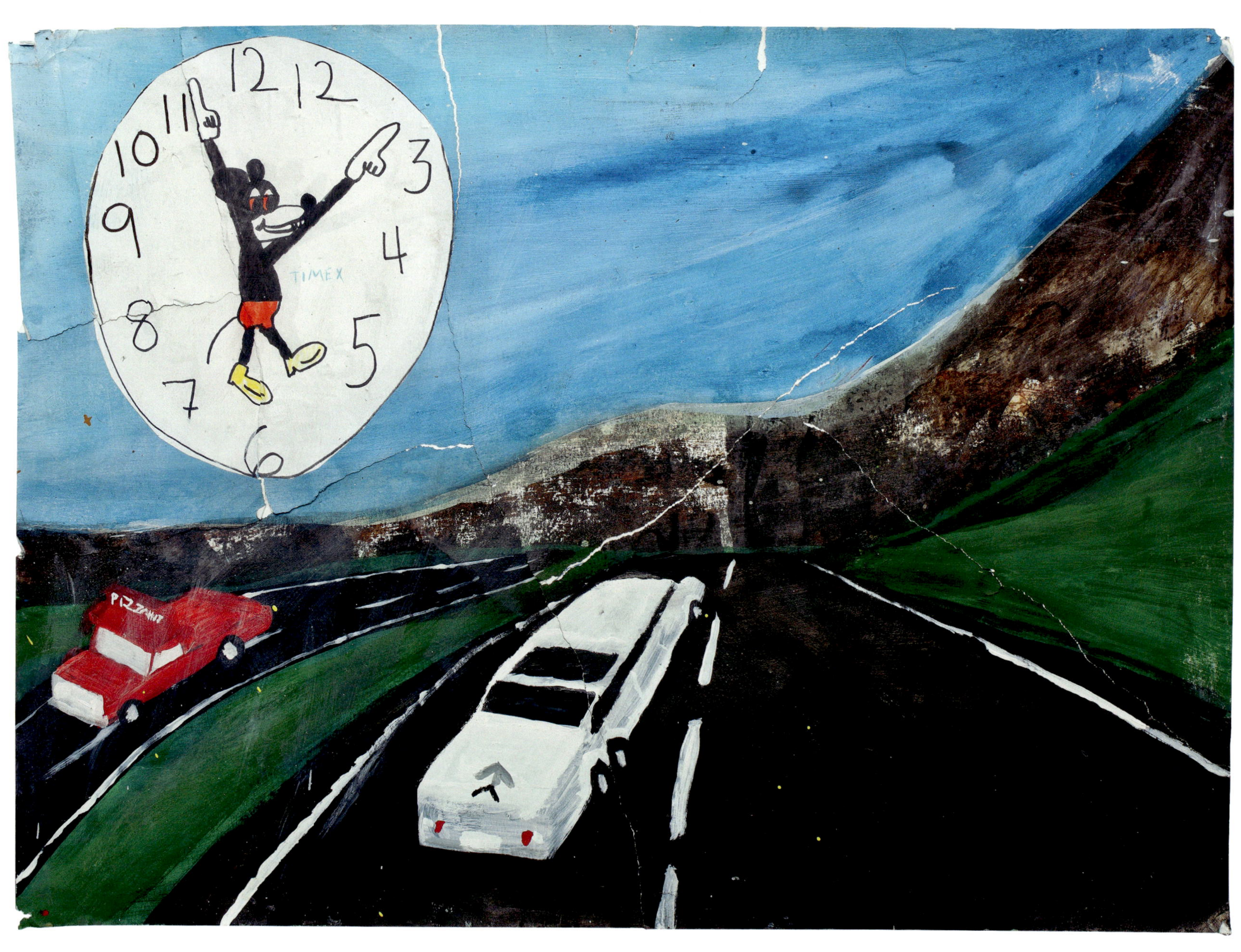

Rip in Time, 2012

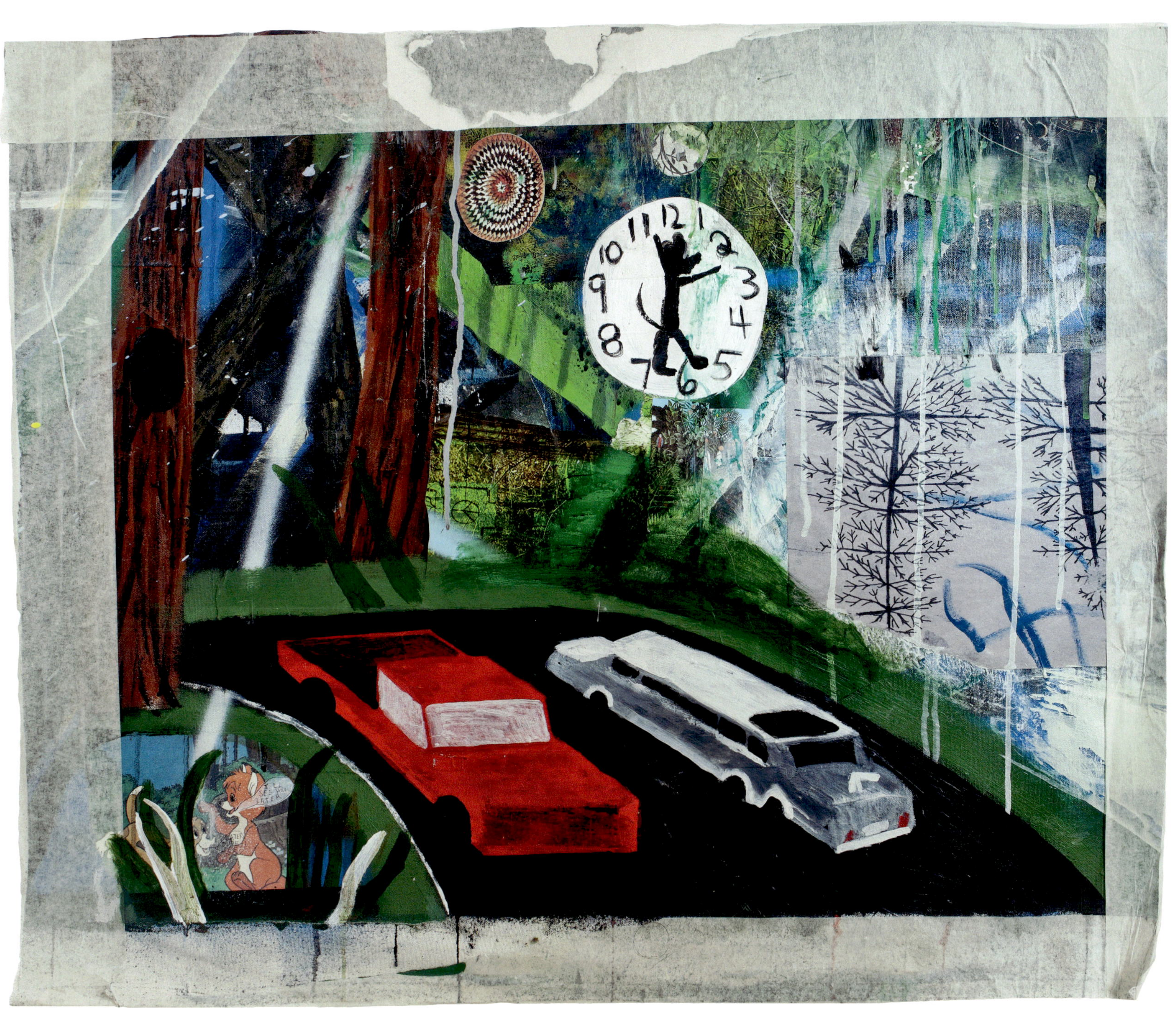

The Great Highway, 2012

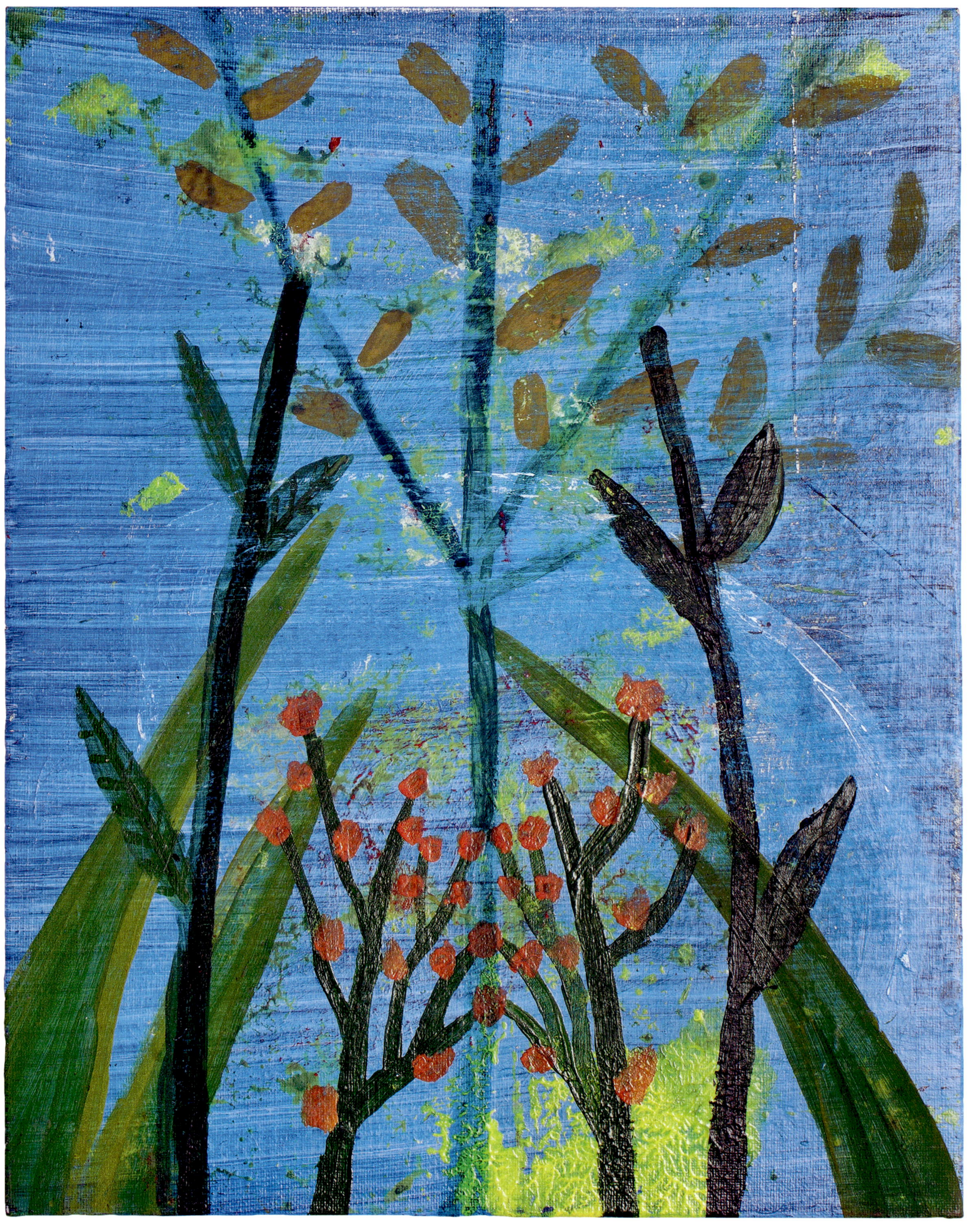

Flowers, 2012

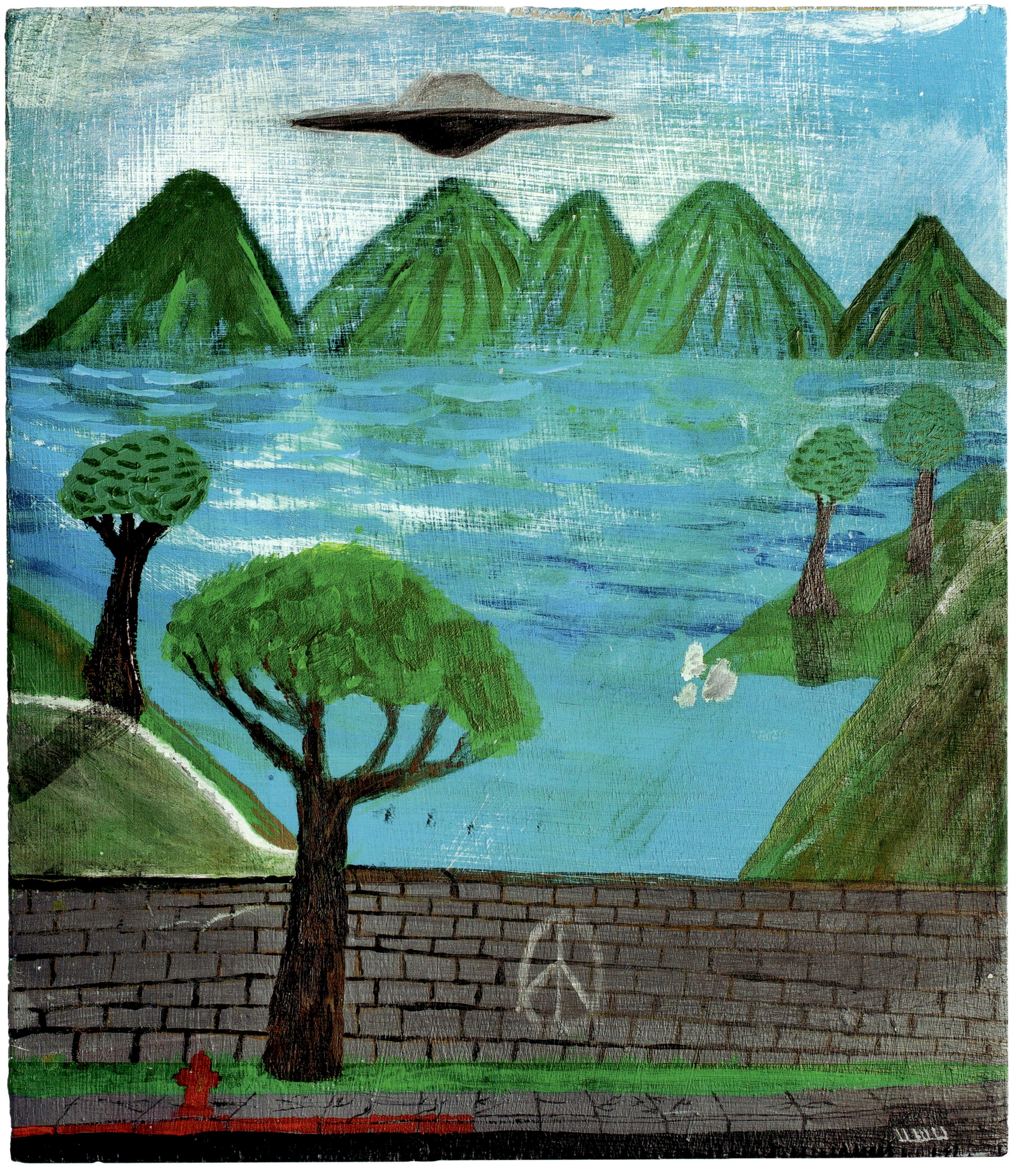

Blue Dream, 2009

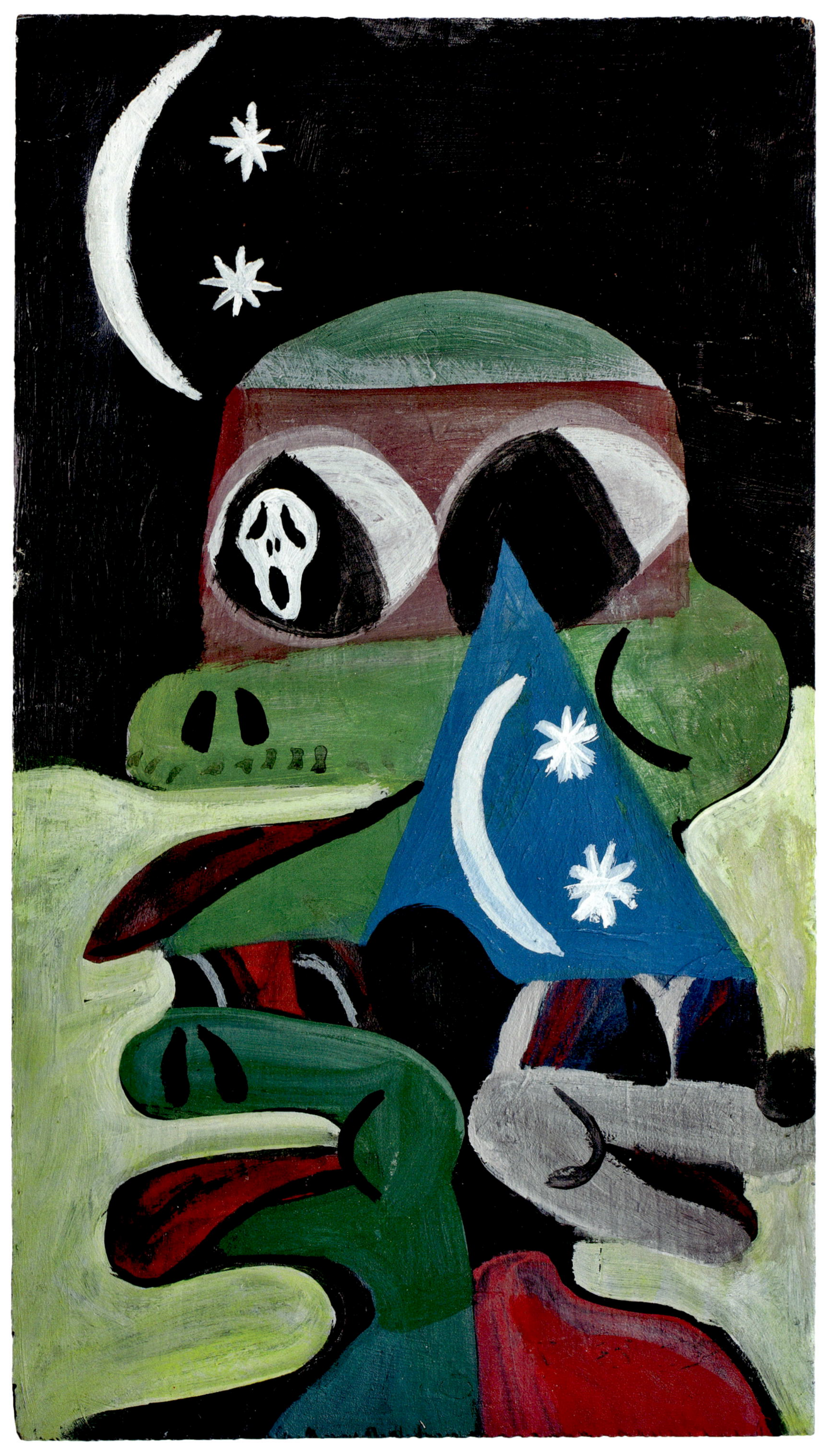

Night Trip, 2012

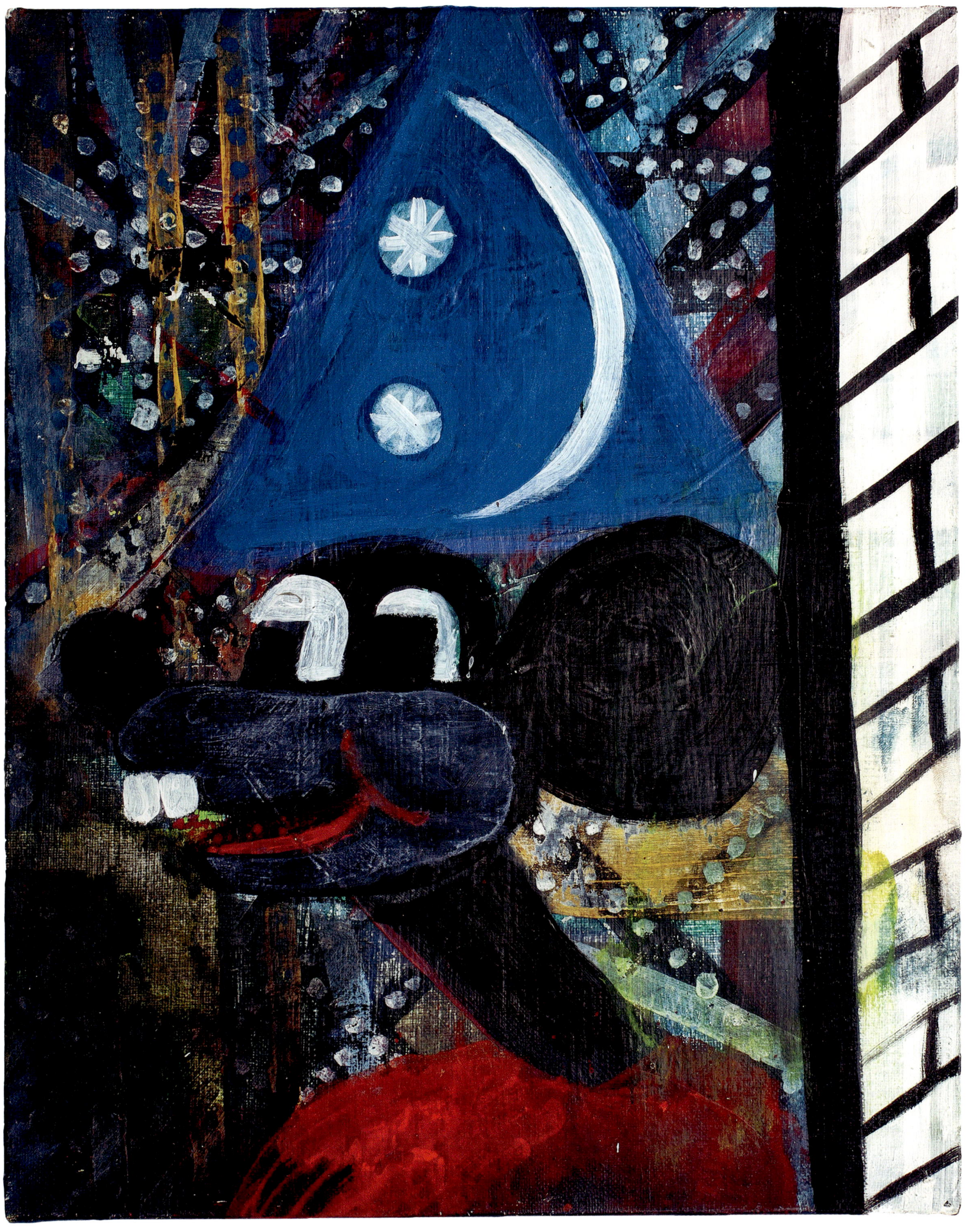

Splinter, 2012

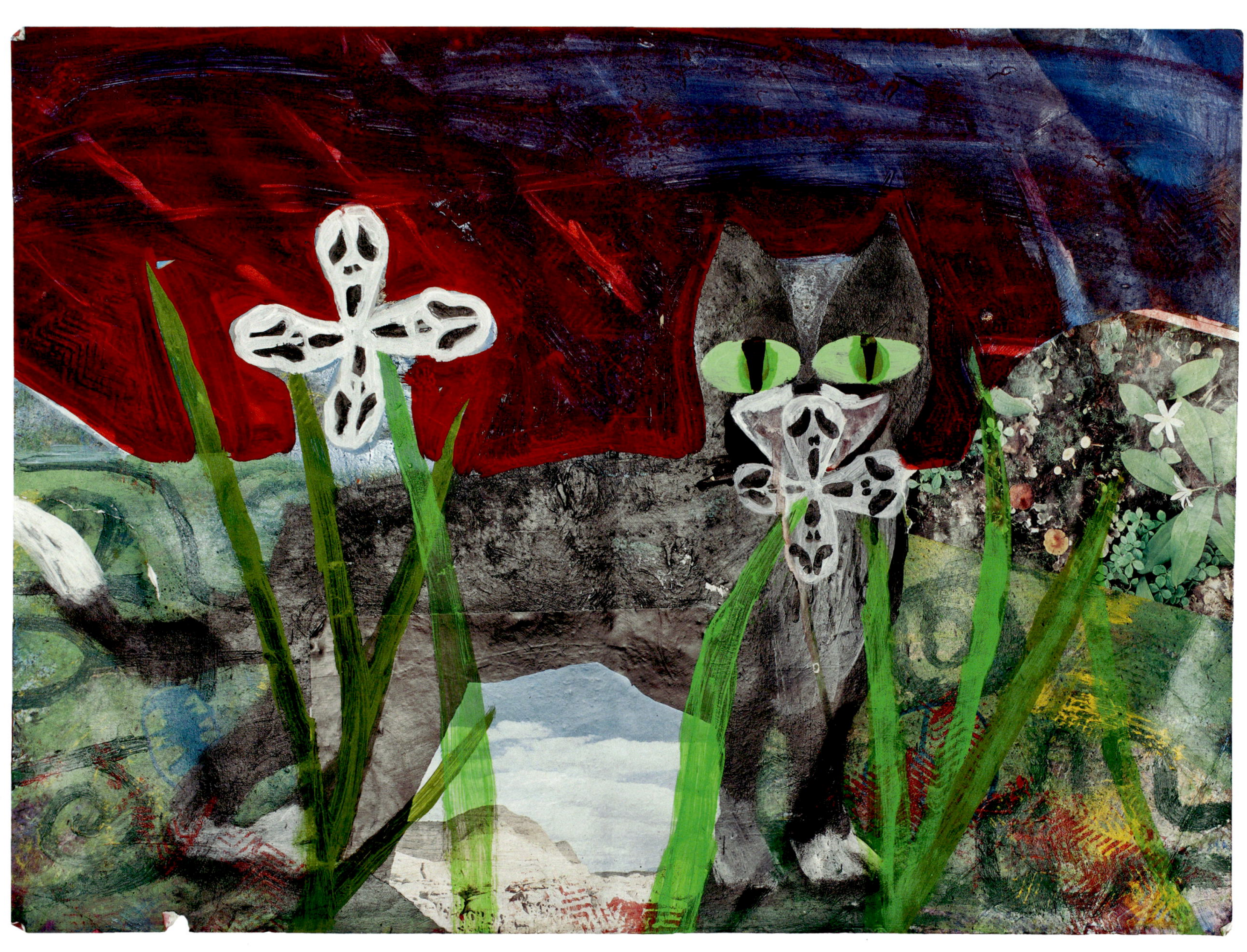

The Search for Adventure, 2014

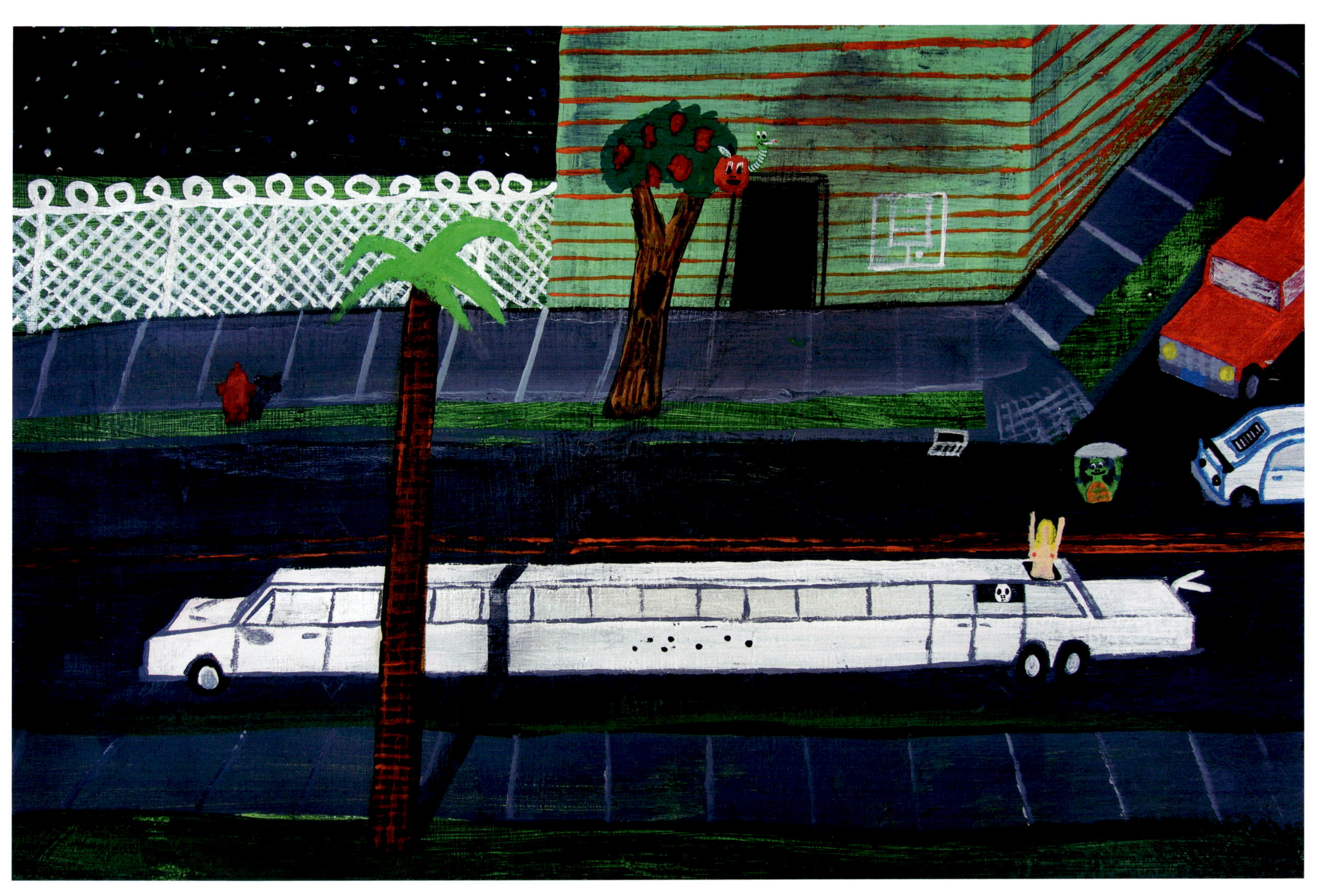

Homecoming, 2010

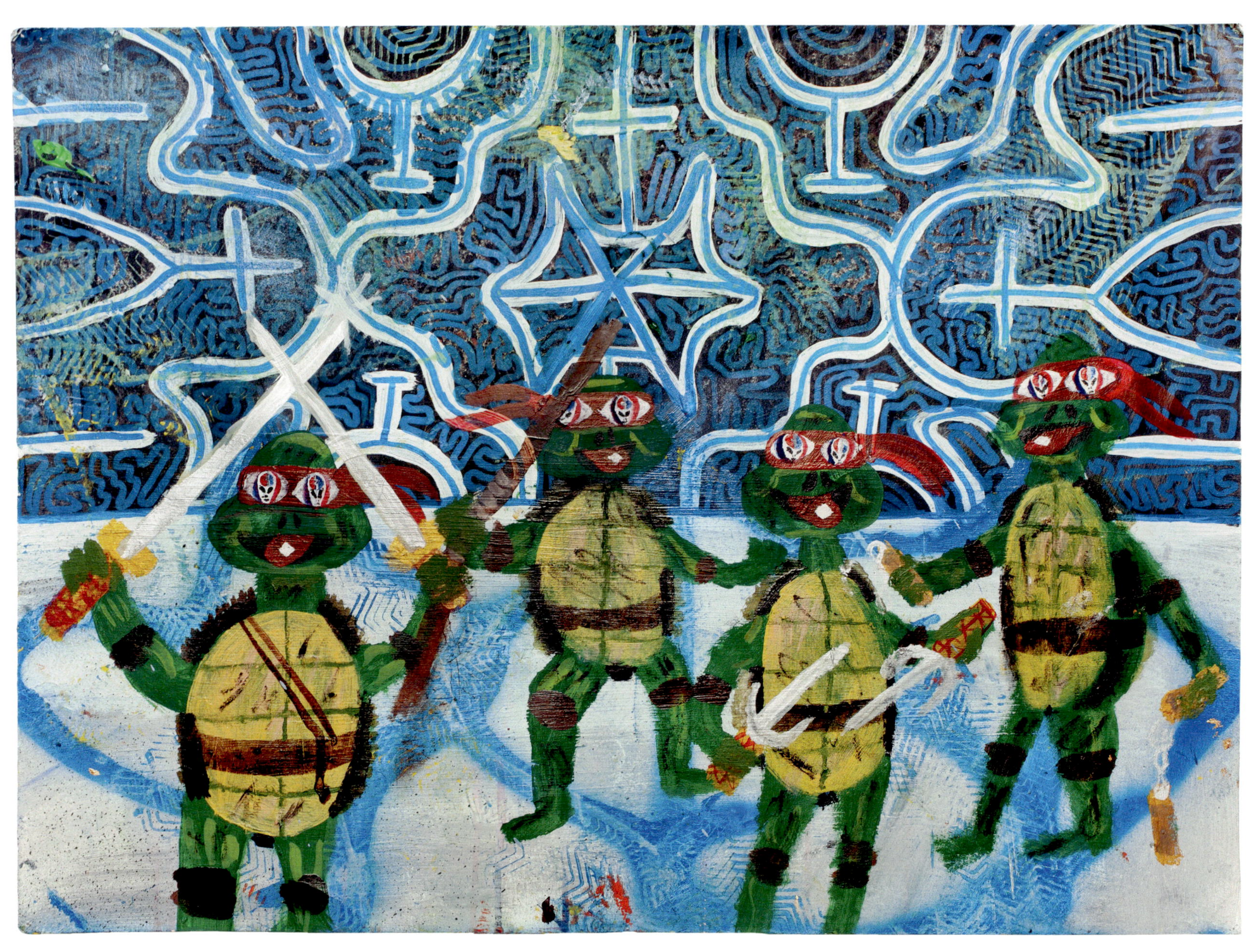

Group Vision, 2013

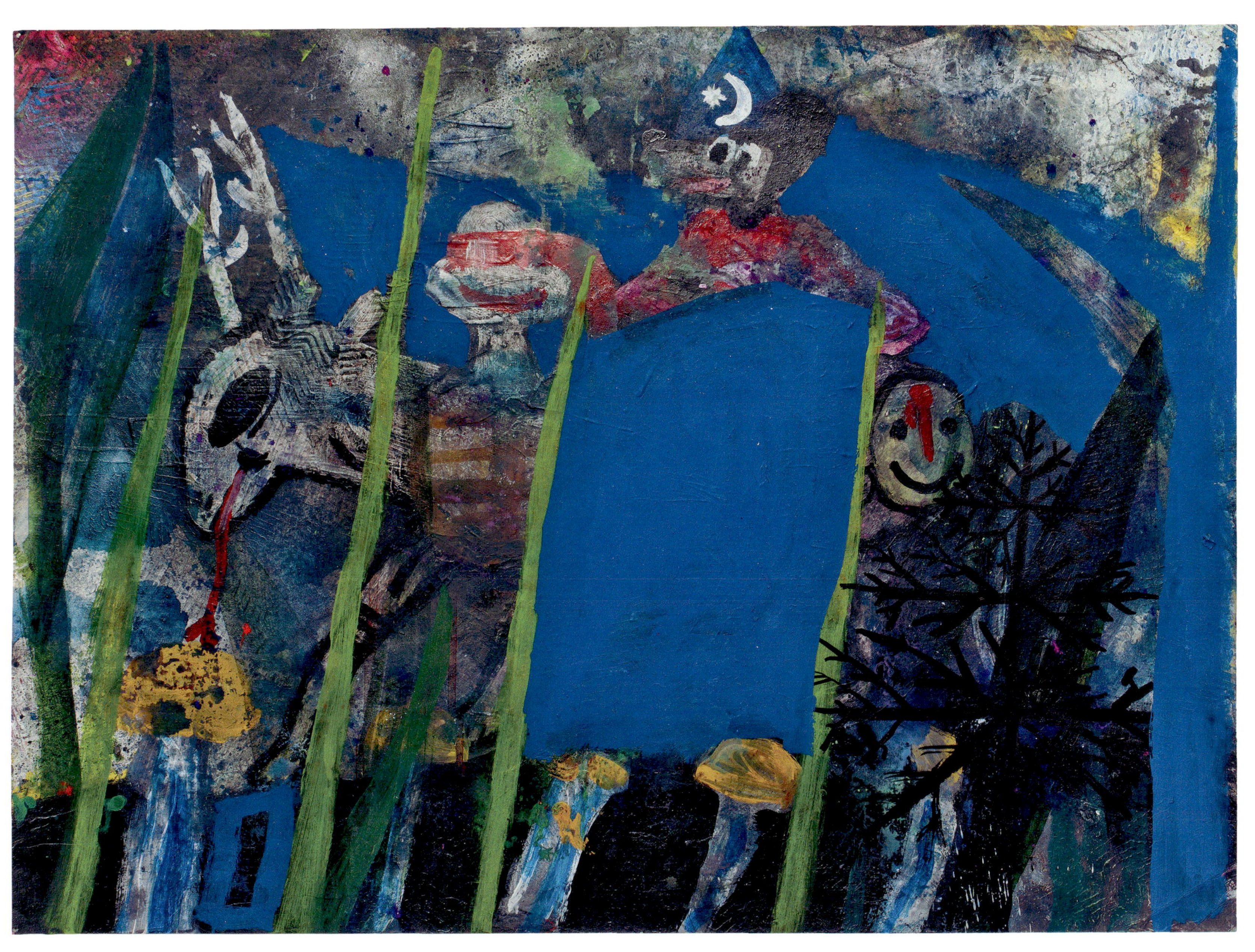

Unfolding Time, 2013

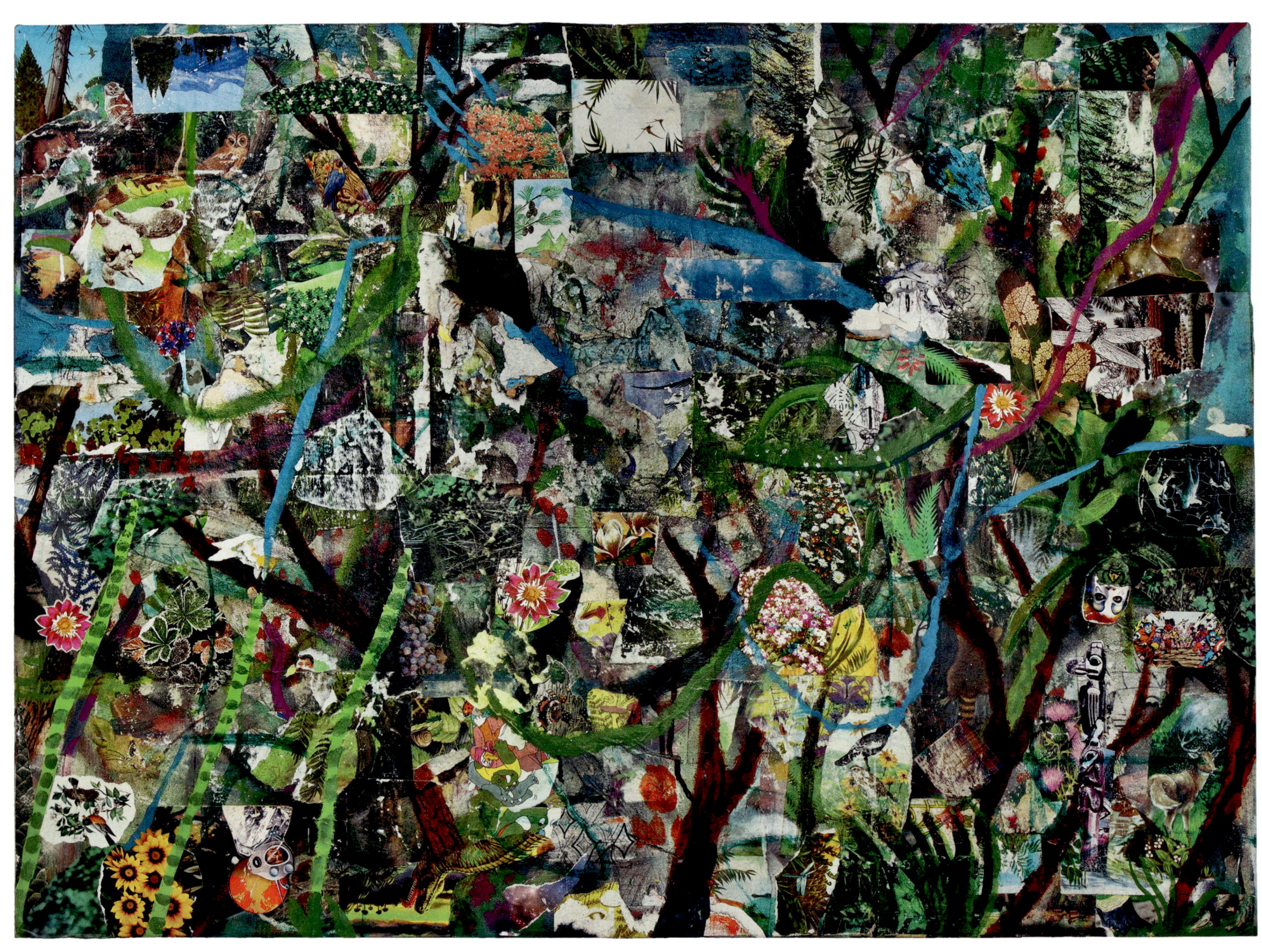

Shamen's Cookbook, 2012

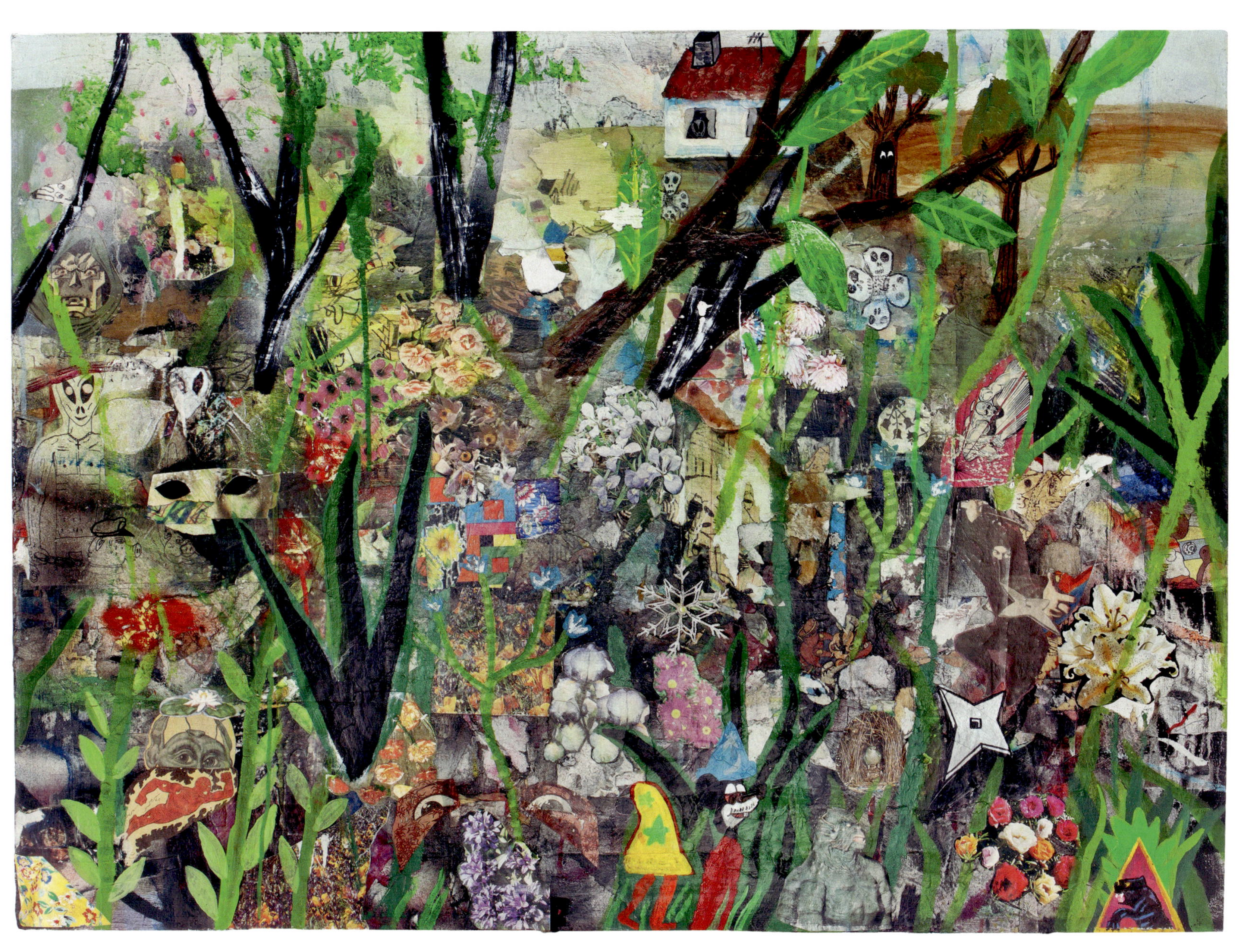

The Edge of Magic, 2012

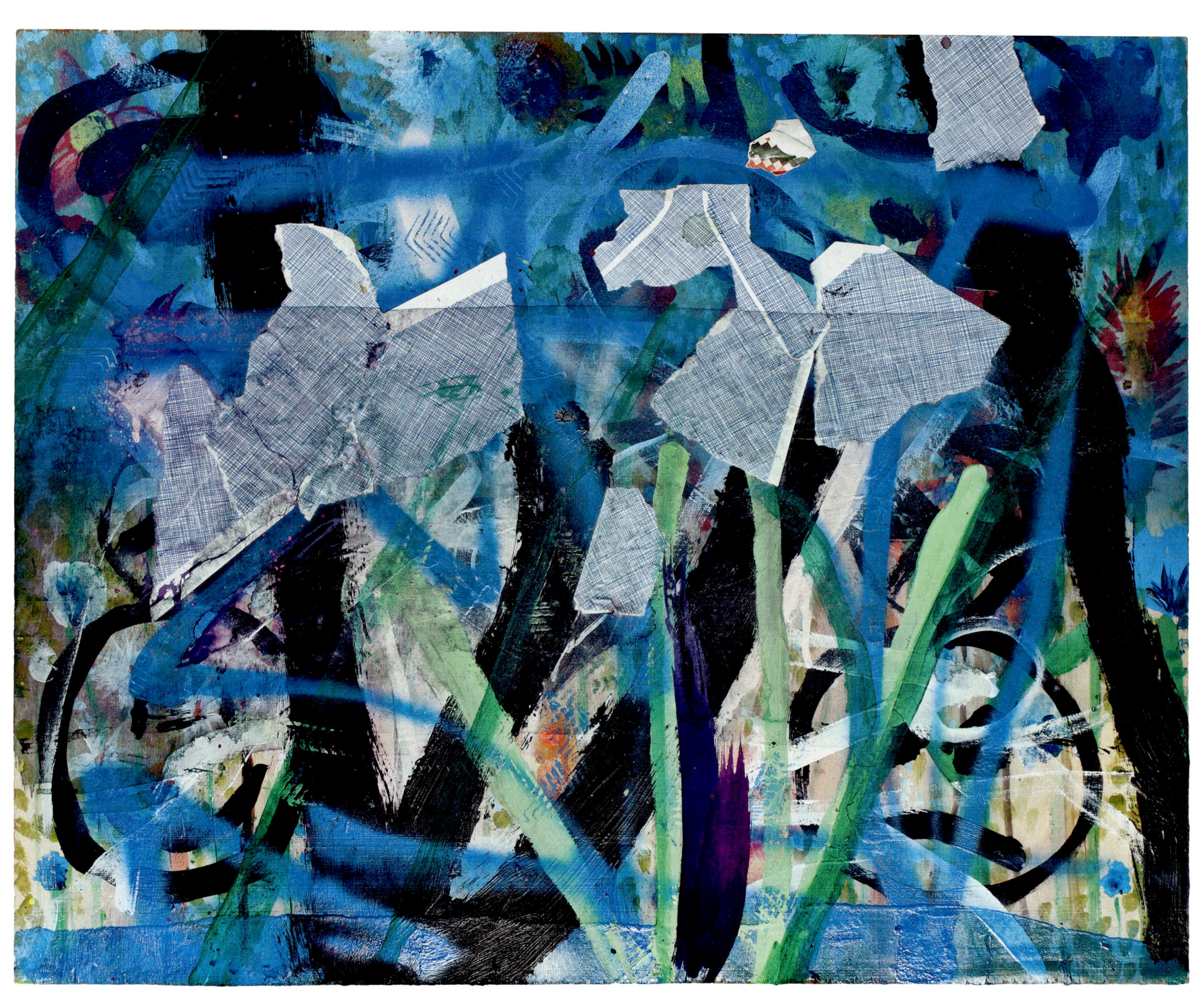

Flowers in Bloom, 2013

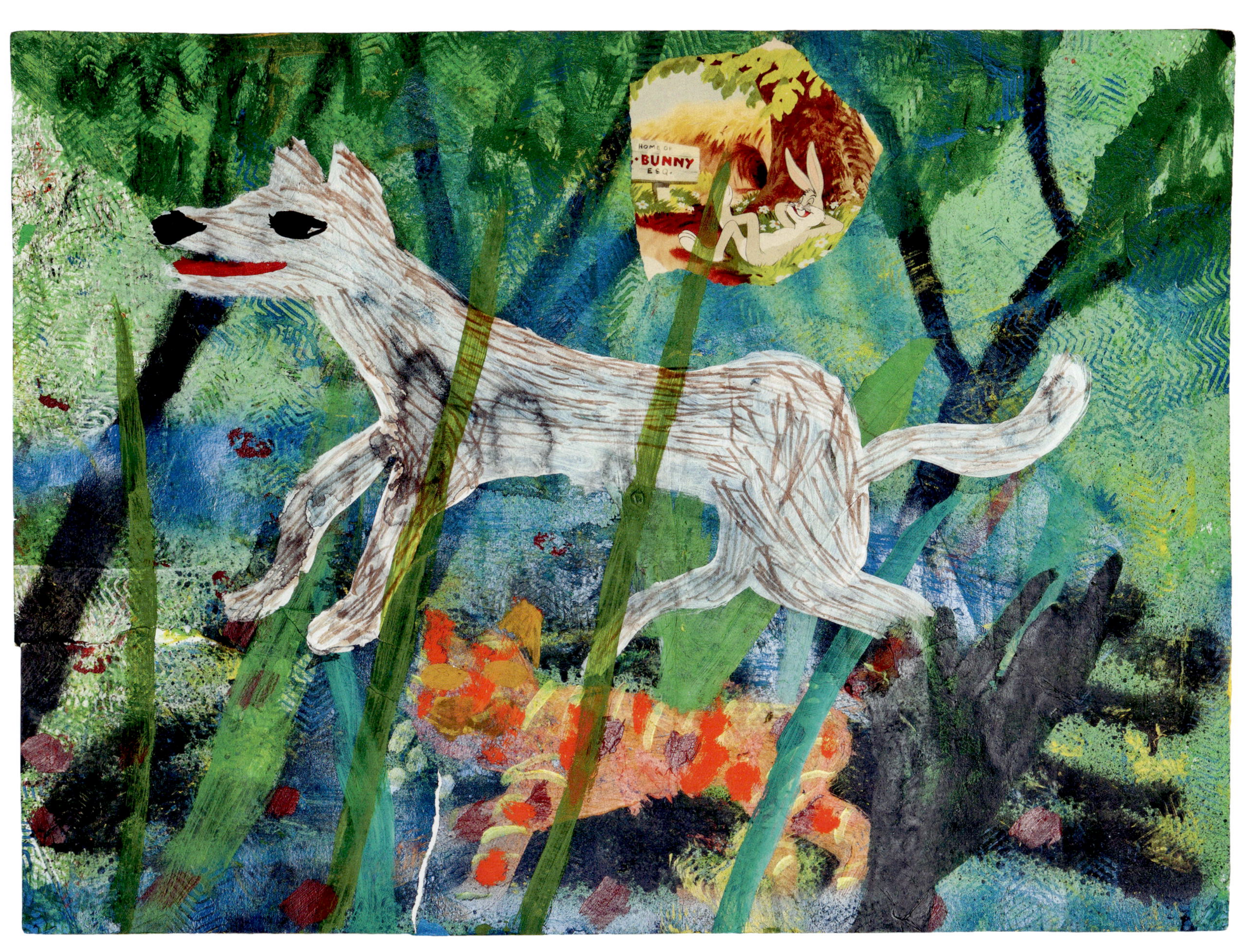

Woods, 2014

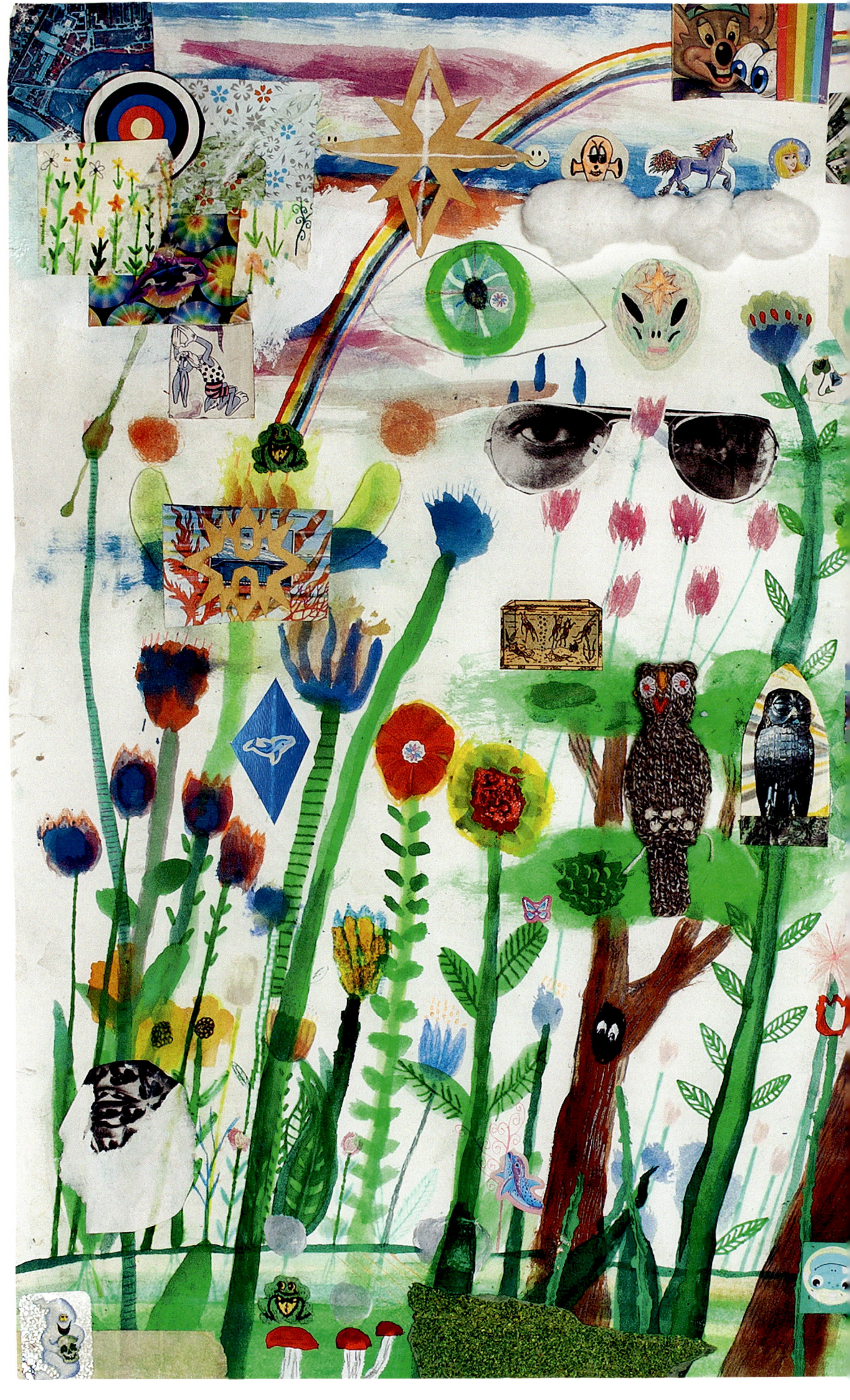

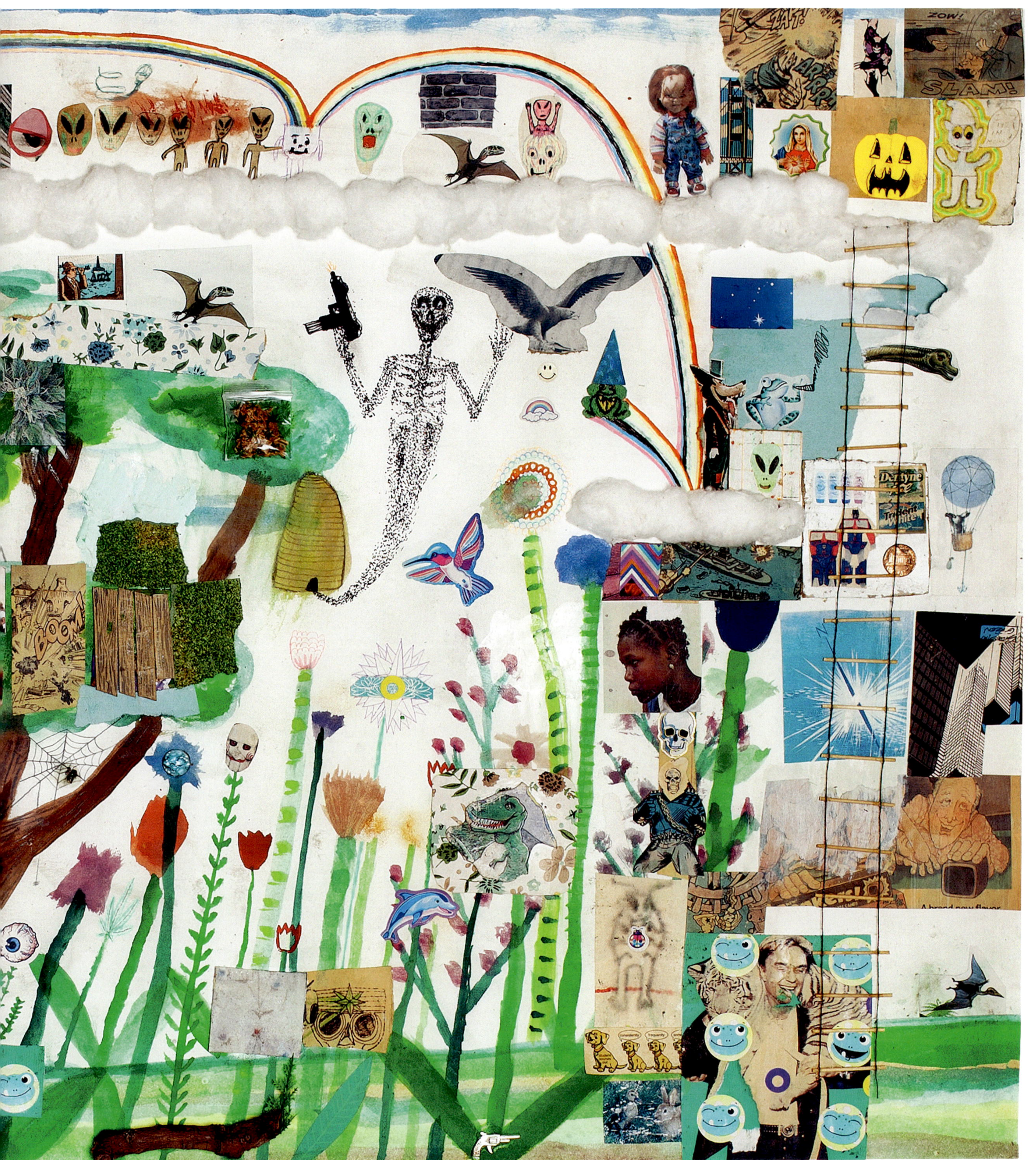

Hidden Jungle, 2009

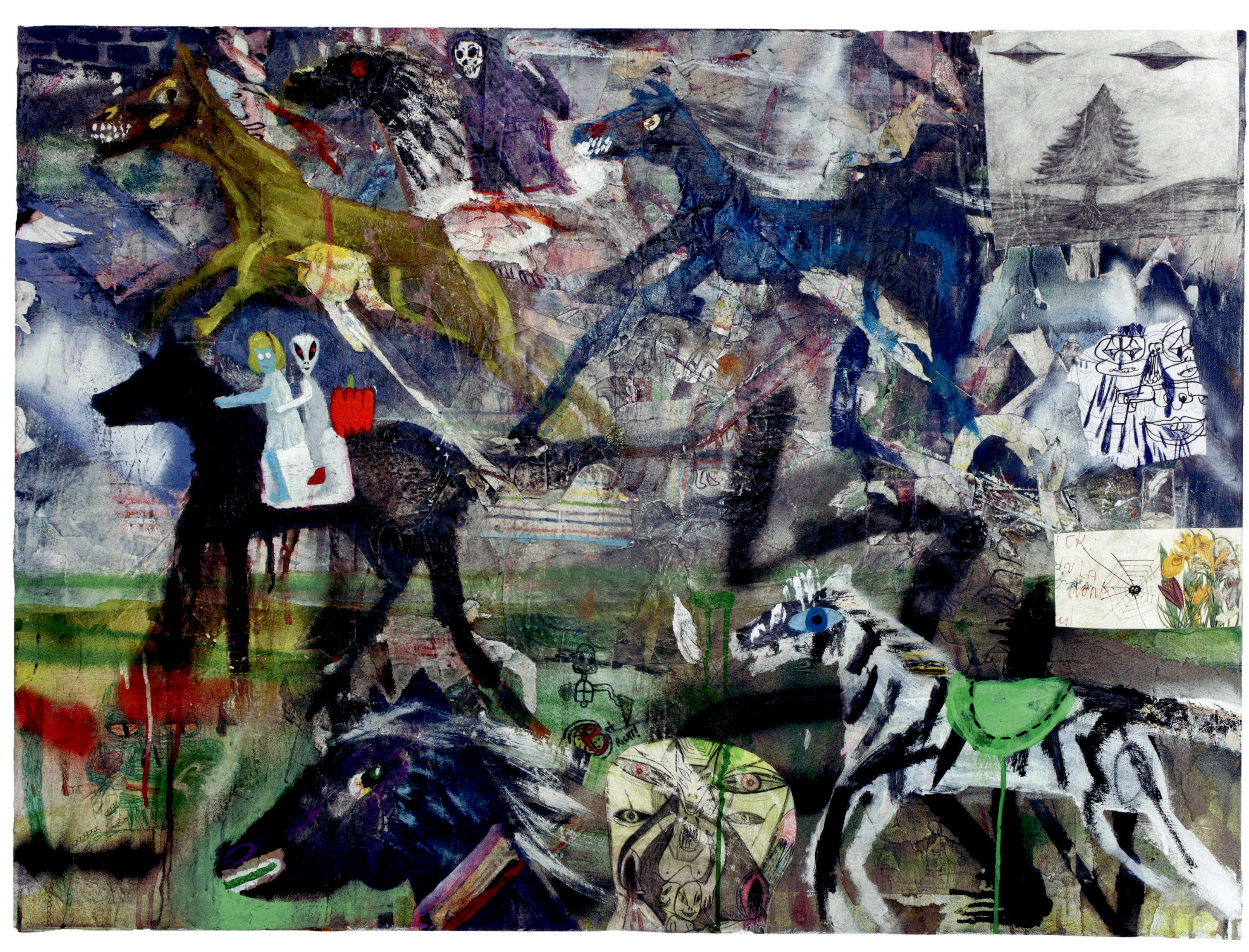

We Are All Friends, 2012

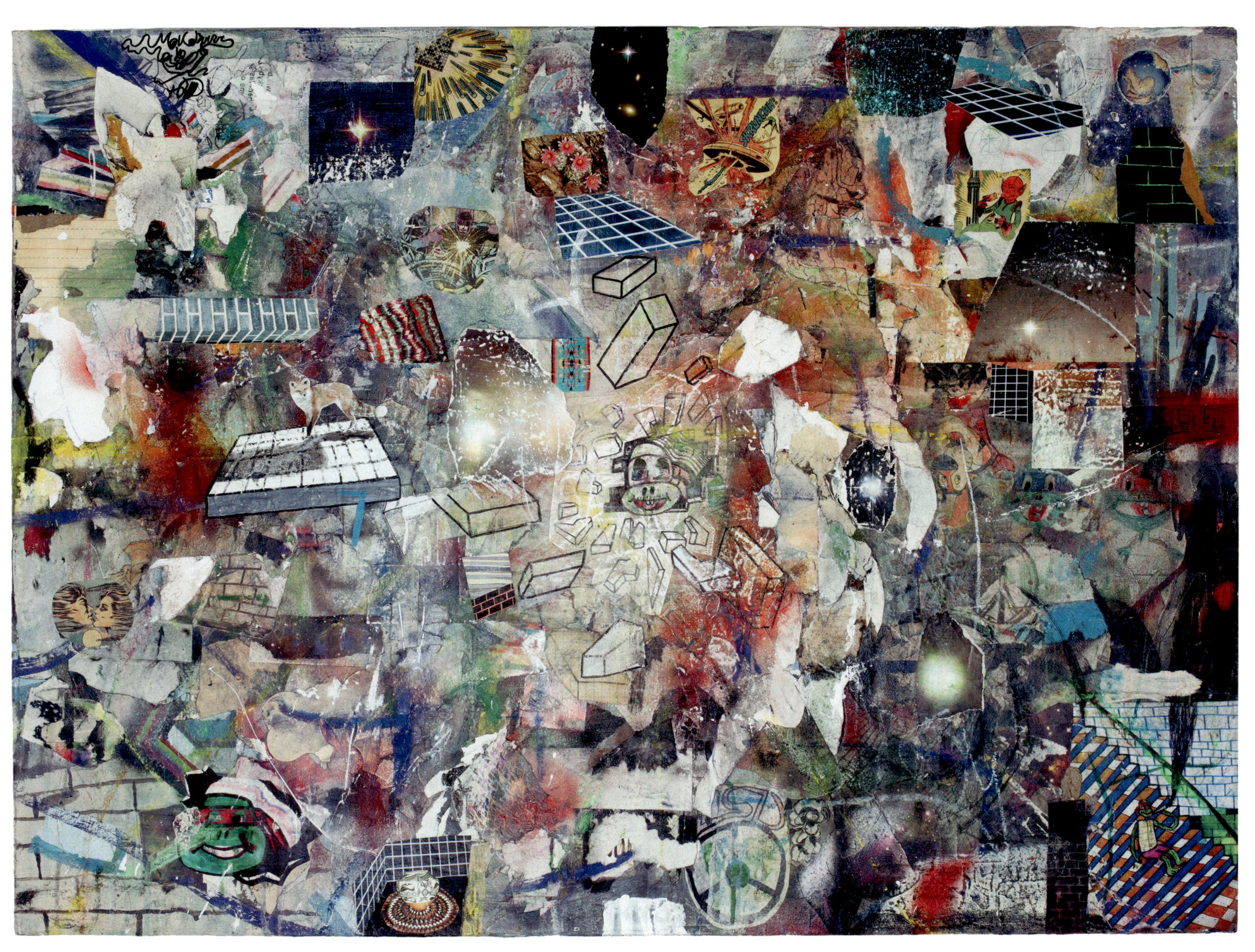

Have You Ever Seen a Portal?, 2012

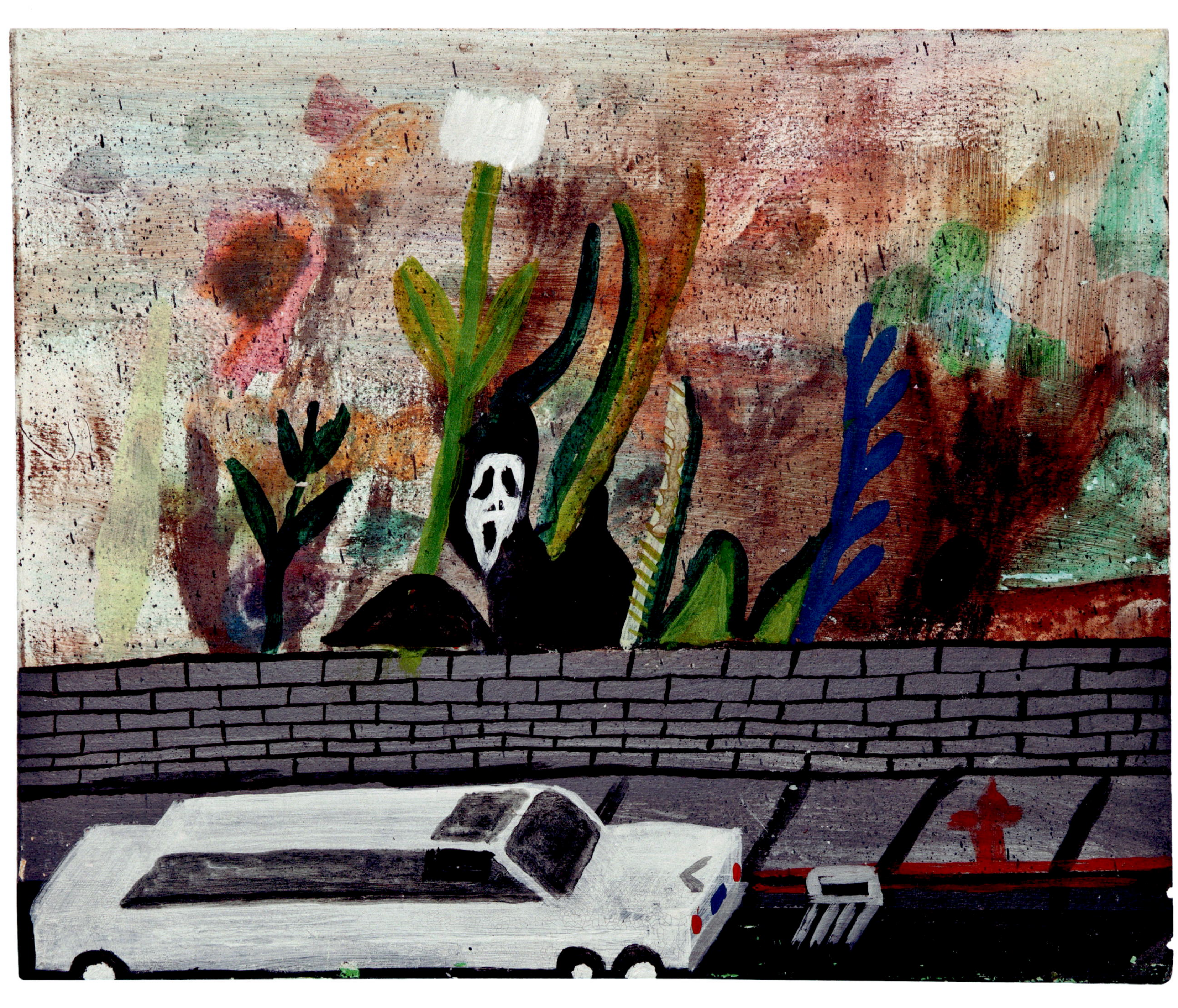

Simple Nightmare, 2013

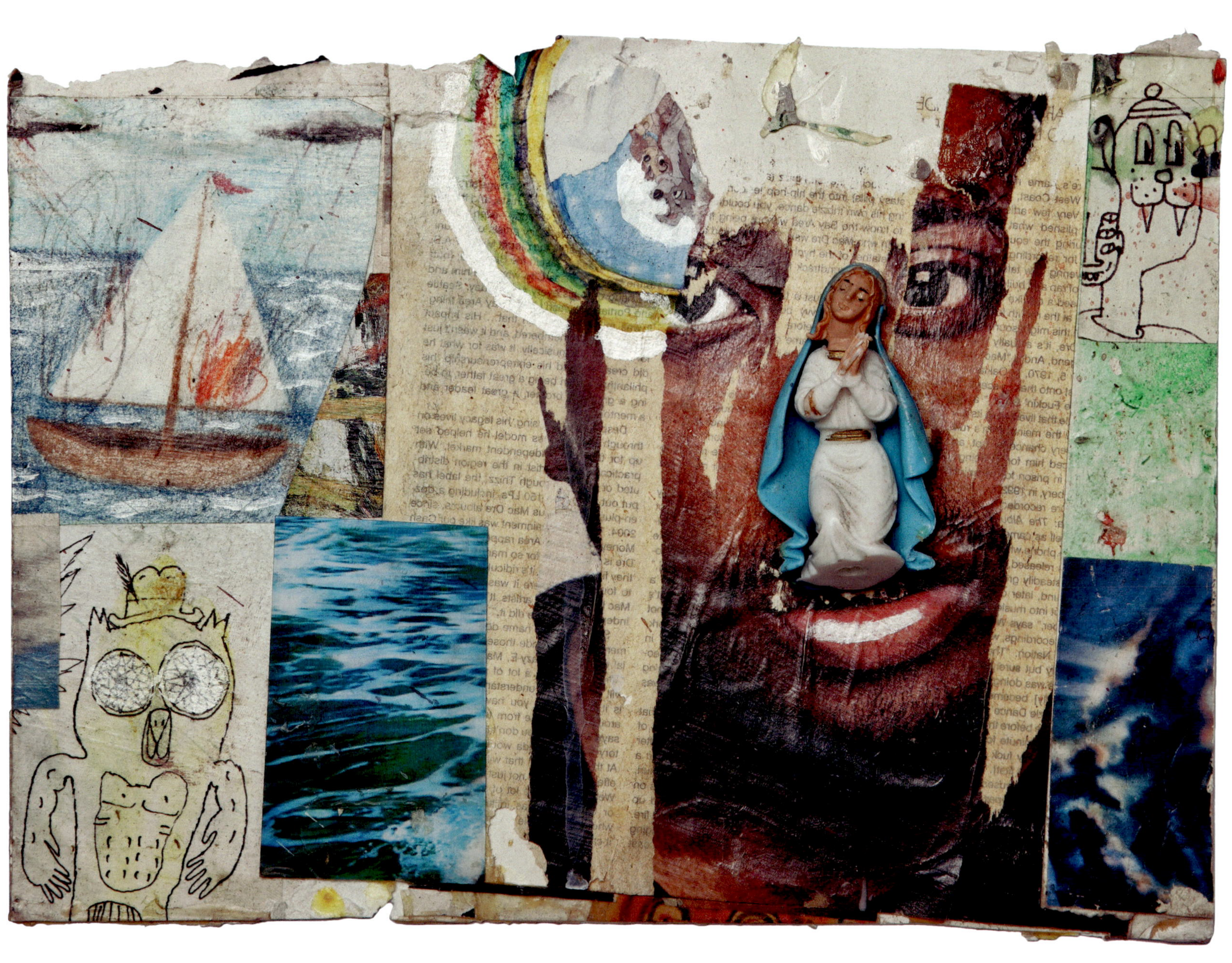

Sup Wit That God, 2012

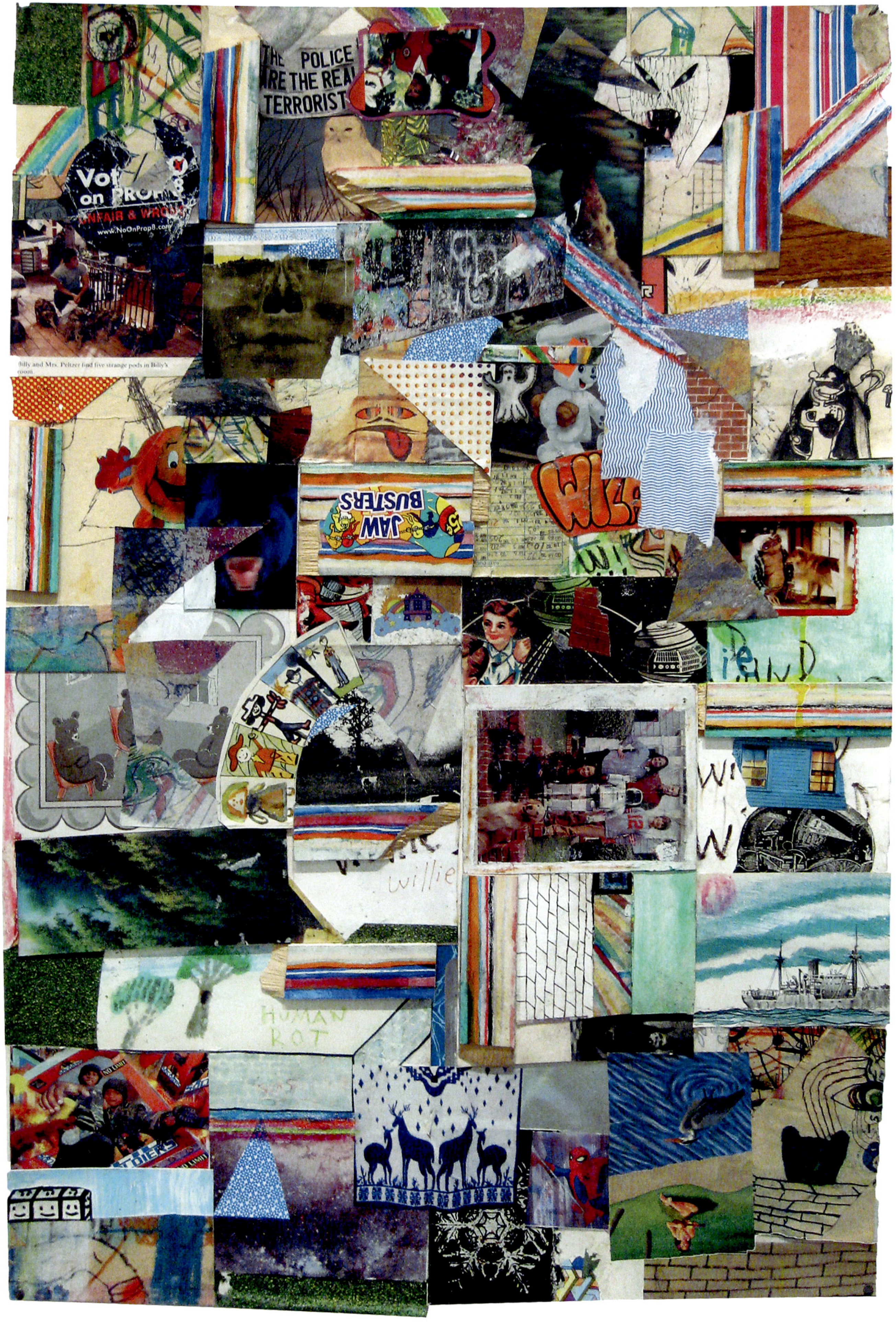

The Real Terrorist, 2010

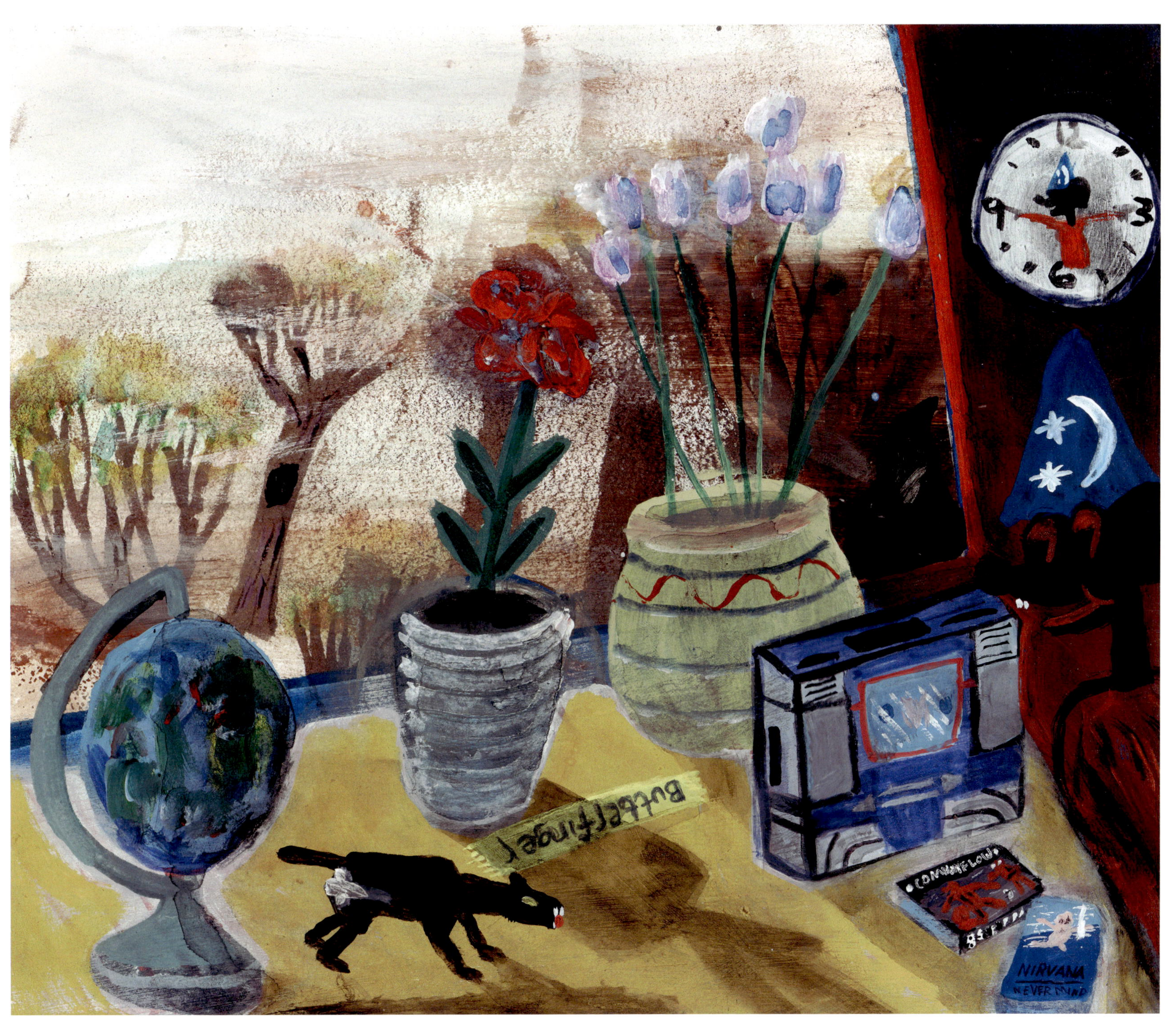

Sound Wave, 2014

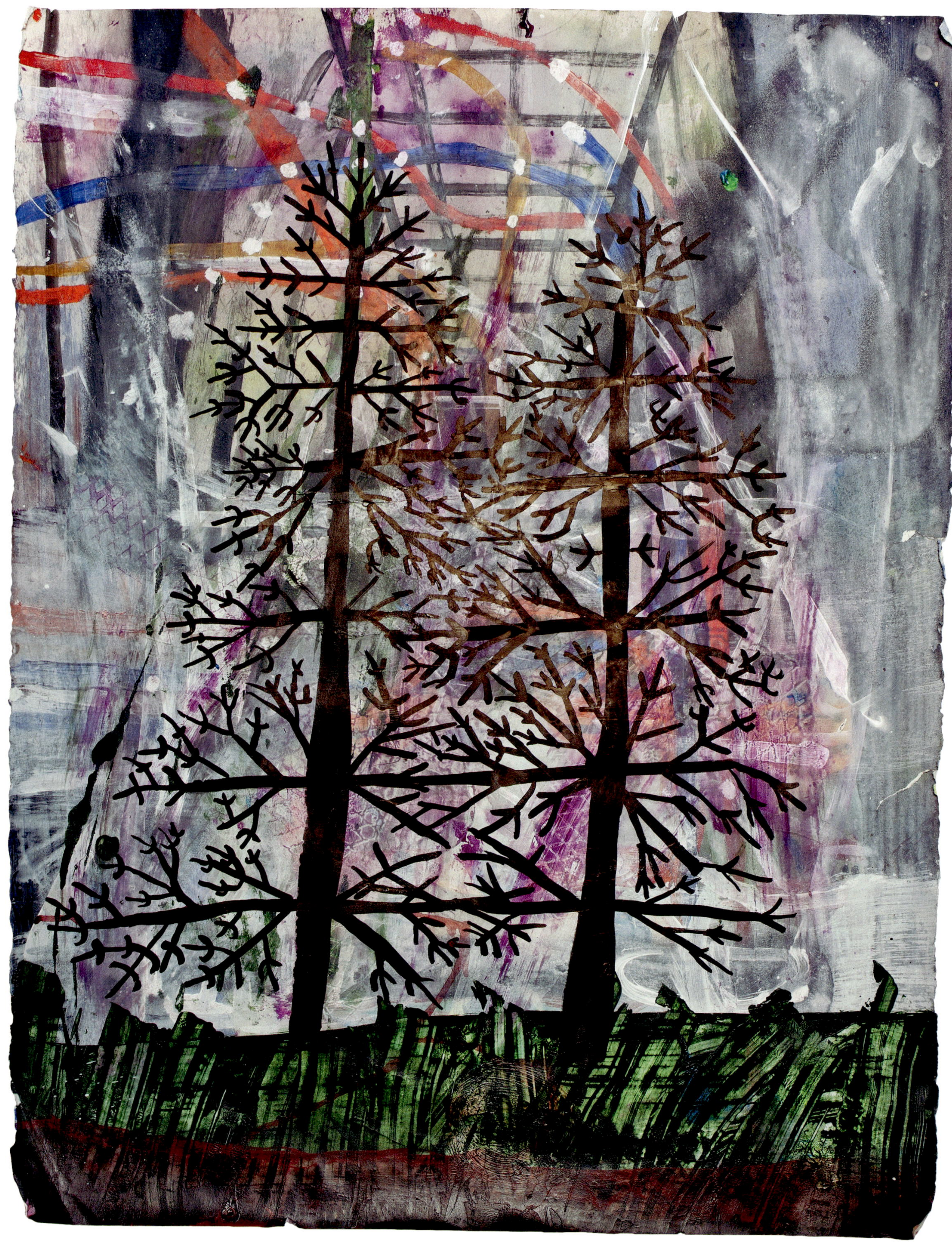

Two Trees, 2014

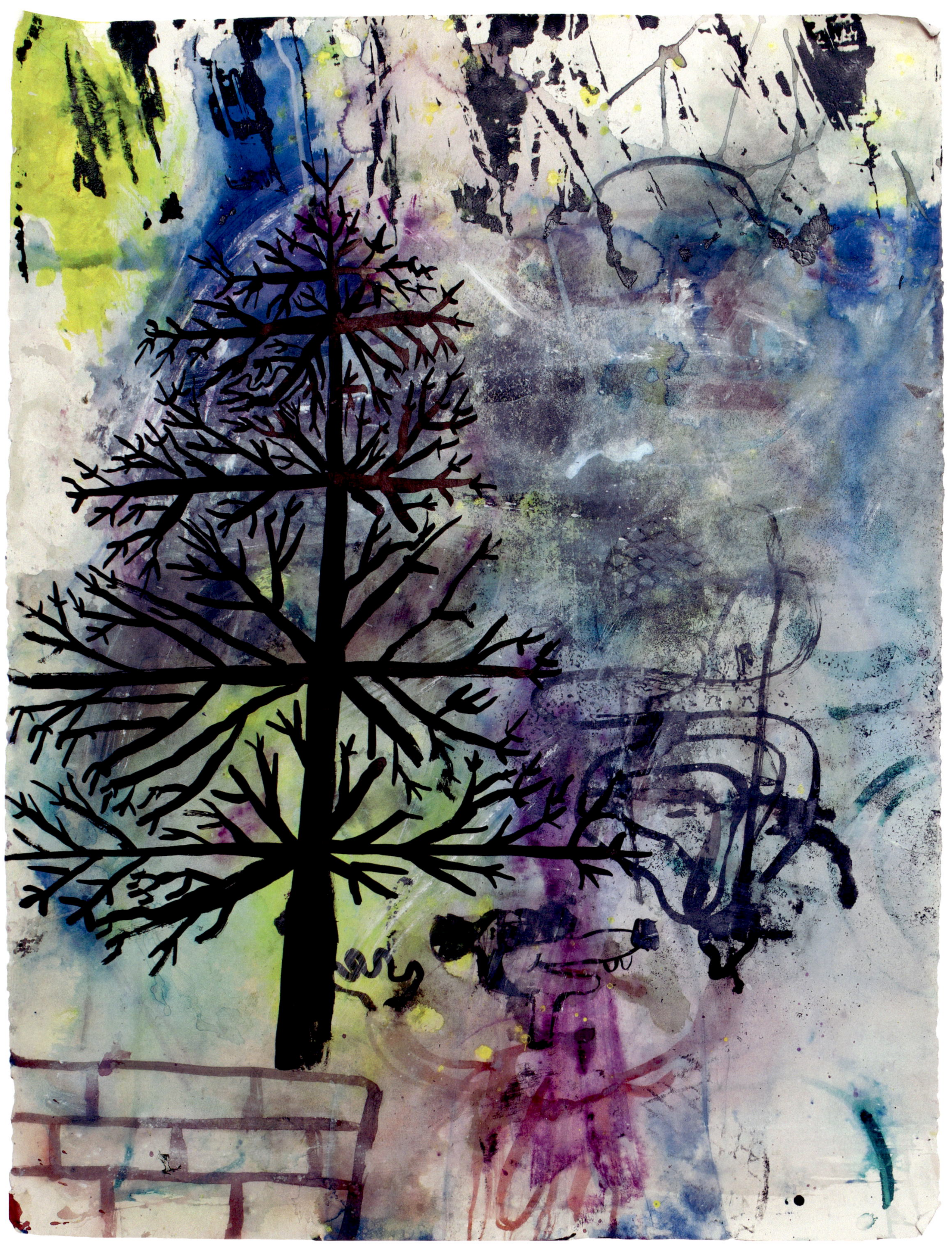

The Natural Order, 2014

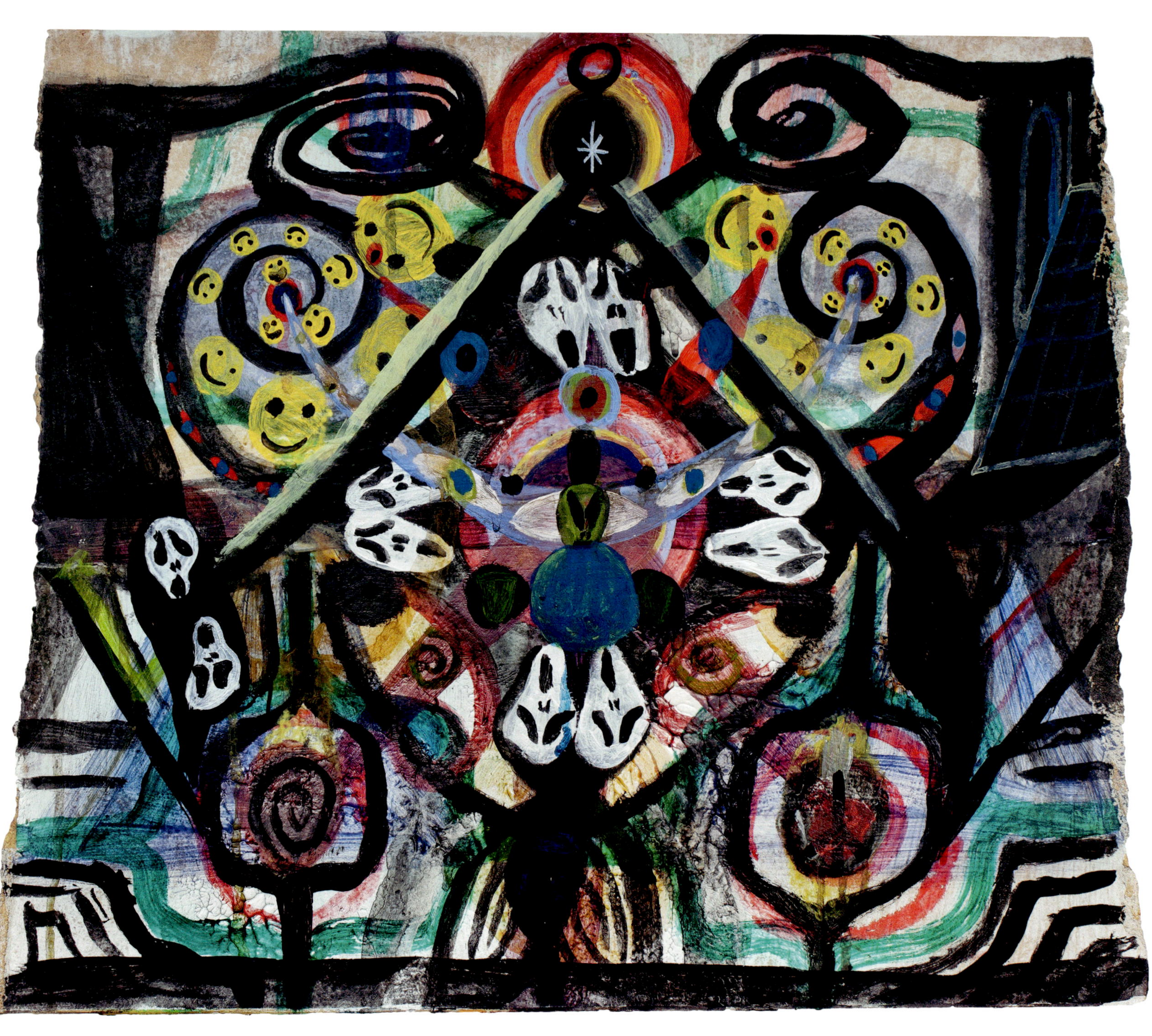

Deep Magic Time 2, 2014

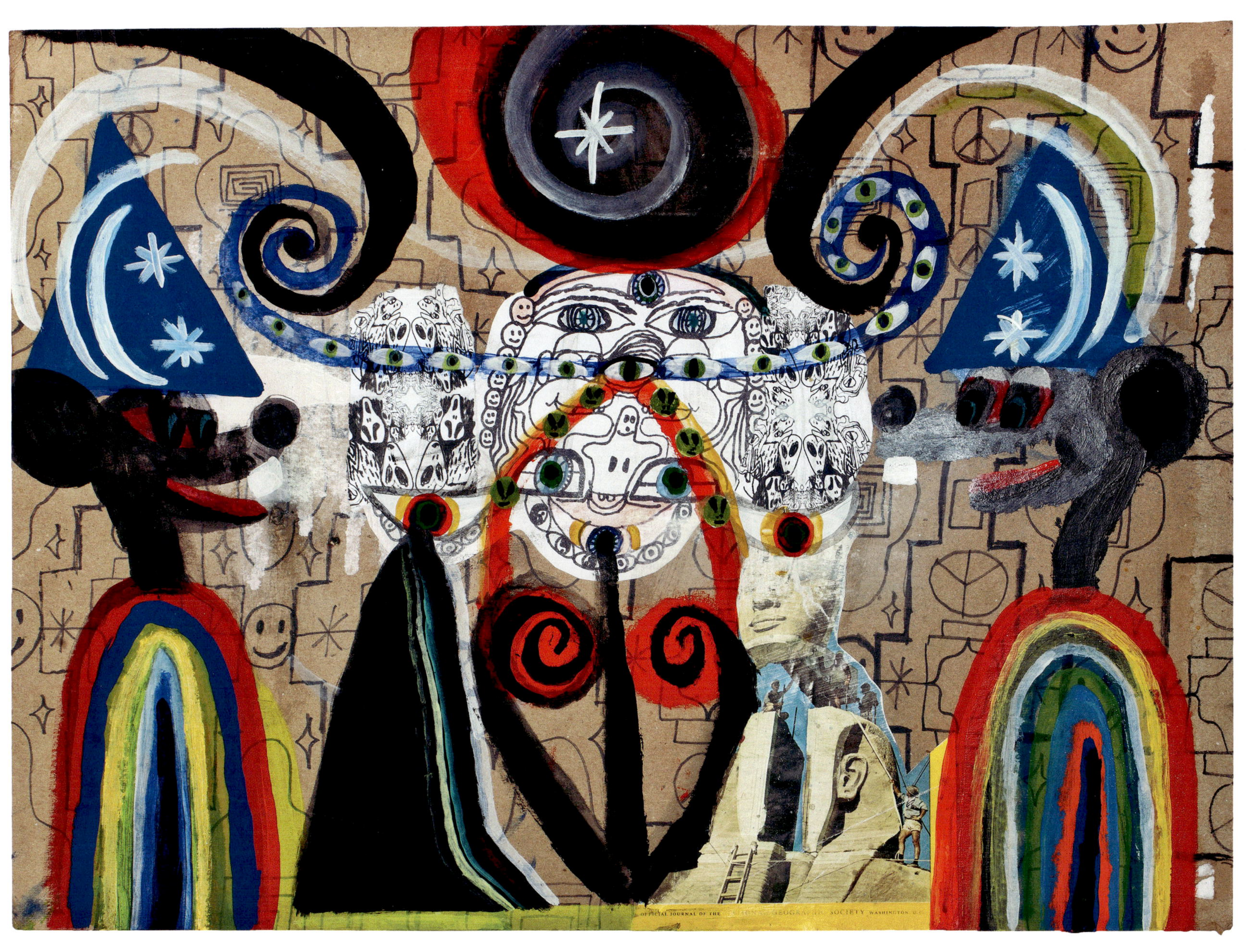

Deep Magic Time, 2014

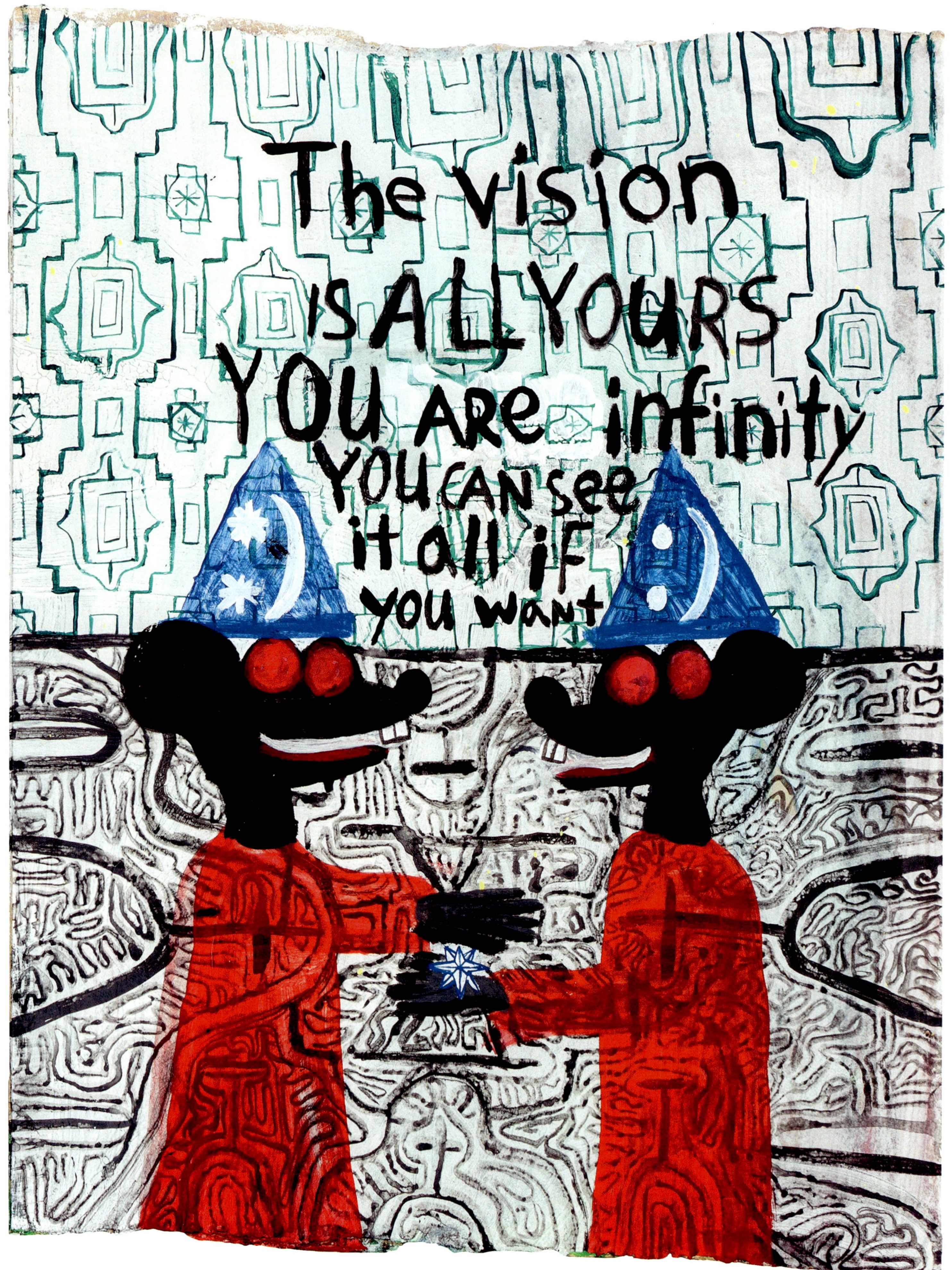

Vision Quest 2, 2014

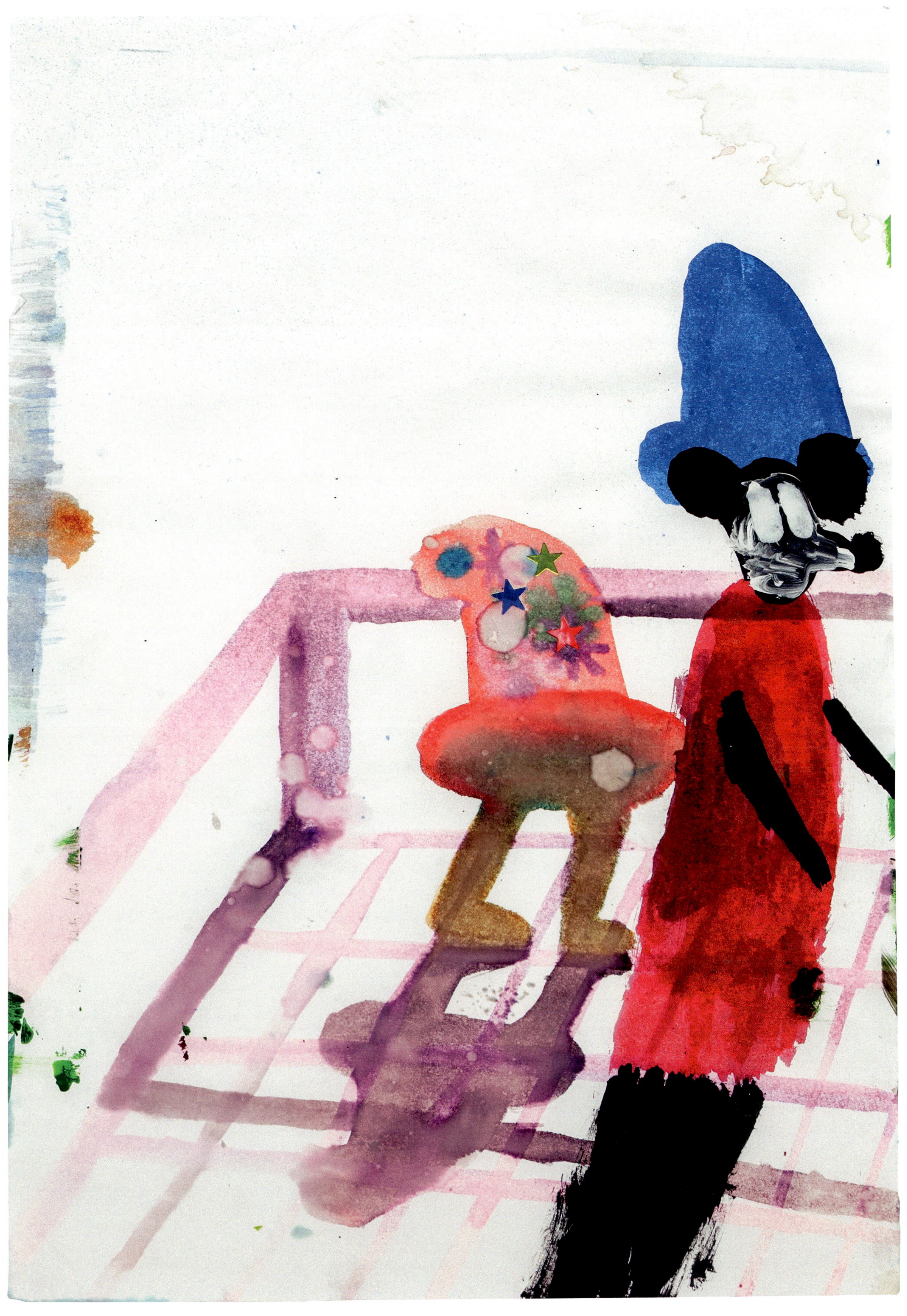

False Profits 2, 2012

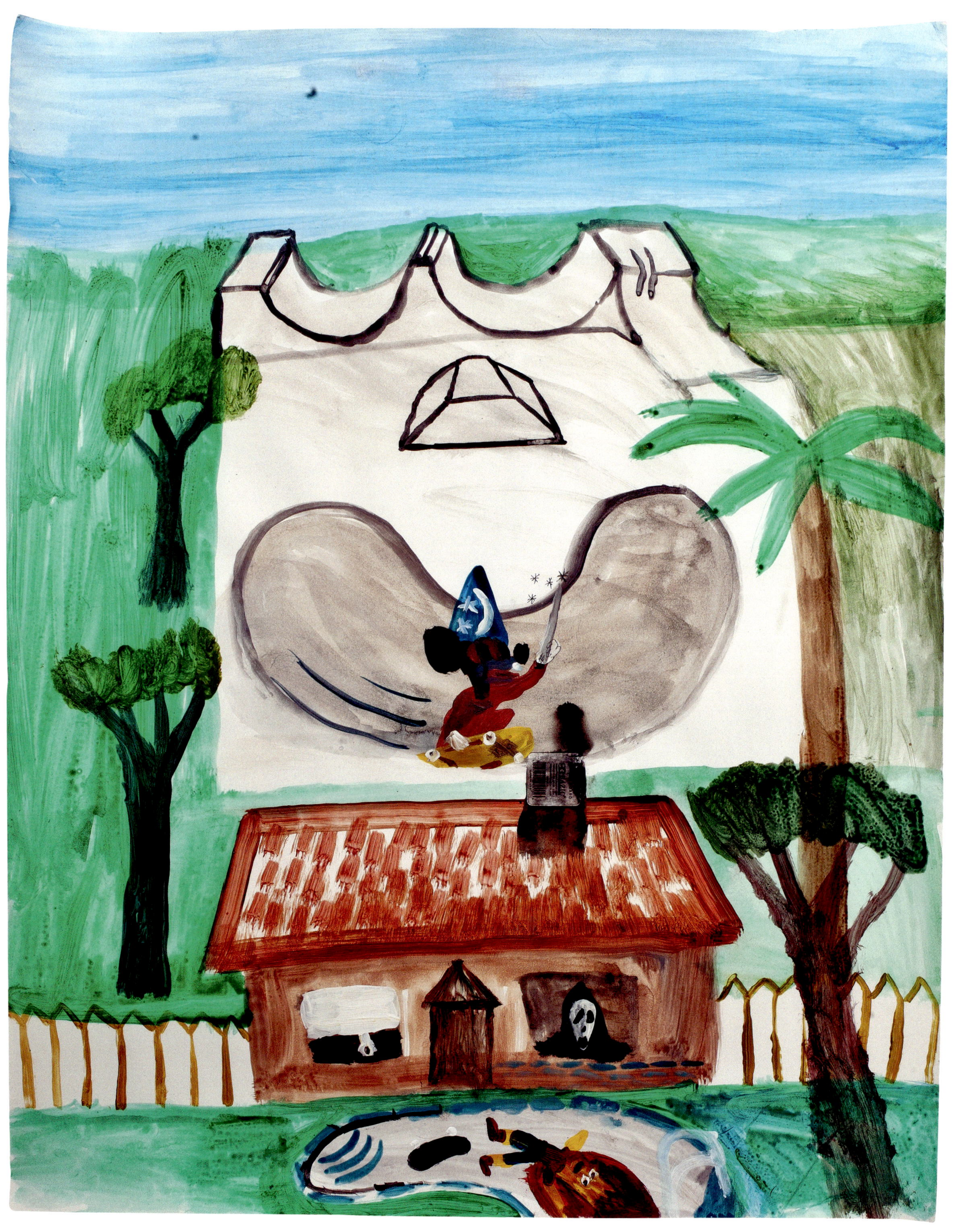

Skatepark, 2014

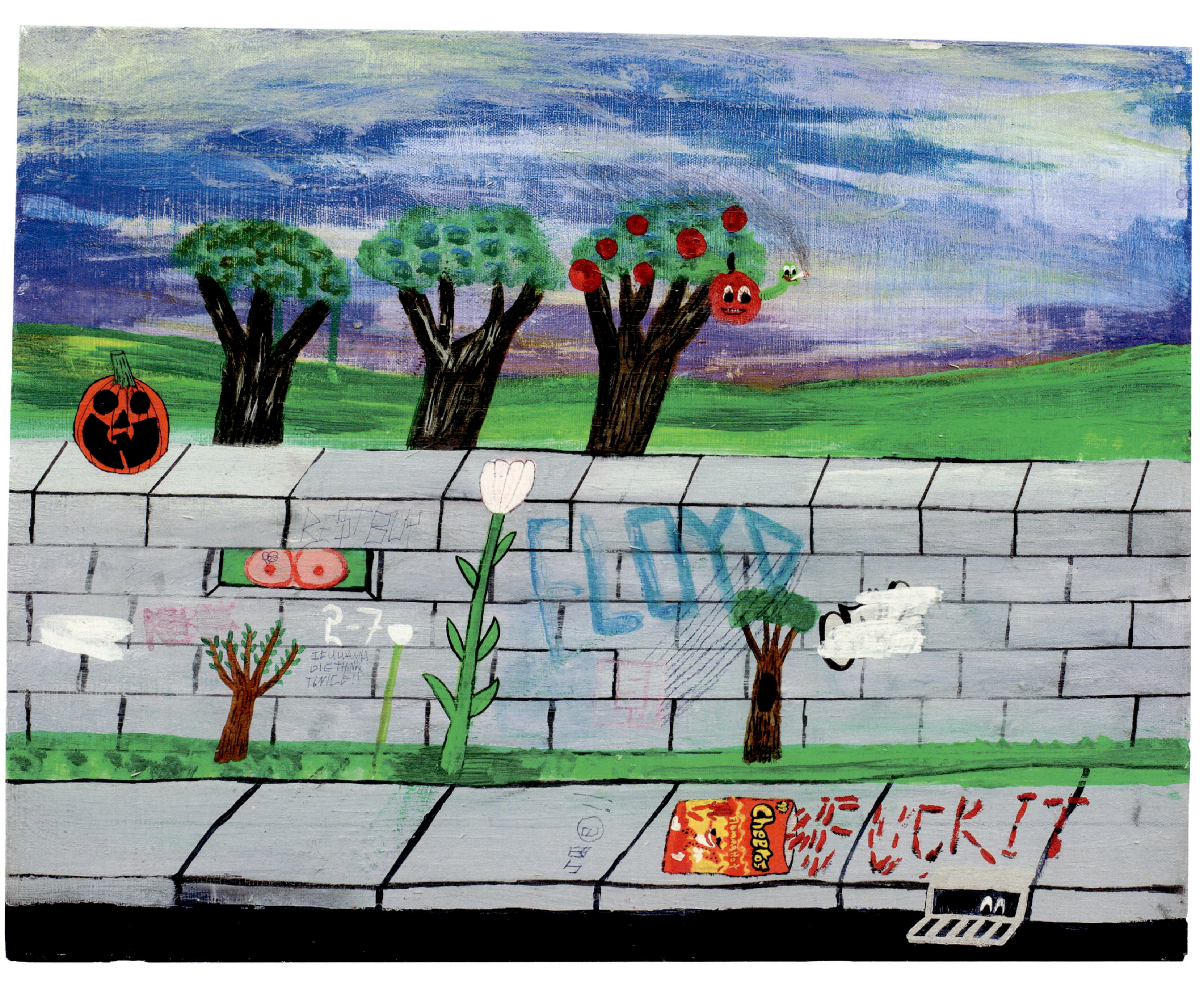

The Walk Home, 2009

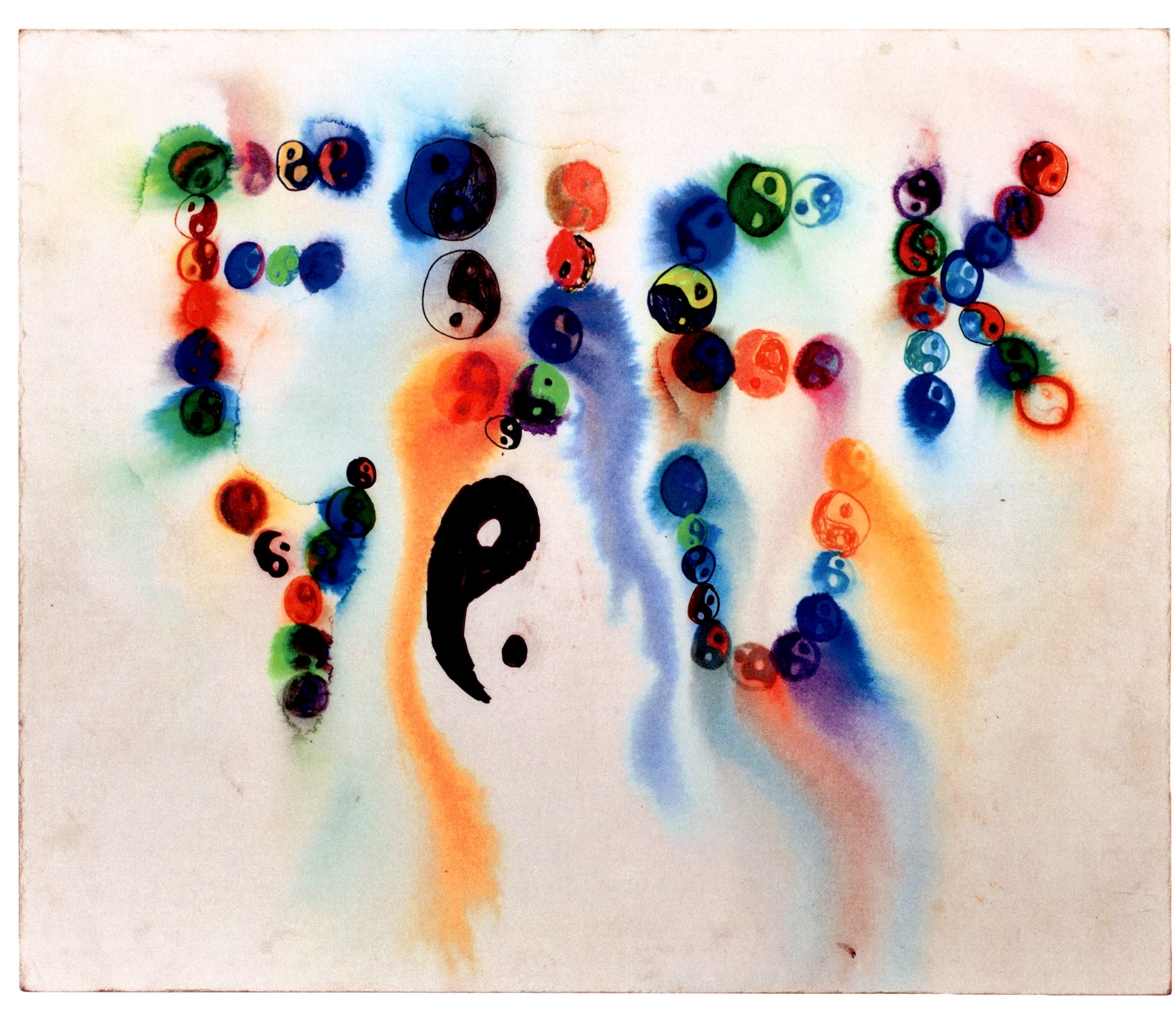

My Acid Trip at Spencer Gifts, 2010

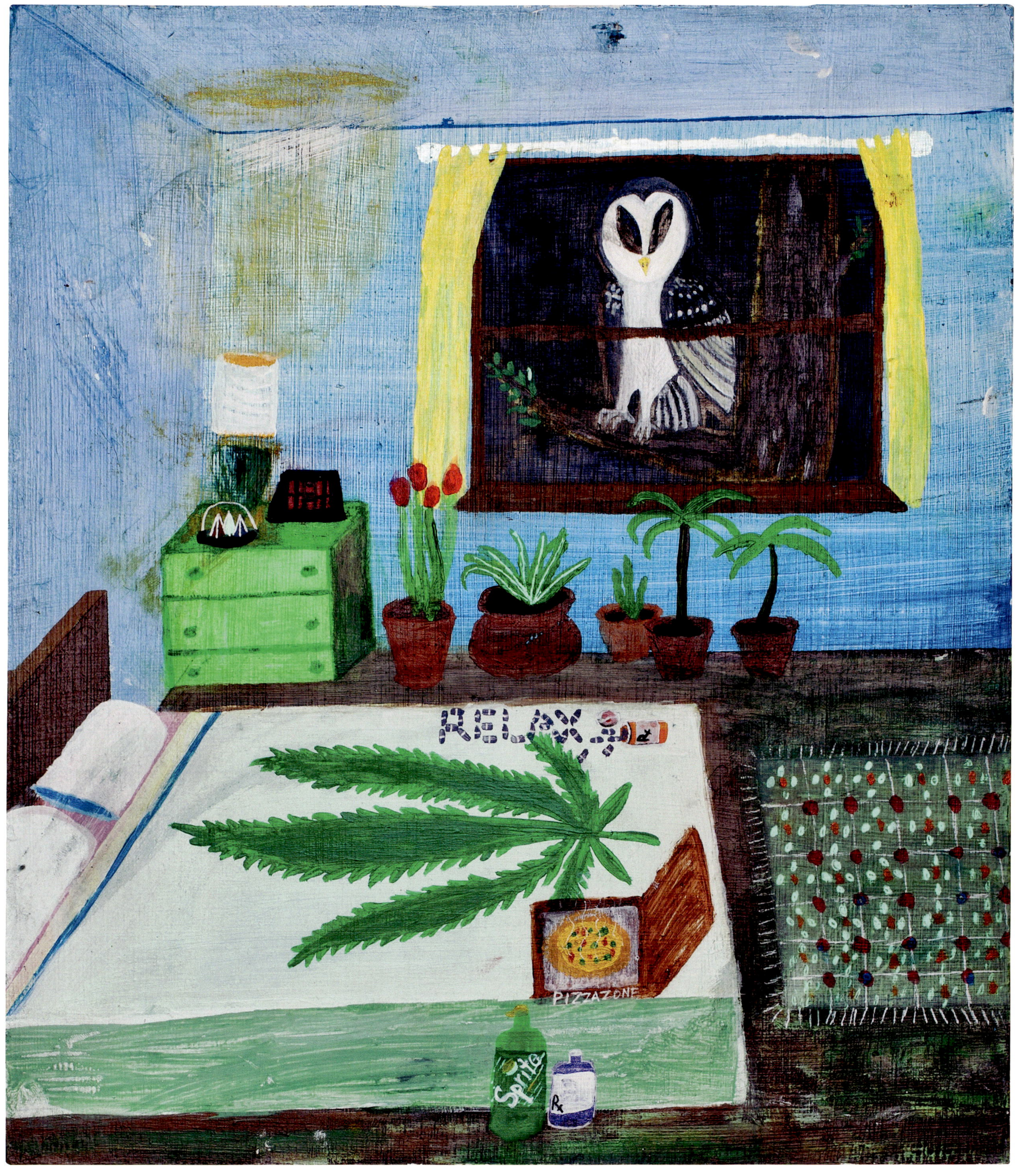

Relax, 2010

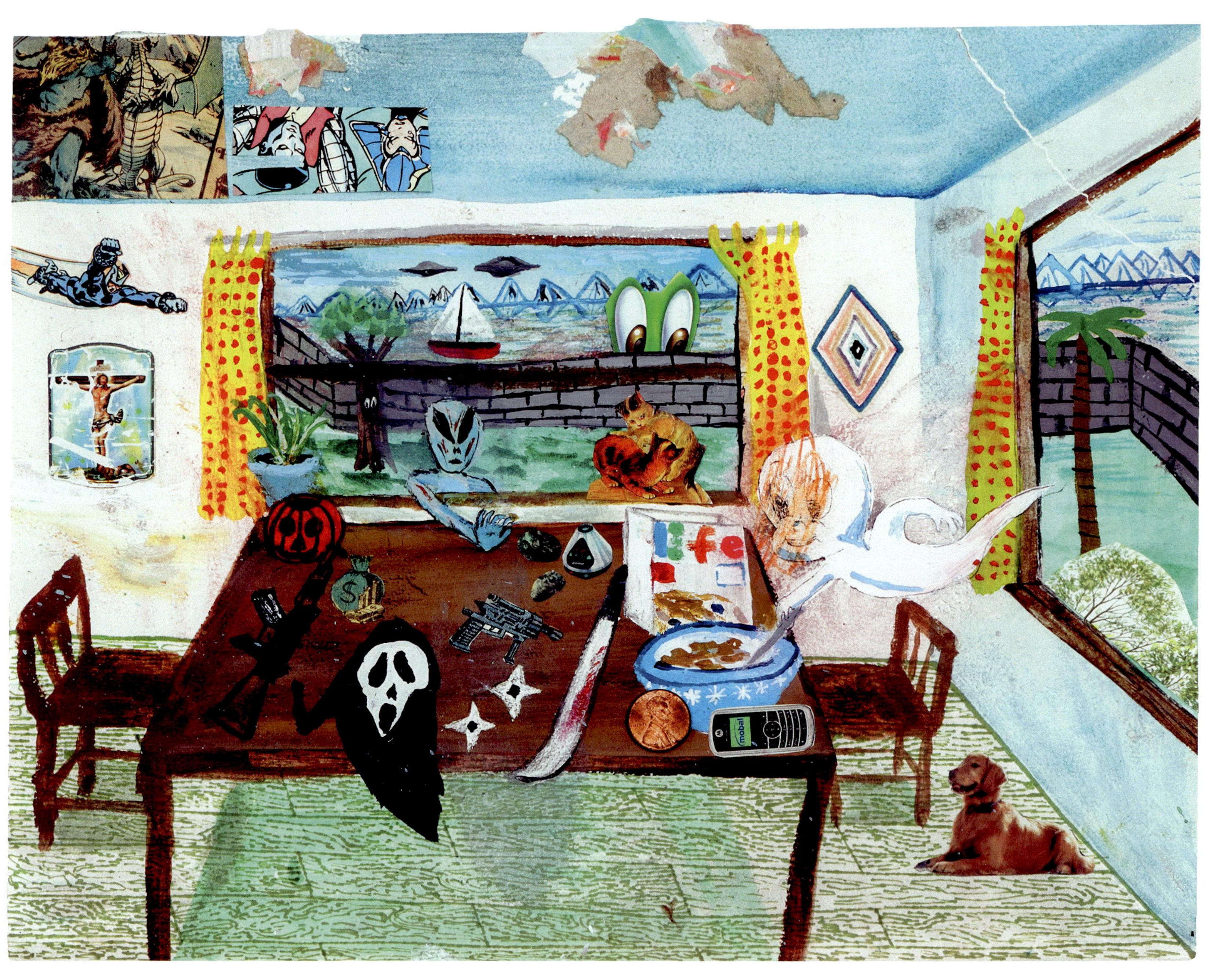

Still Life 1, 2010

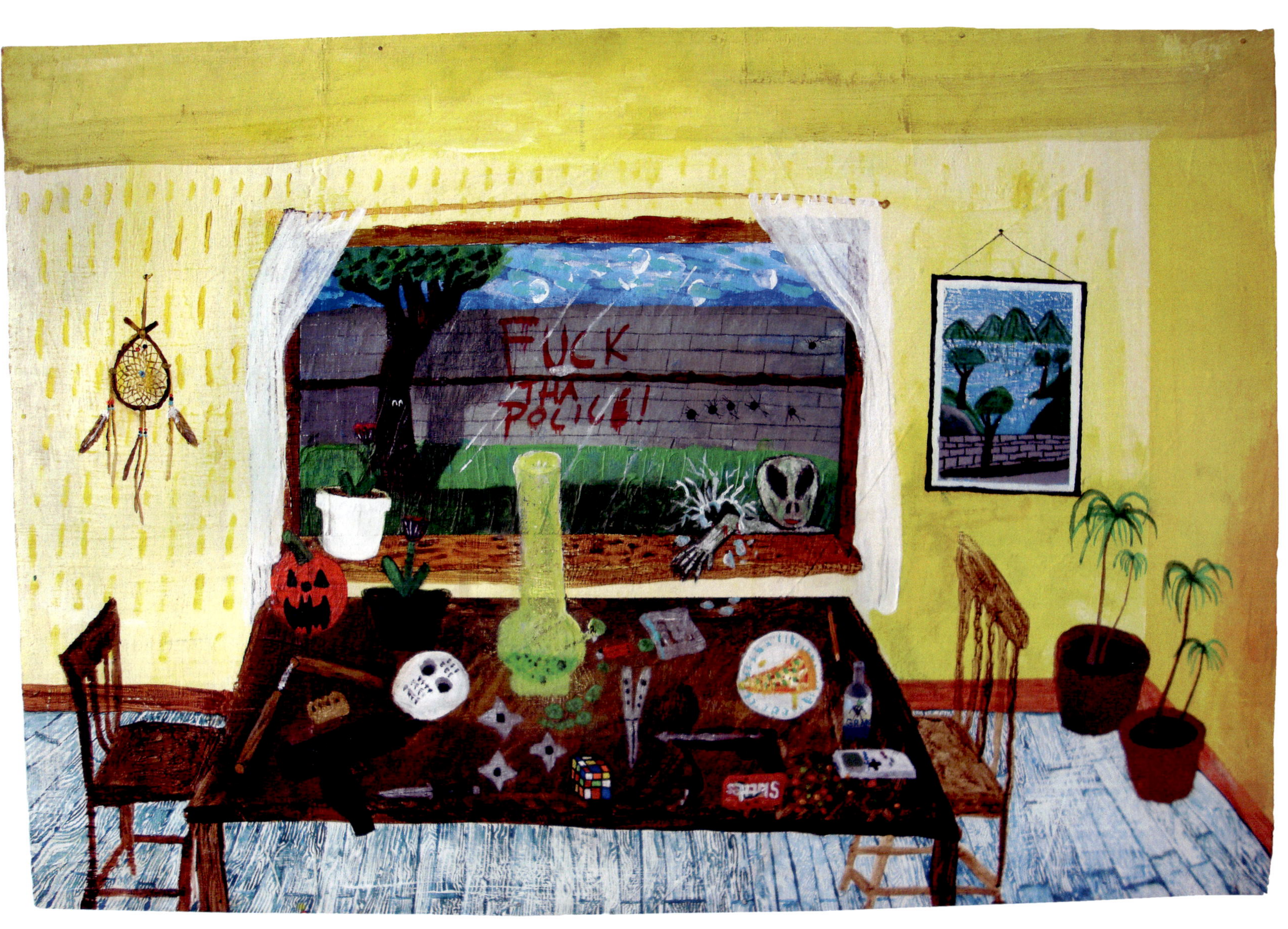

Staba's House, 2009

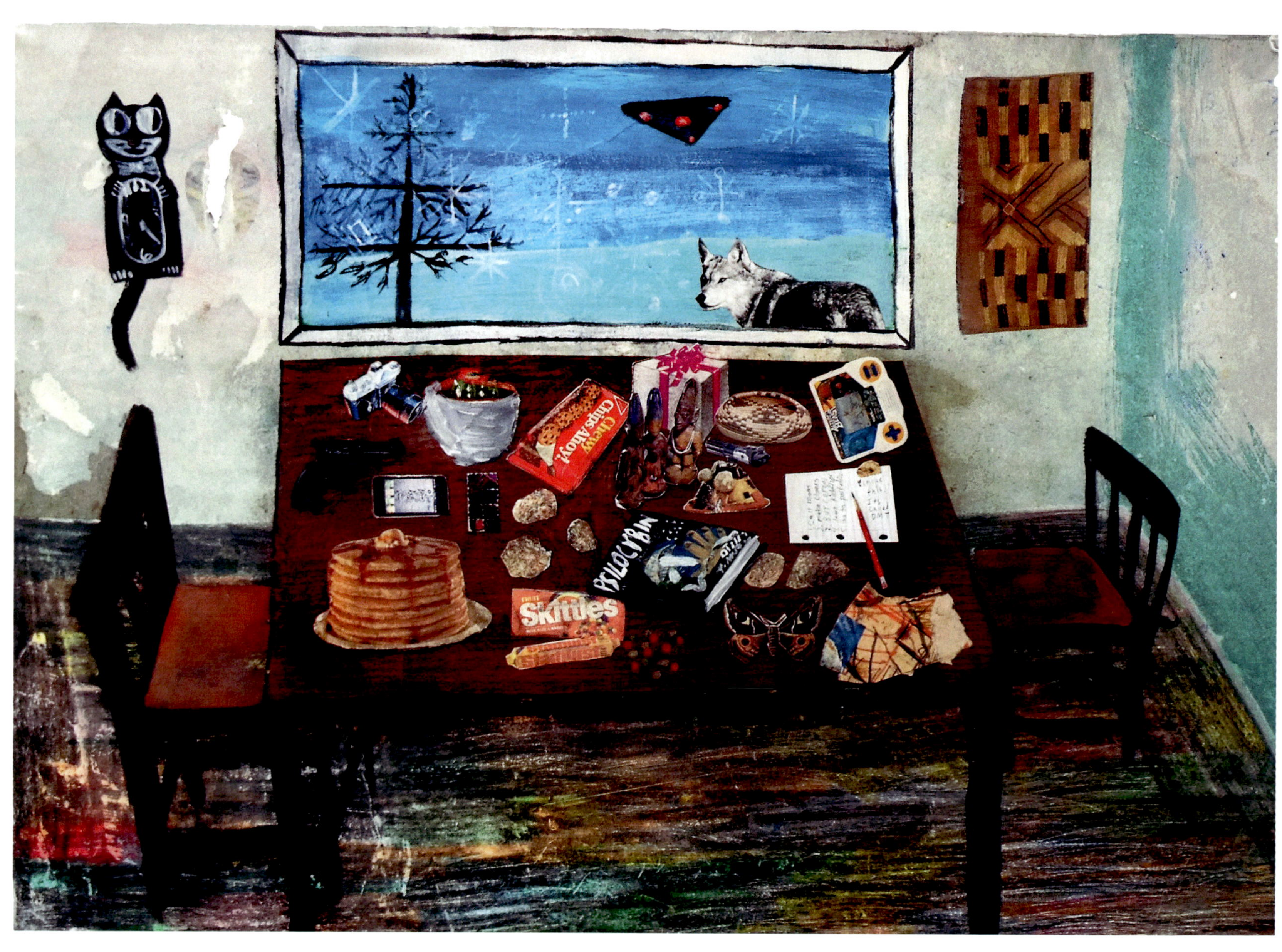

Still Life 2, 2012

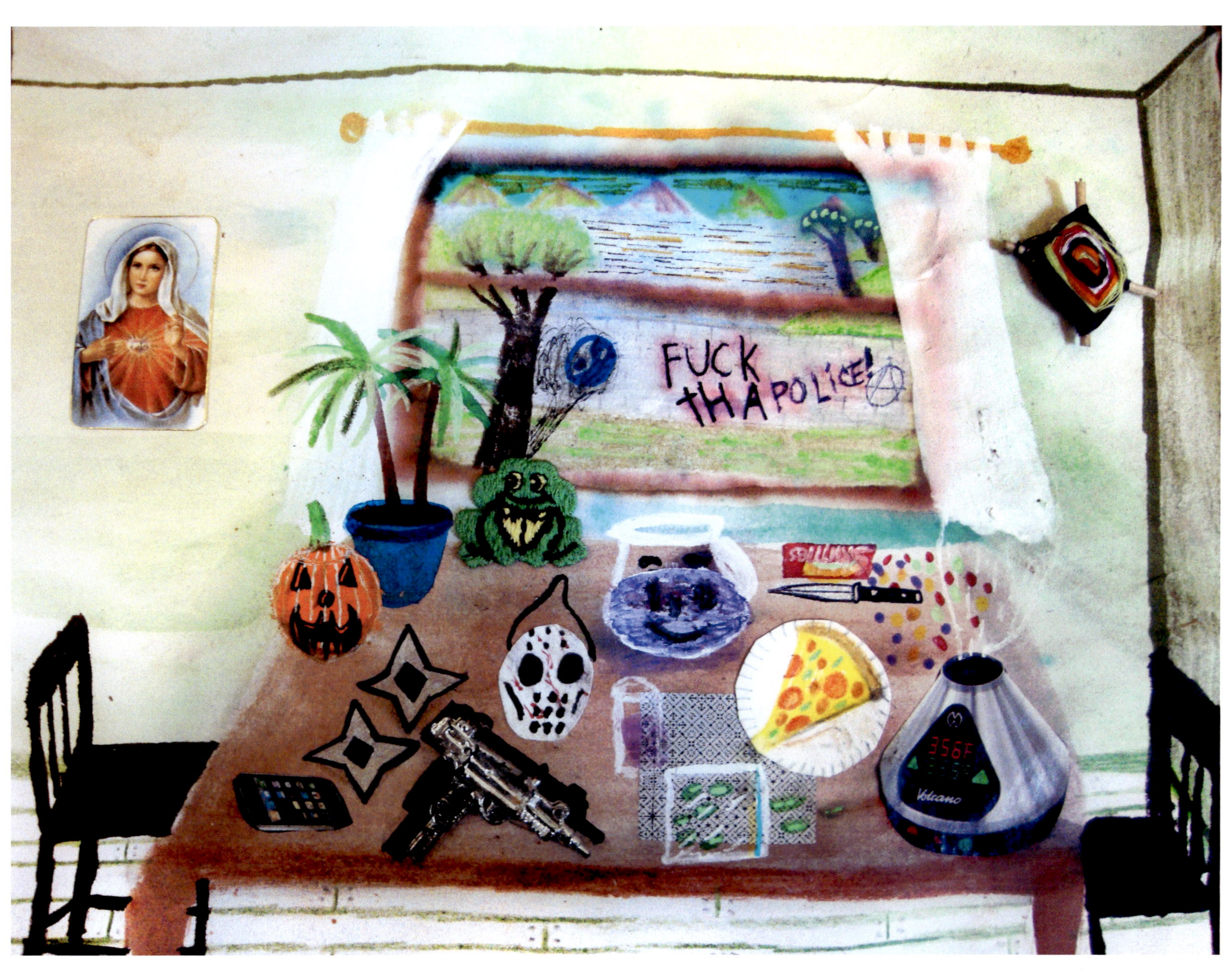

Still Life 3, 2009

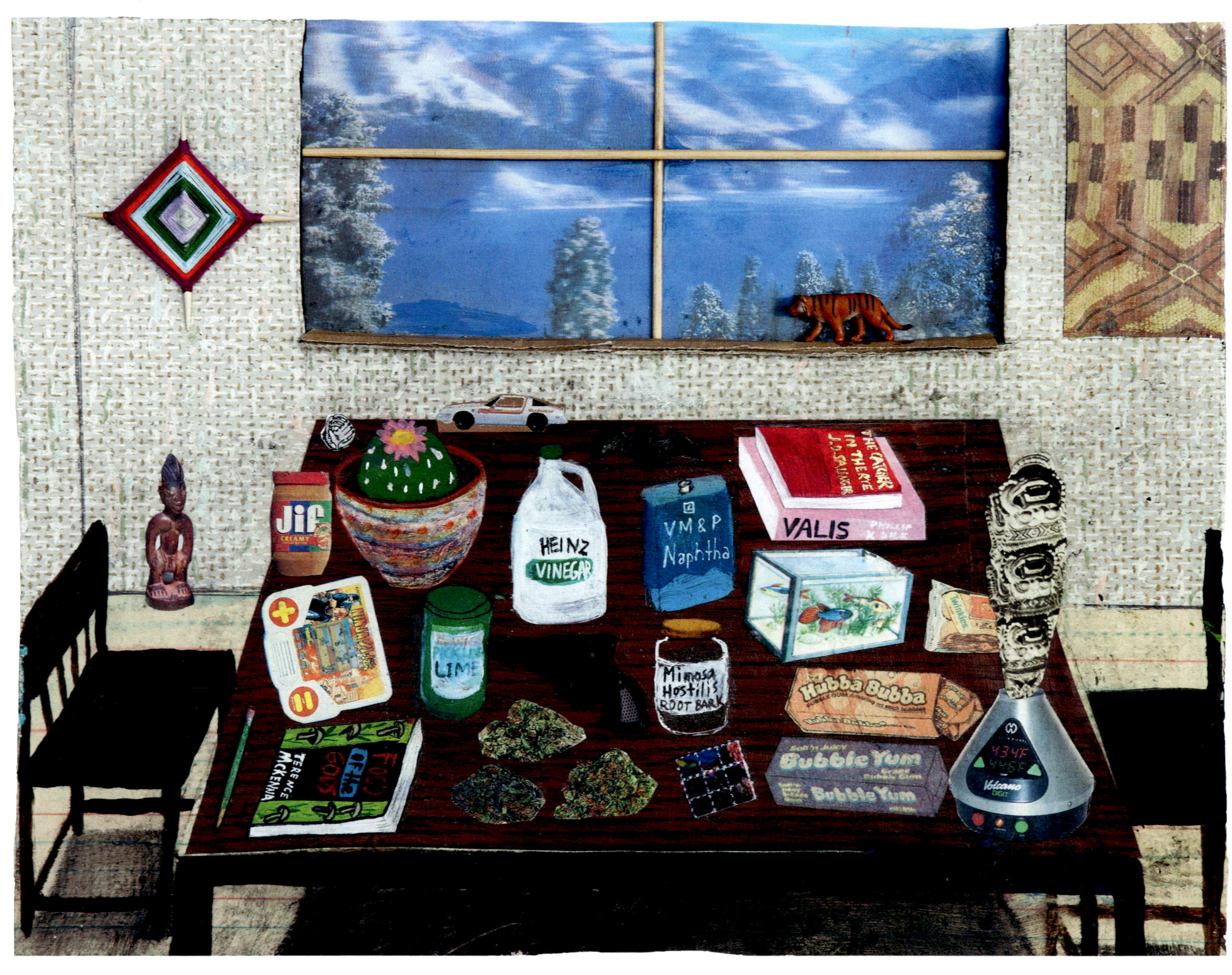

Still Life 7, 2014

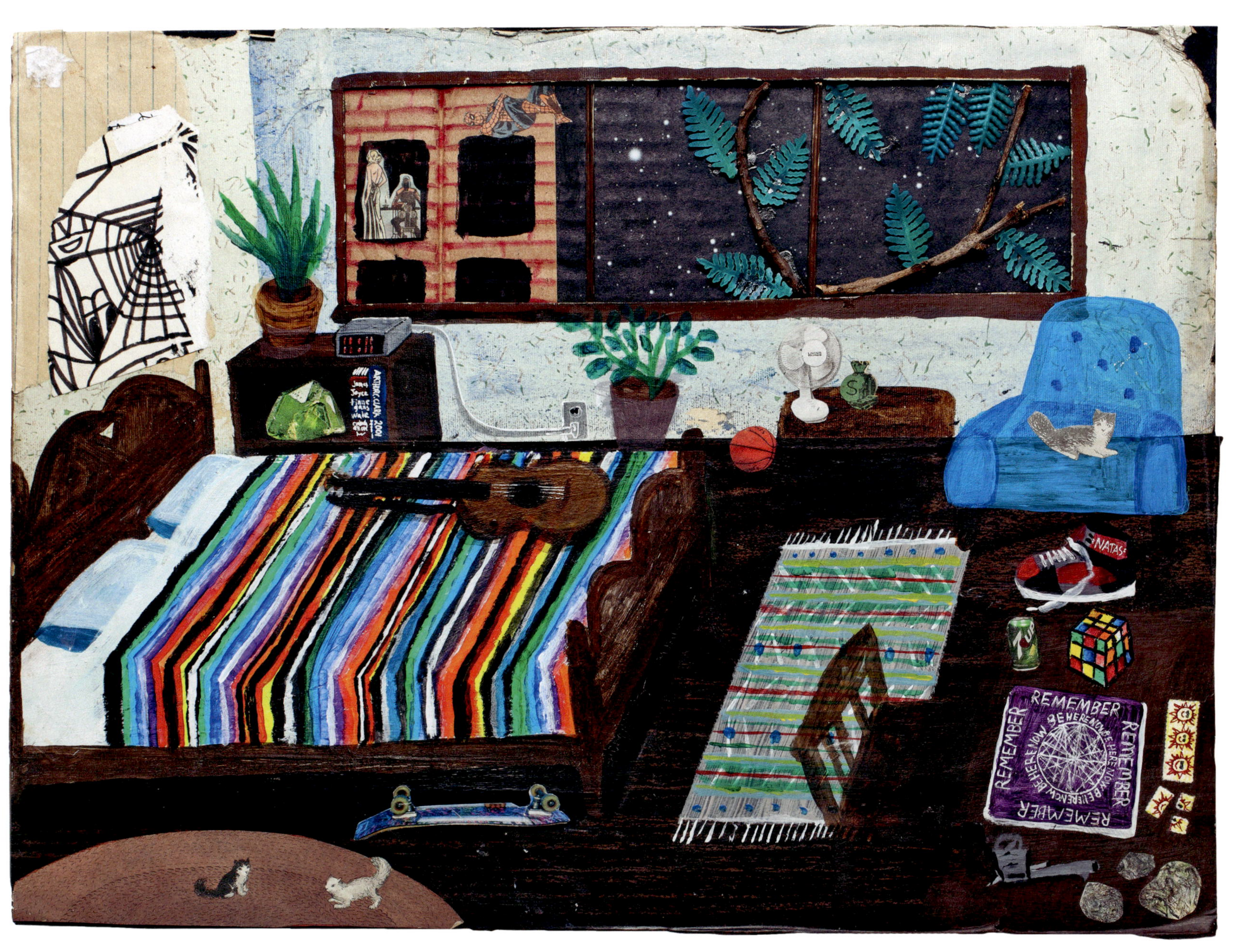

Bedroom, 2014

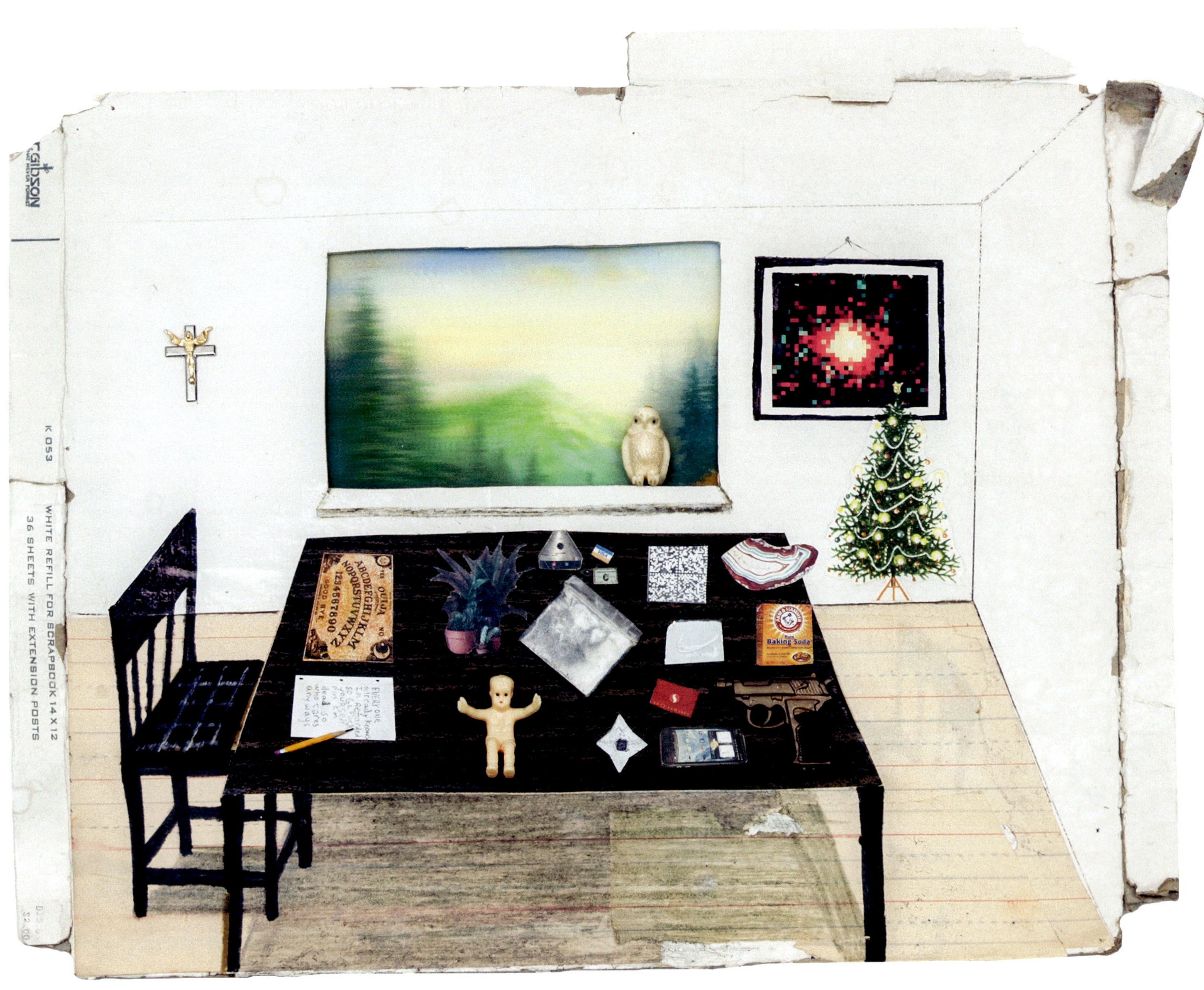

Holiday Season, 2010

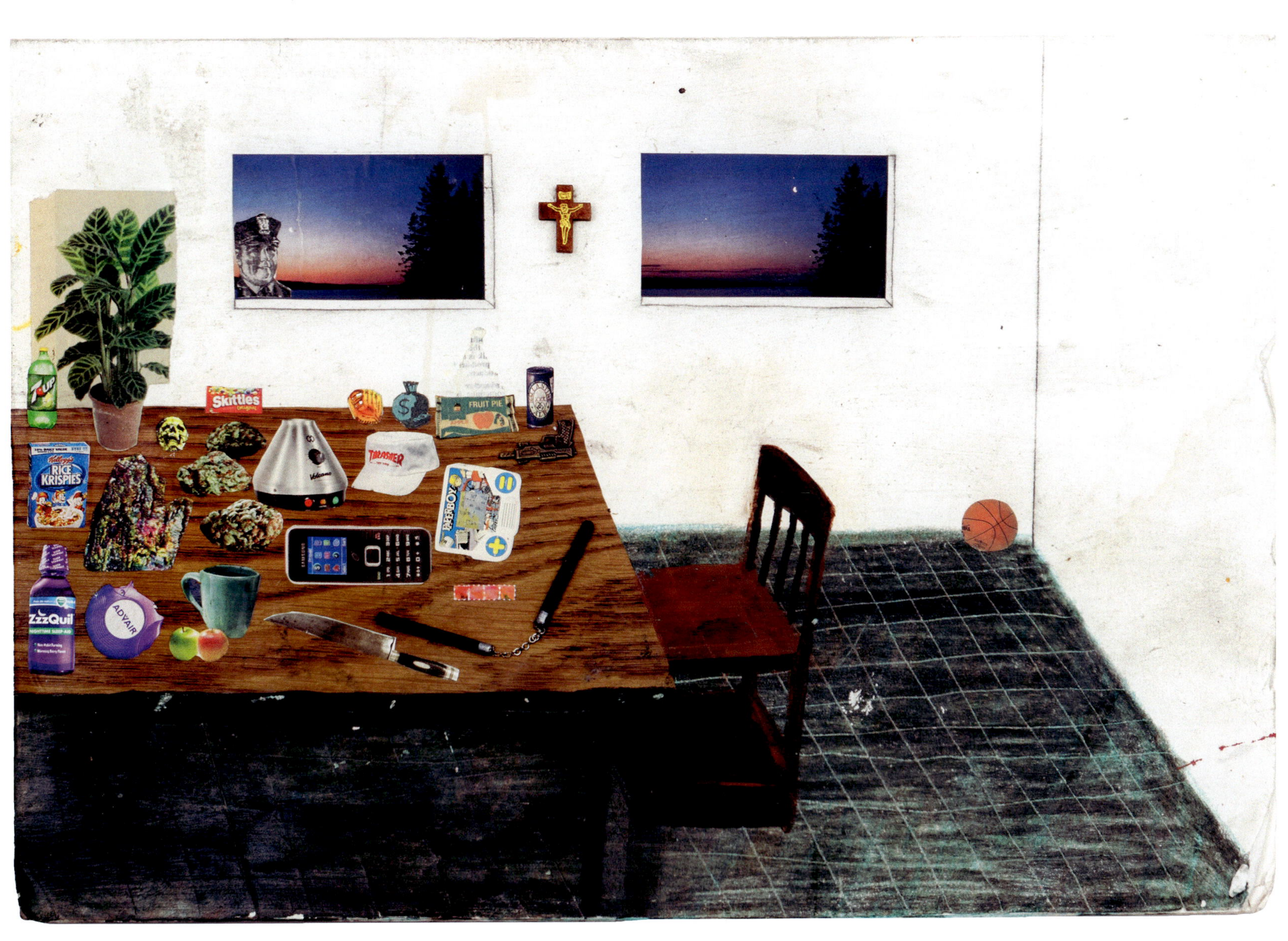

Still Life 4, 2010

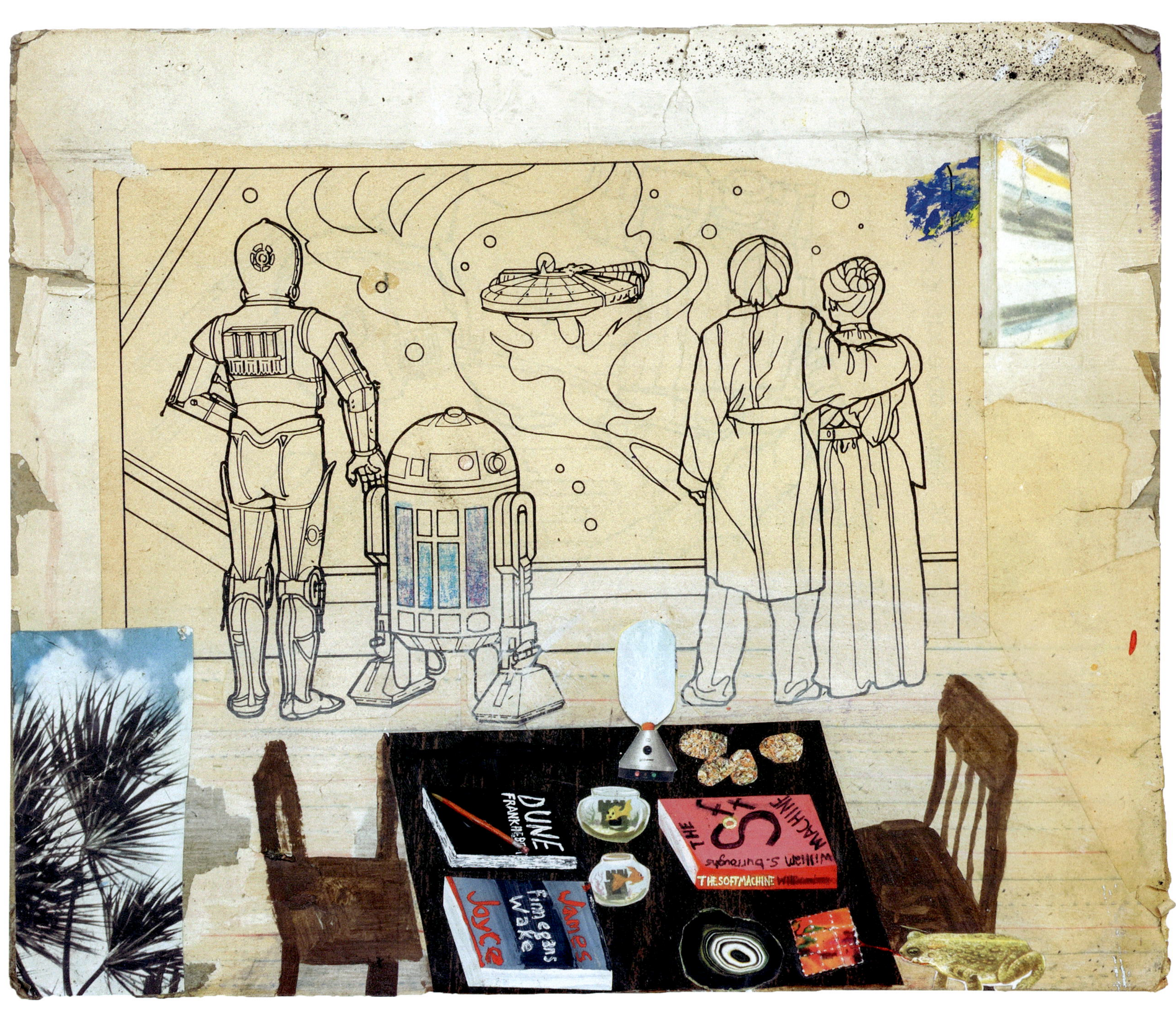

Book Club, 2014

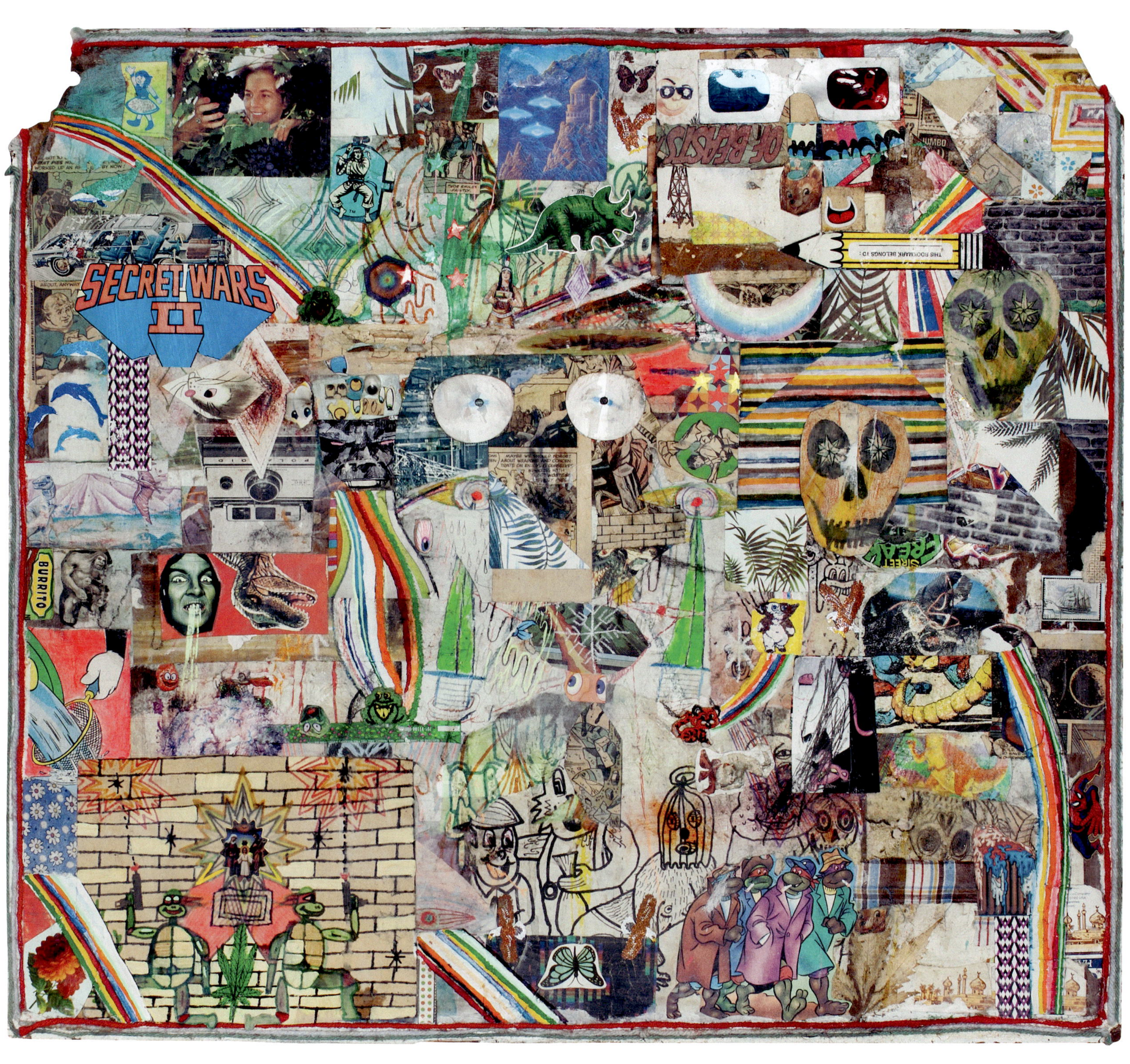

History of Summer, 2008

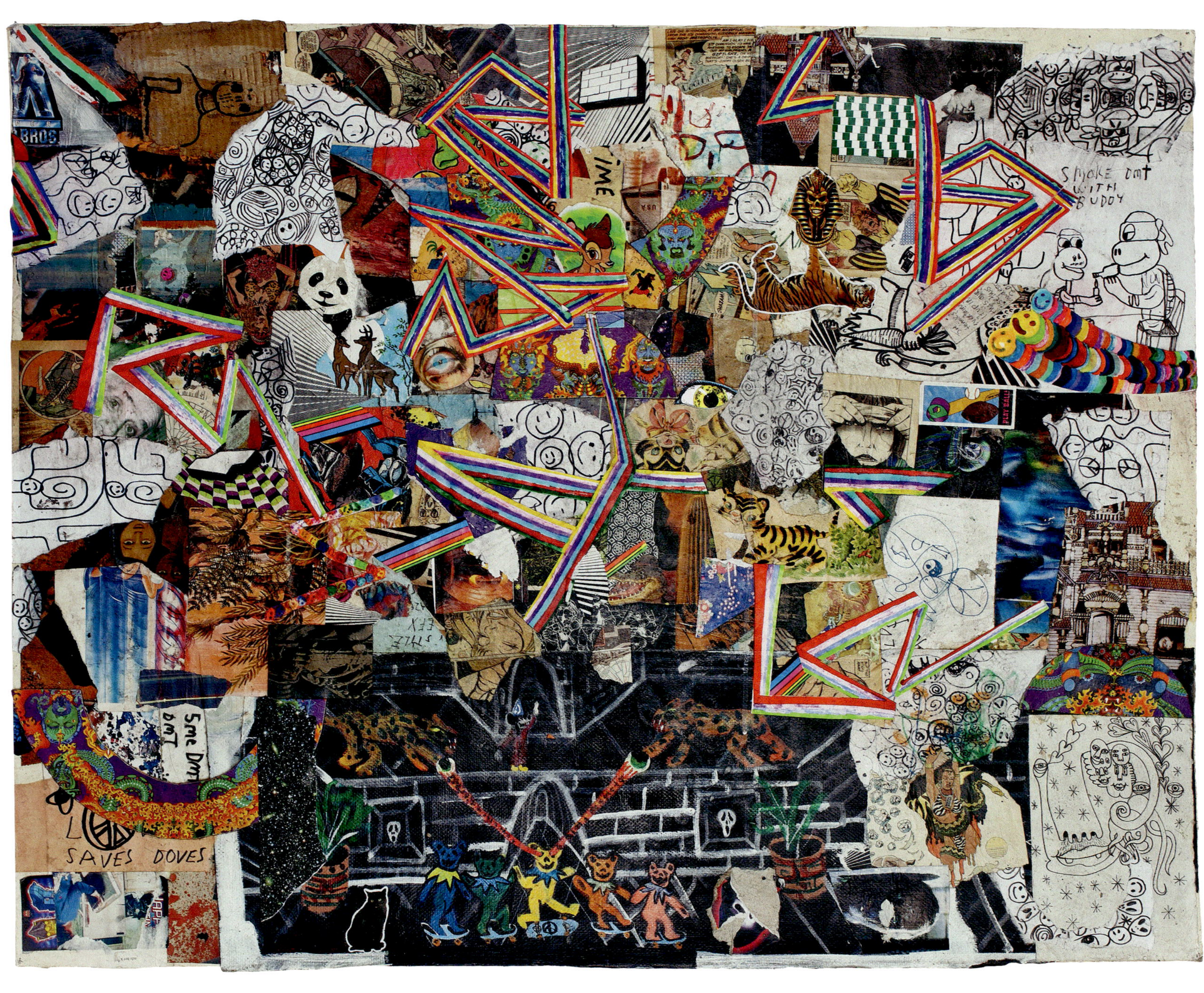

Section of *New Club*, 2014

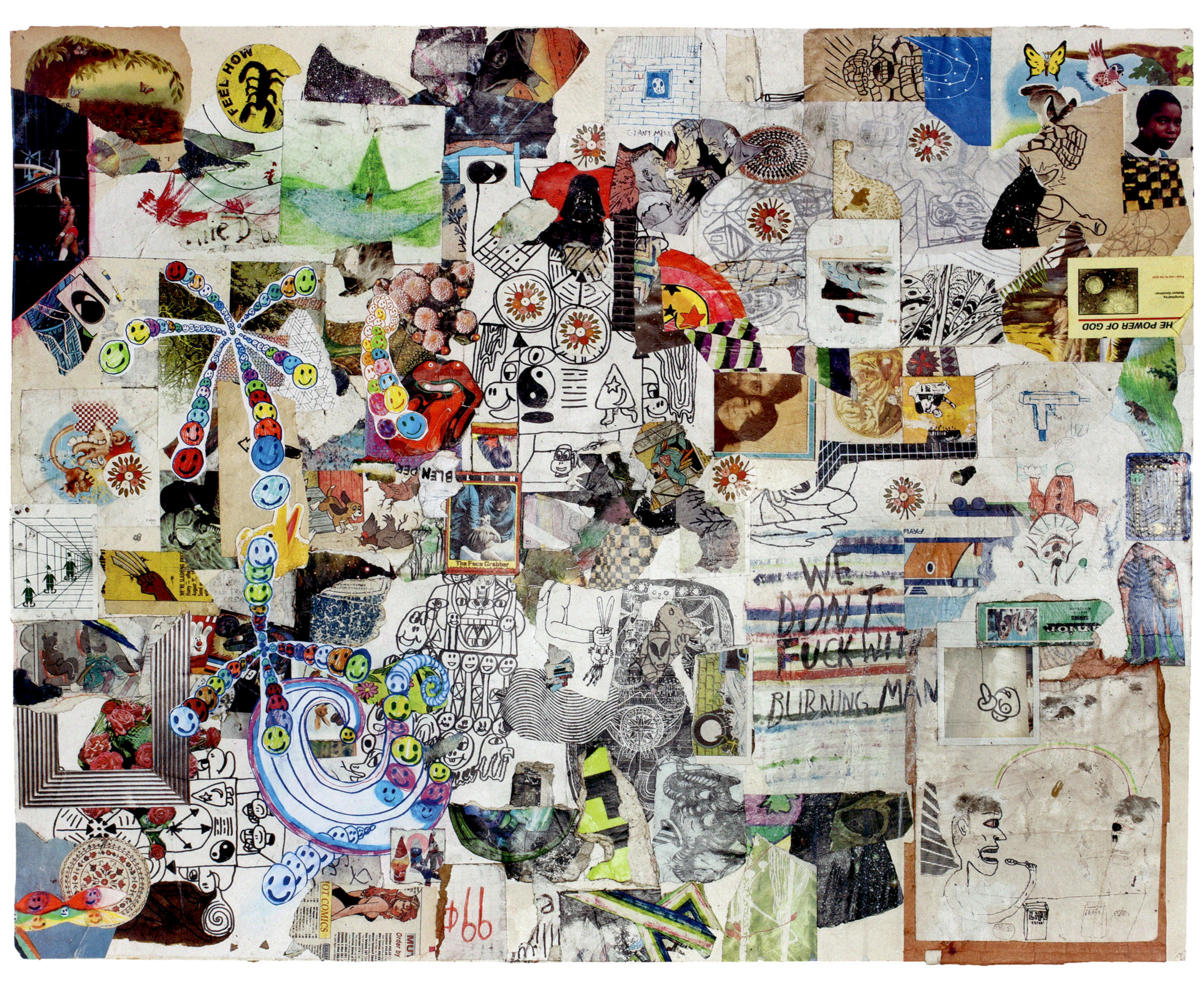

Abyss, 2014

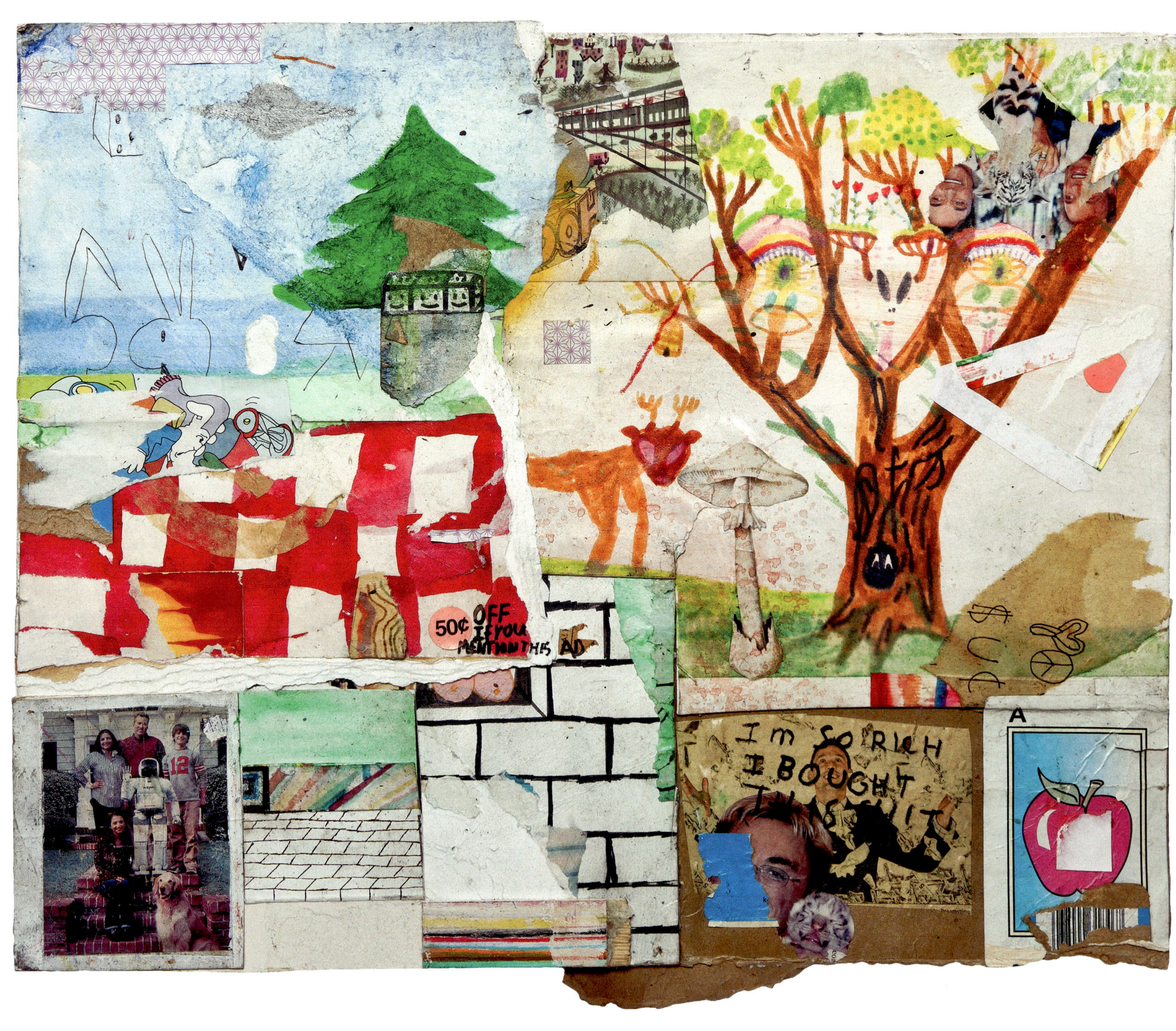

Picnic Lunch, 2011

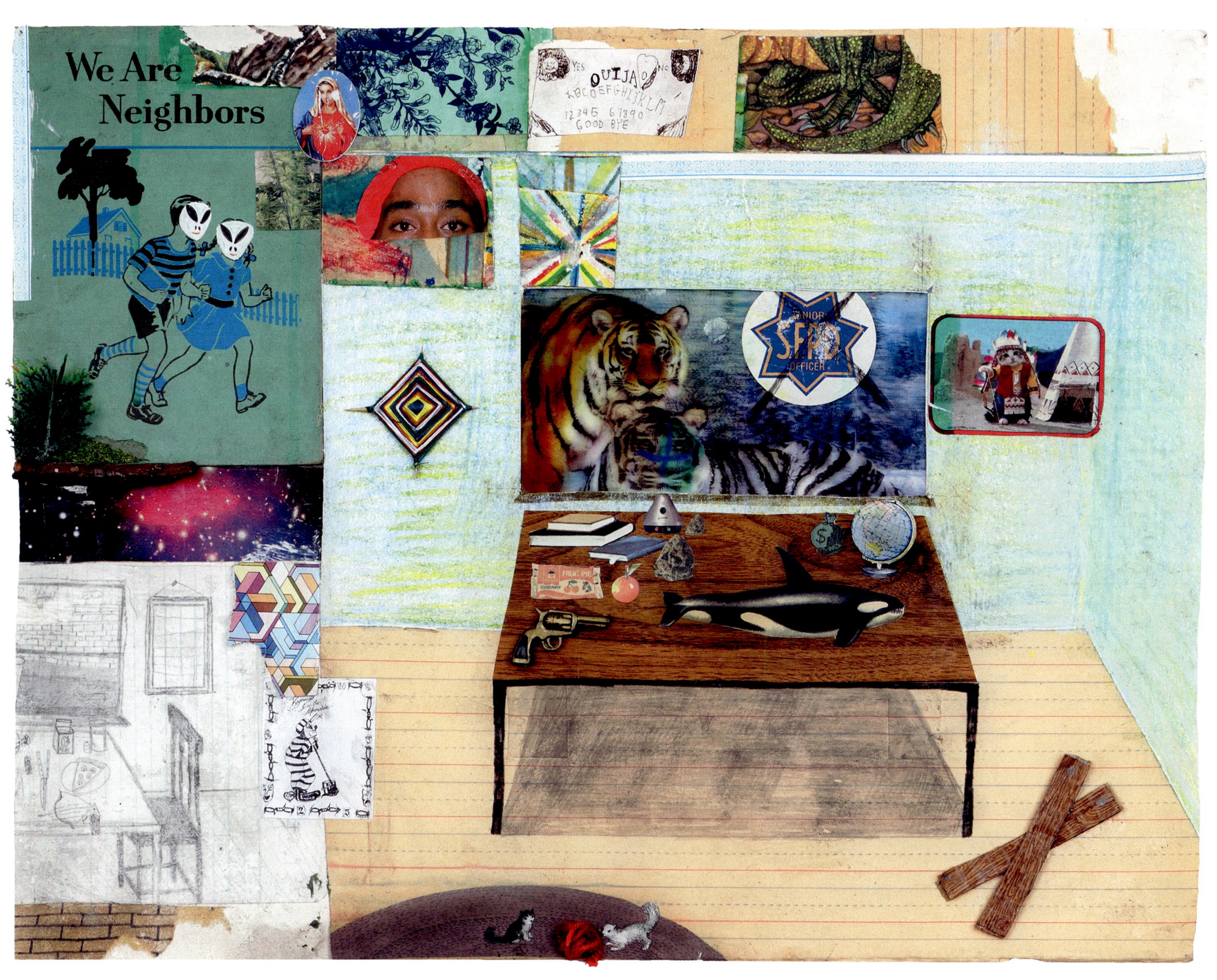

We Are Neighboors, 2010

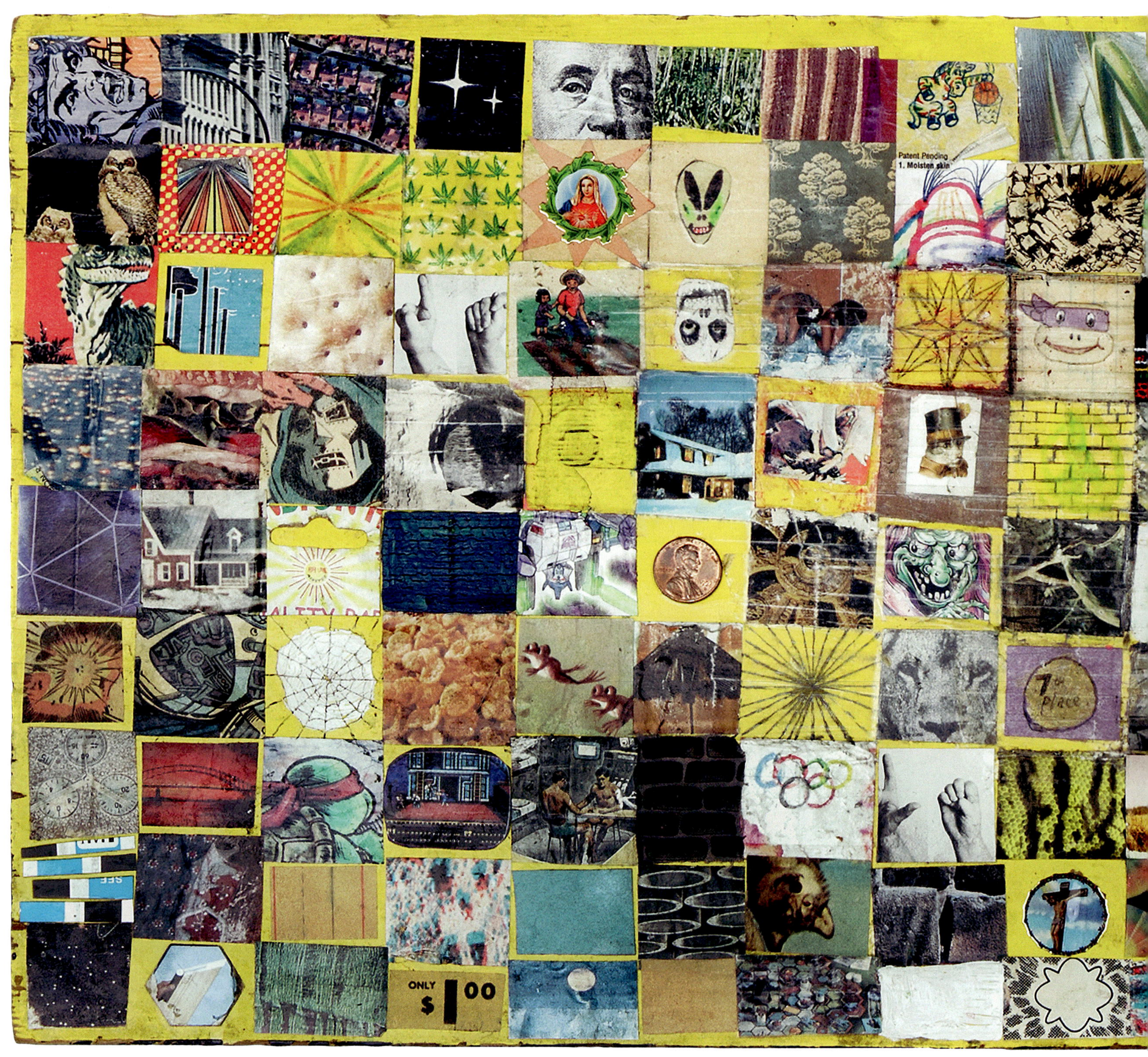

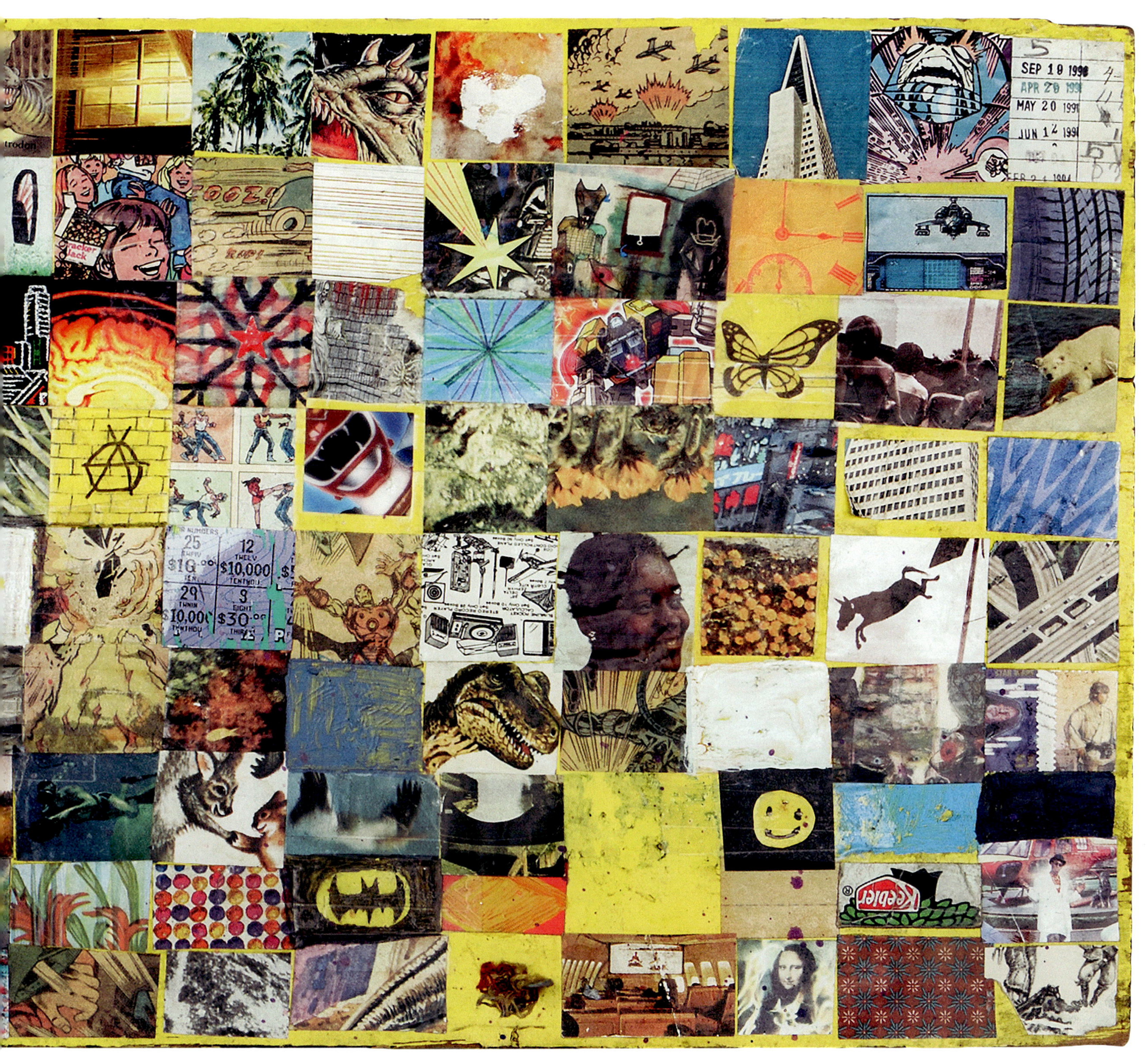

Map of Level Three, 2009

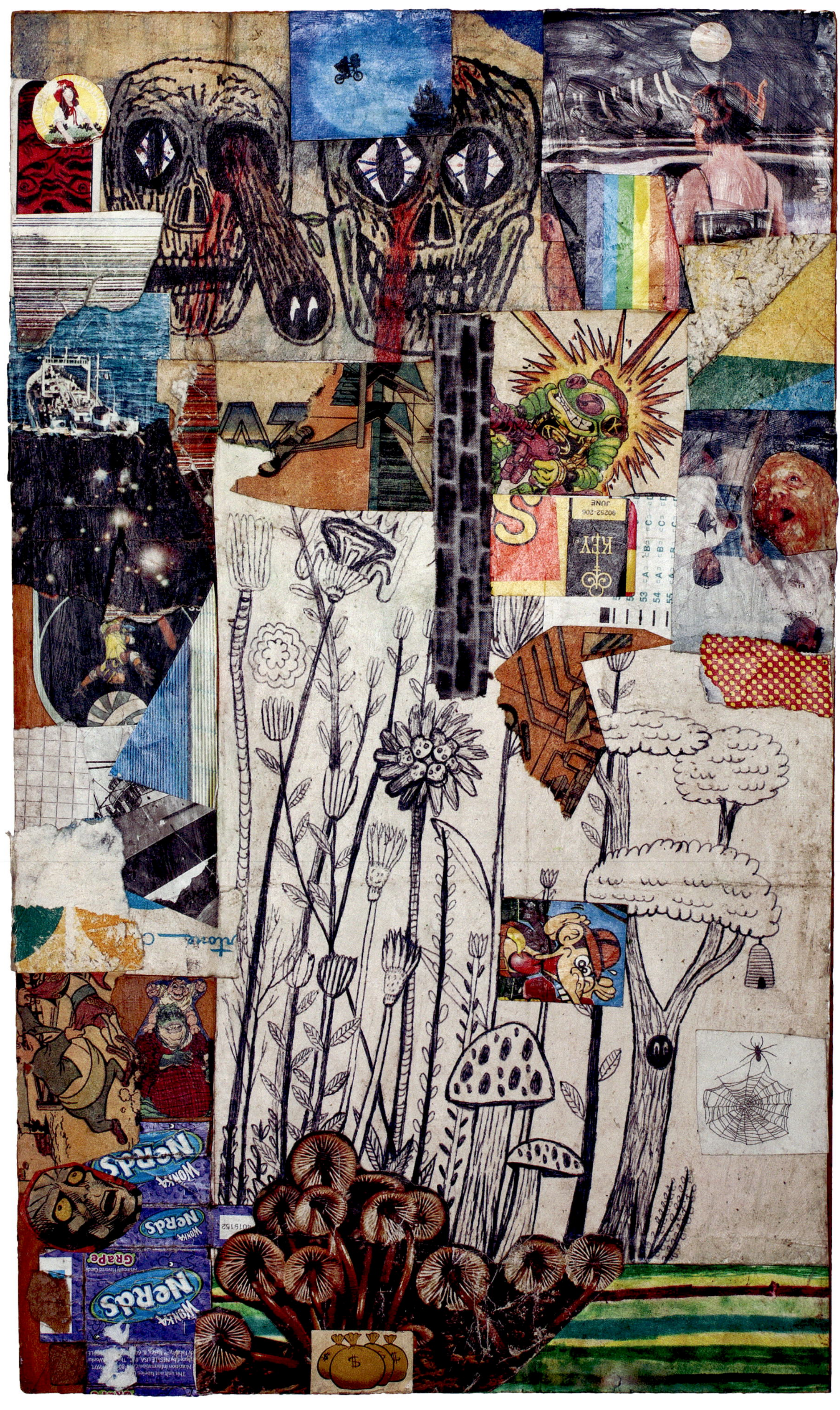

Magic Forest, 2010

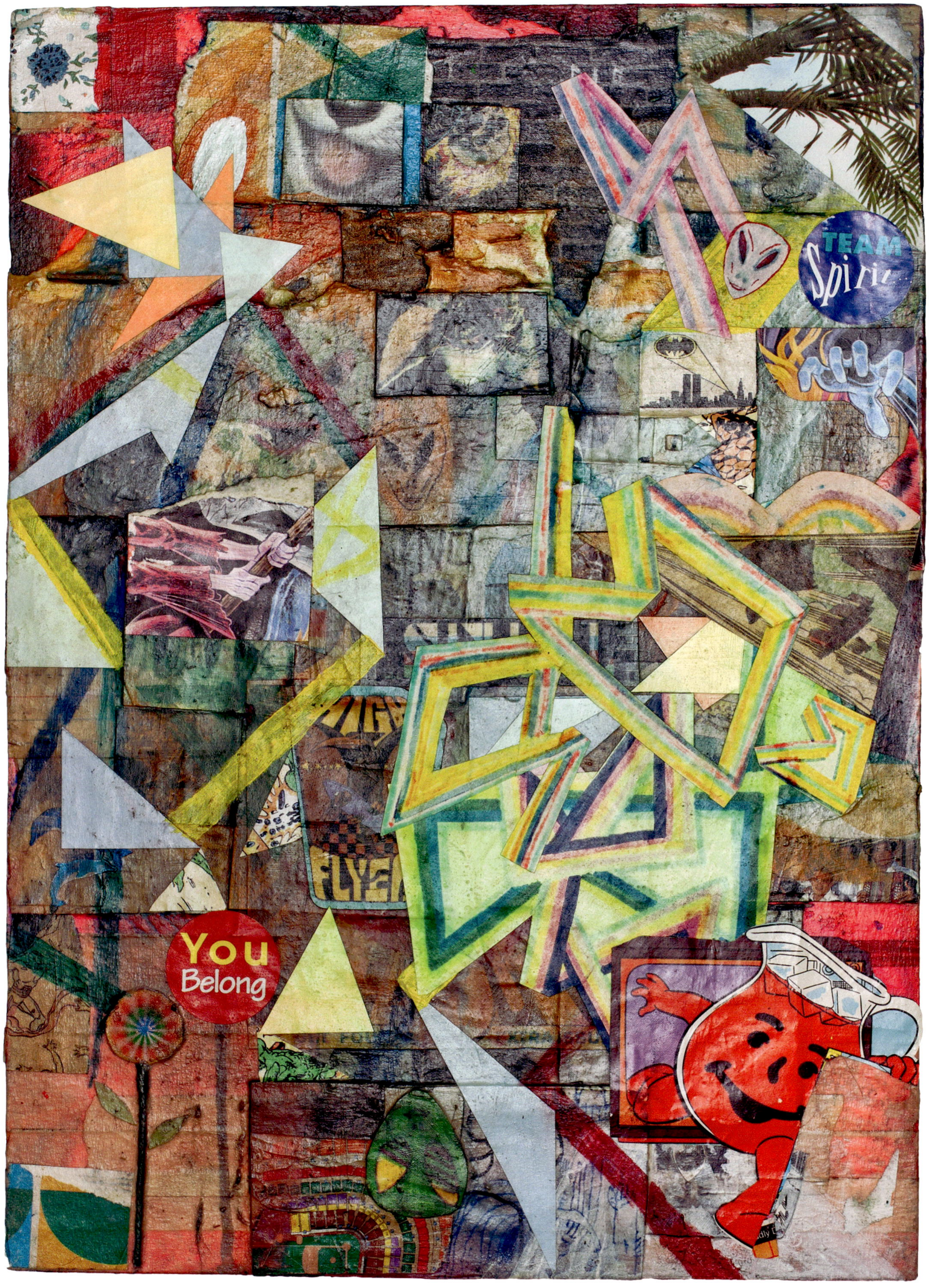

You Belong, 2011

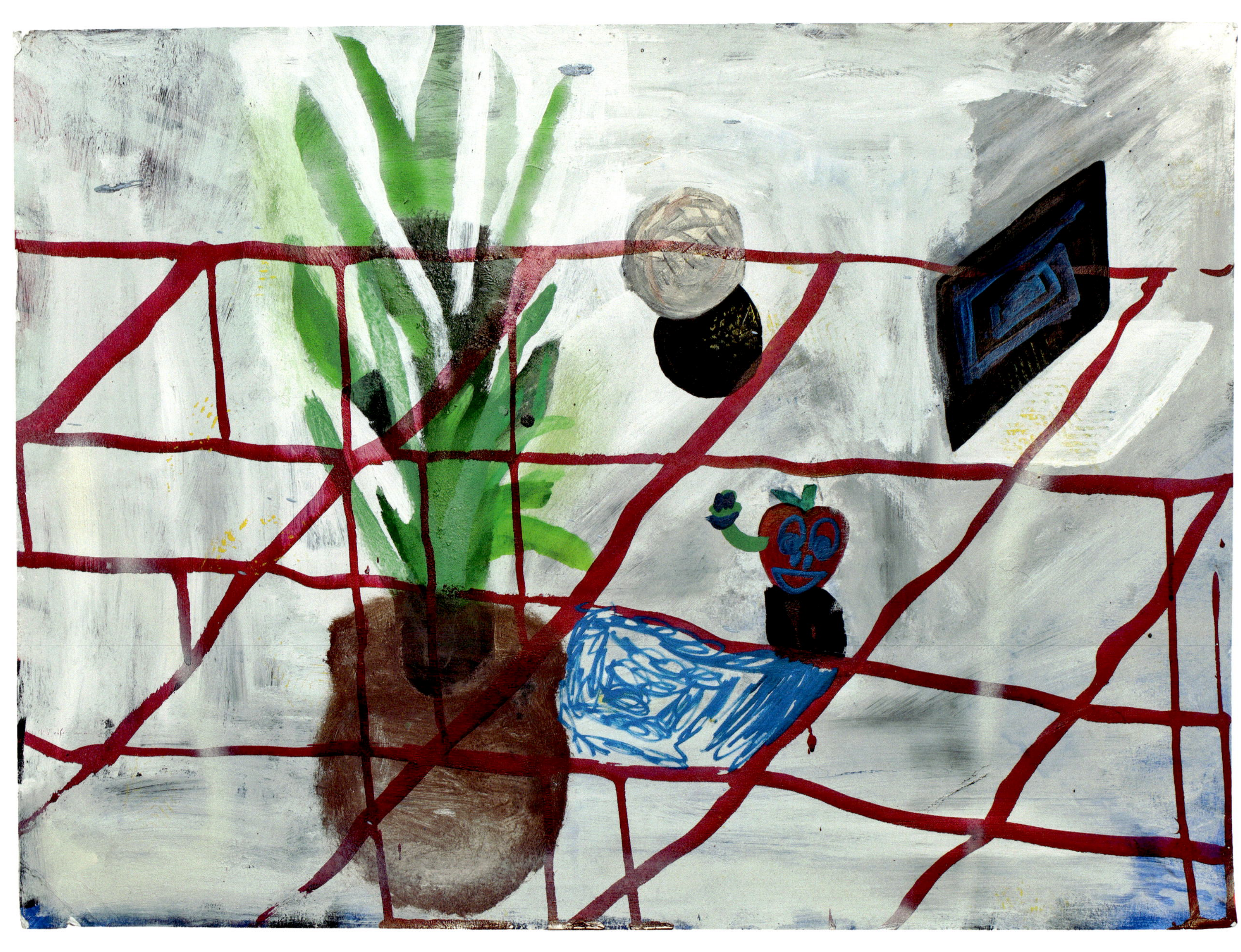

Desktop, 2013

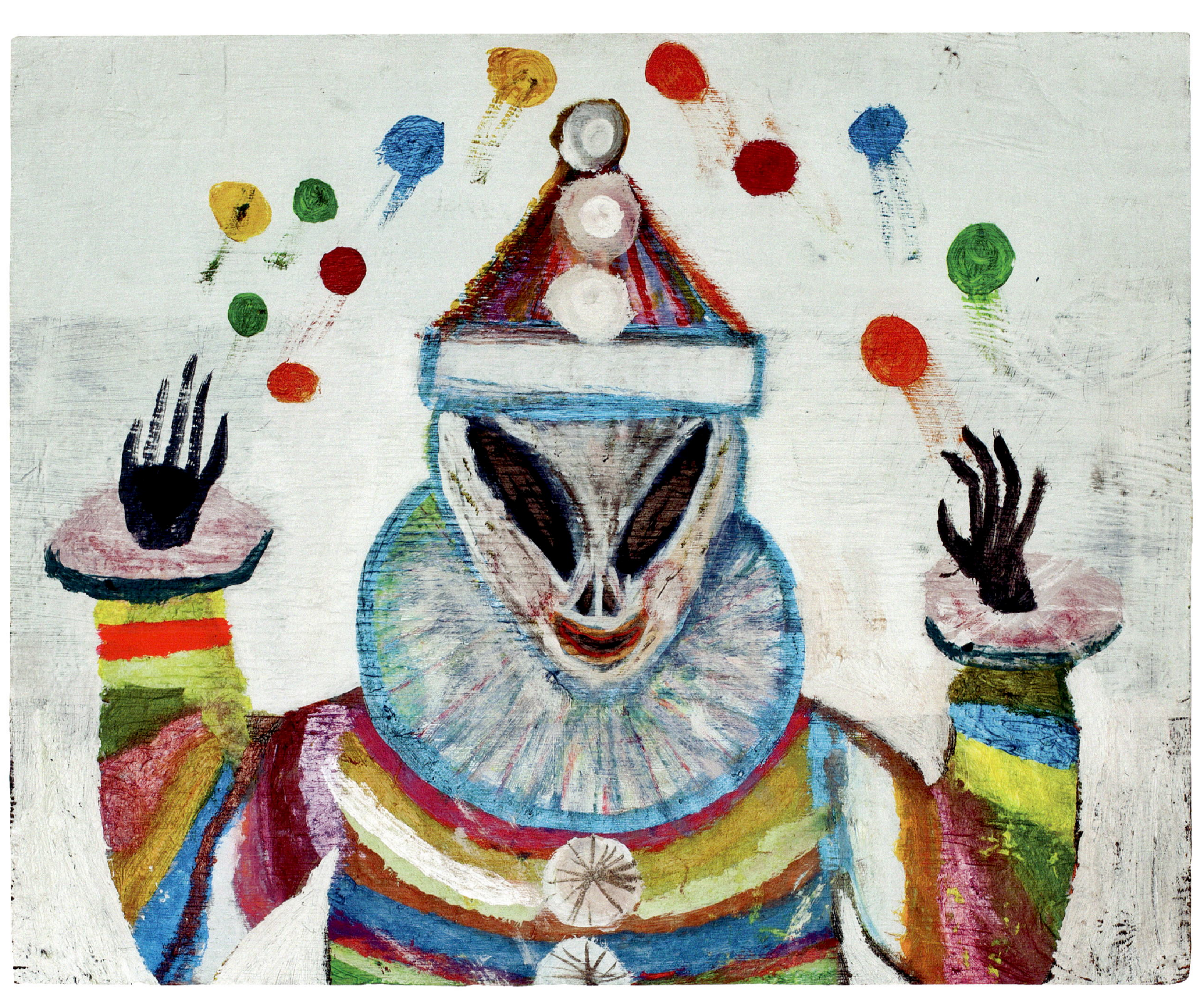

Look a Friendly Stranger, 2010

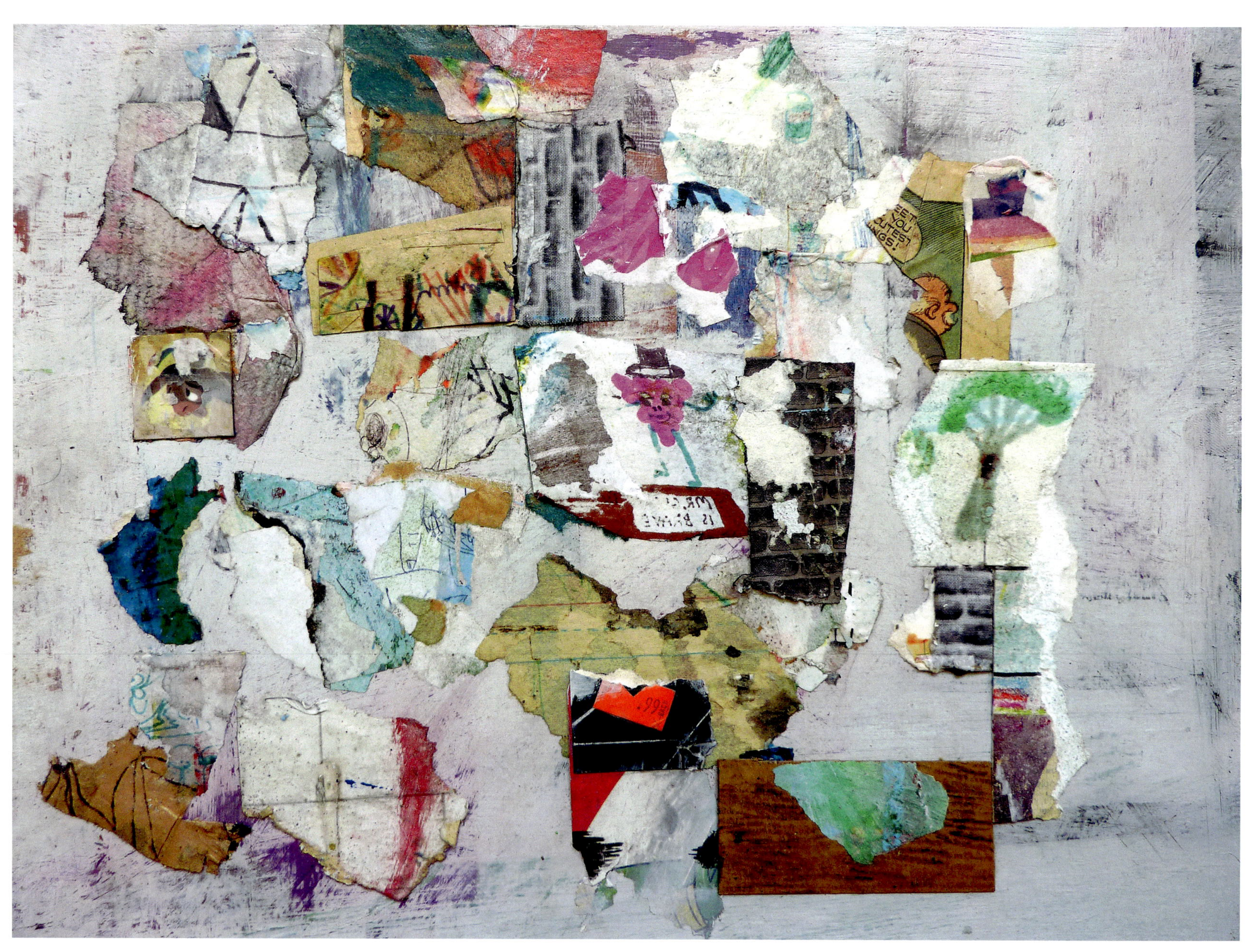

Mister Grape Is Brave, 2011

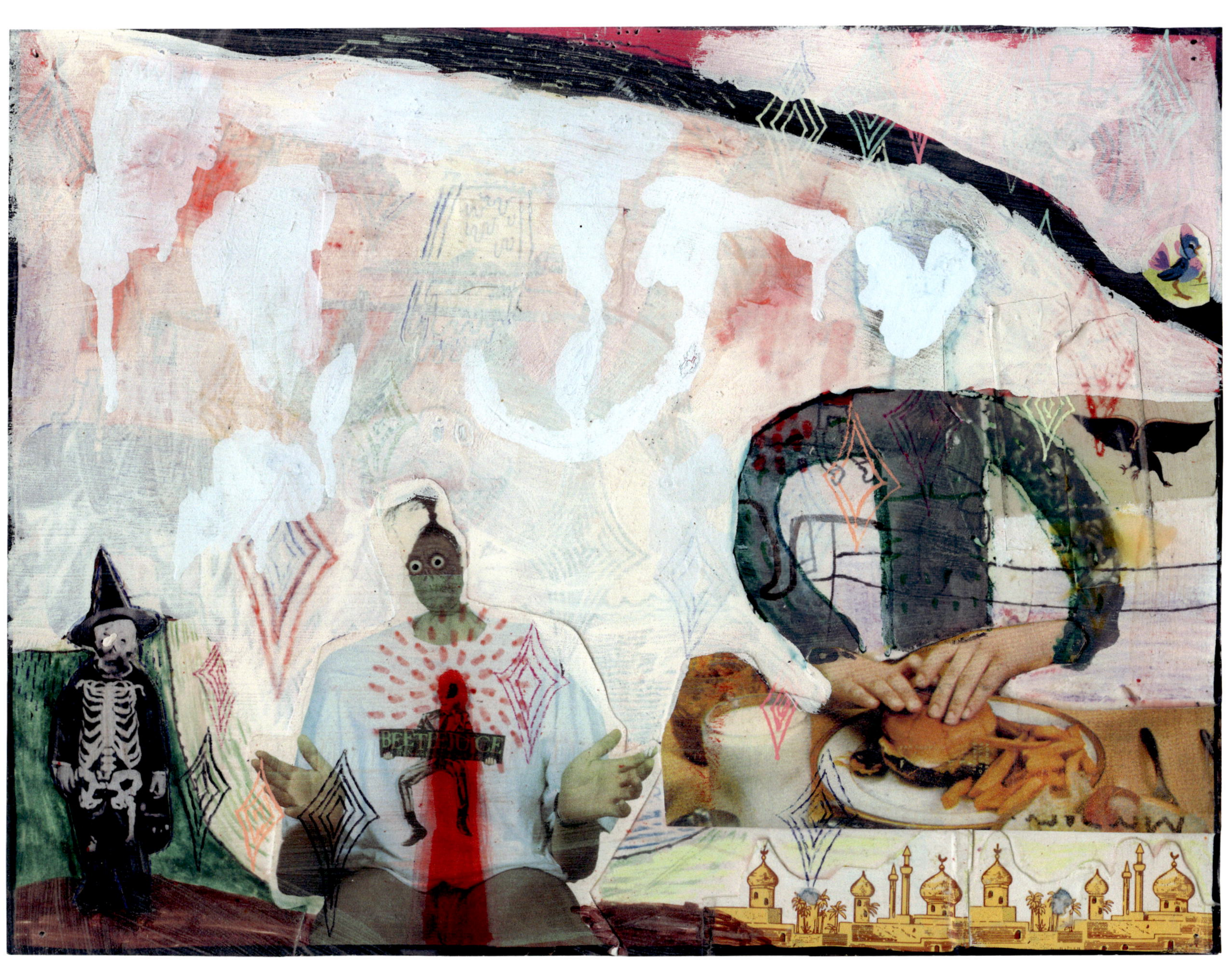

Lunch Break, 2005

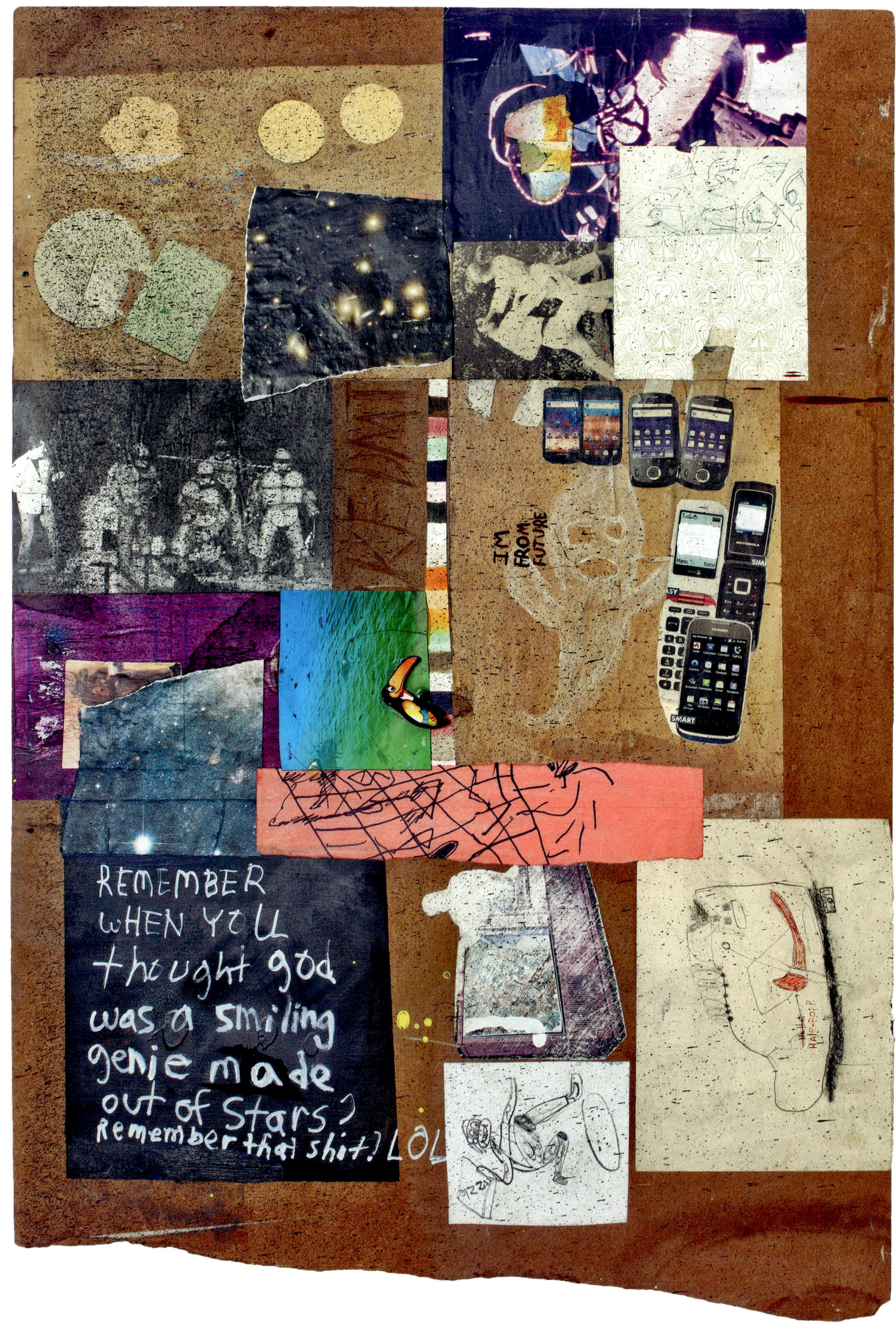

KEMI
IM FROM FUTURE
REMEMBER
WHEN YOU
thought god
was a smiling
genie made
out of stars?
Remember that shit? LOL

Future, 2013

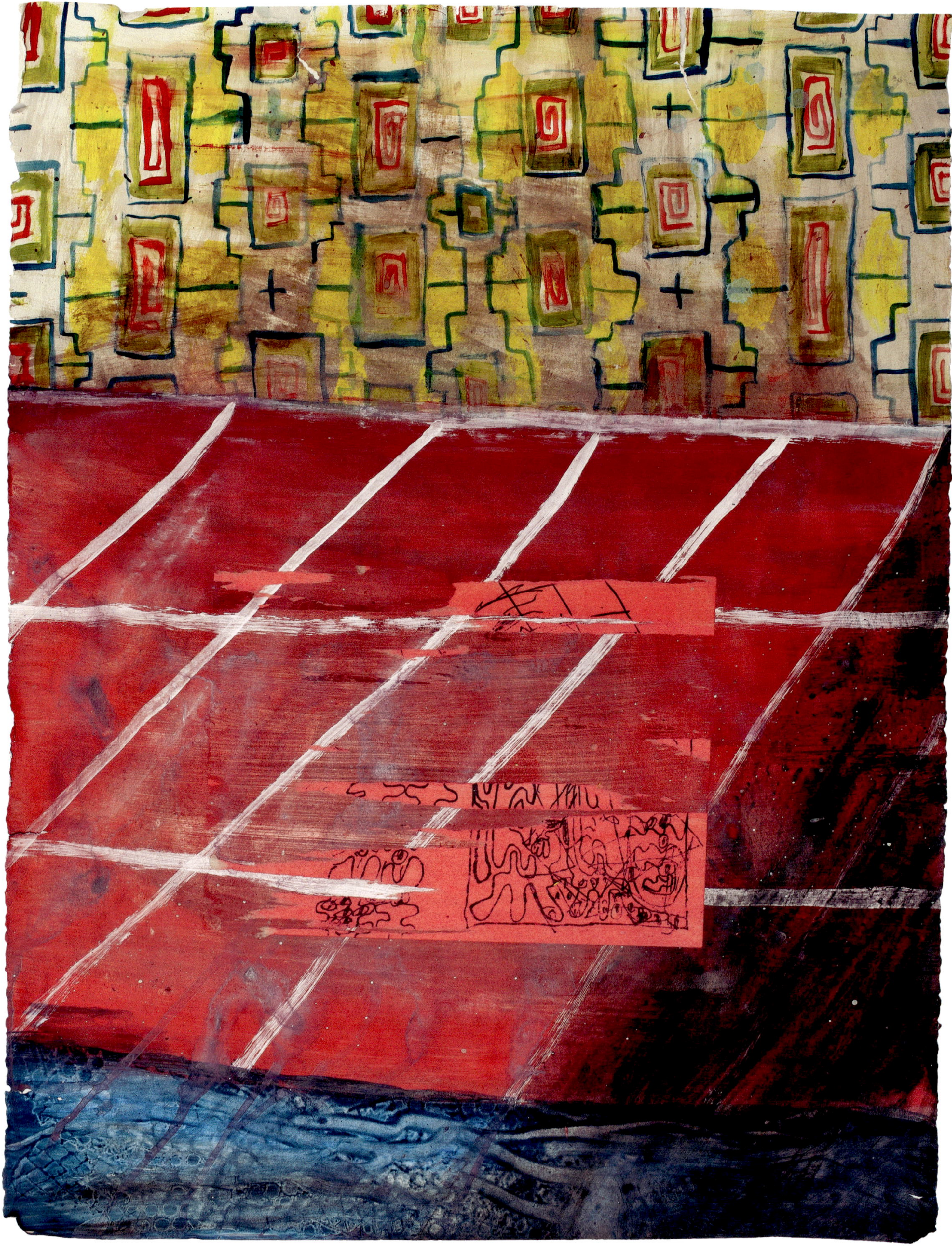

Untitled, 2014

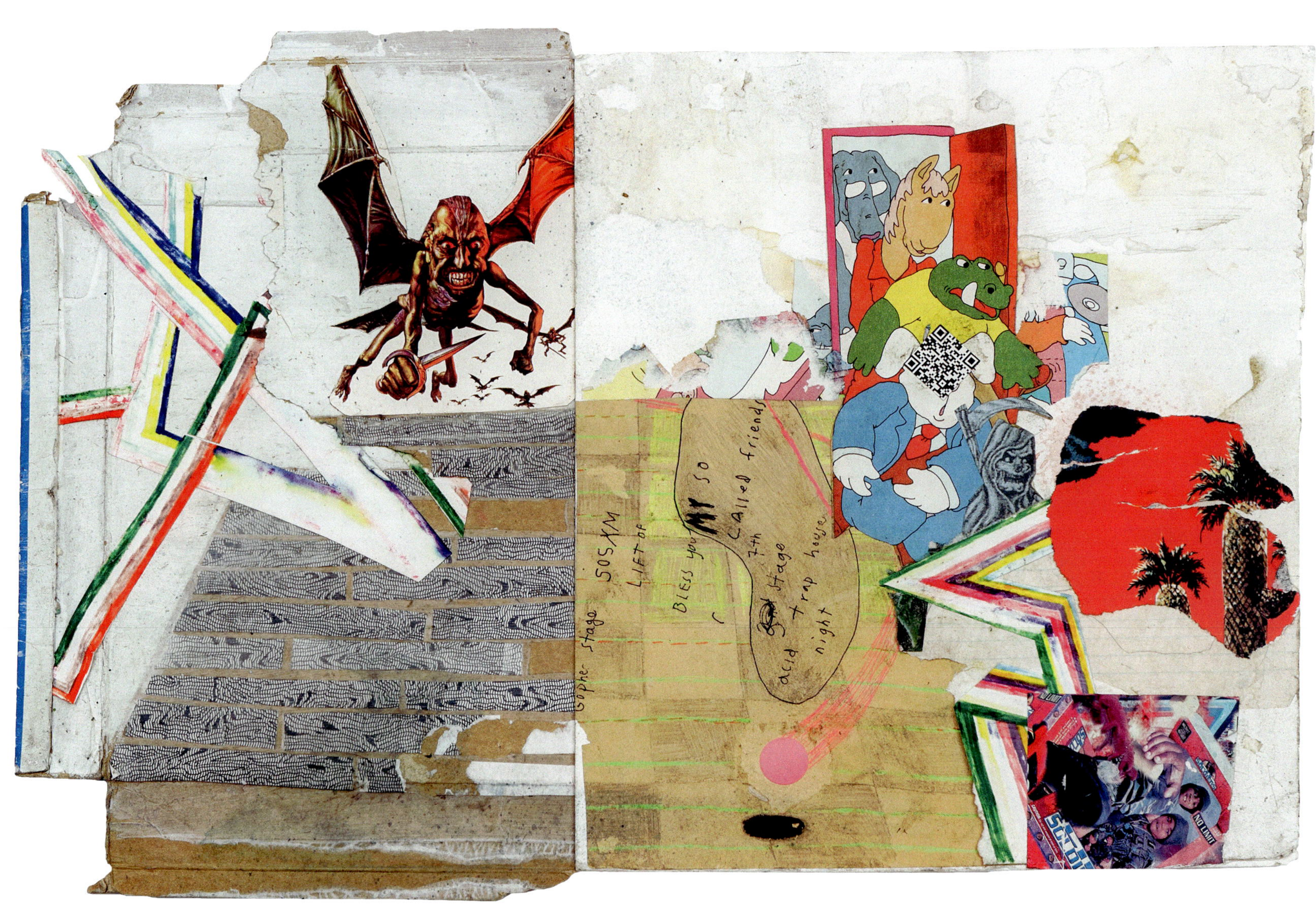

House Party, 2014

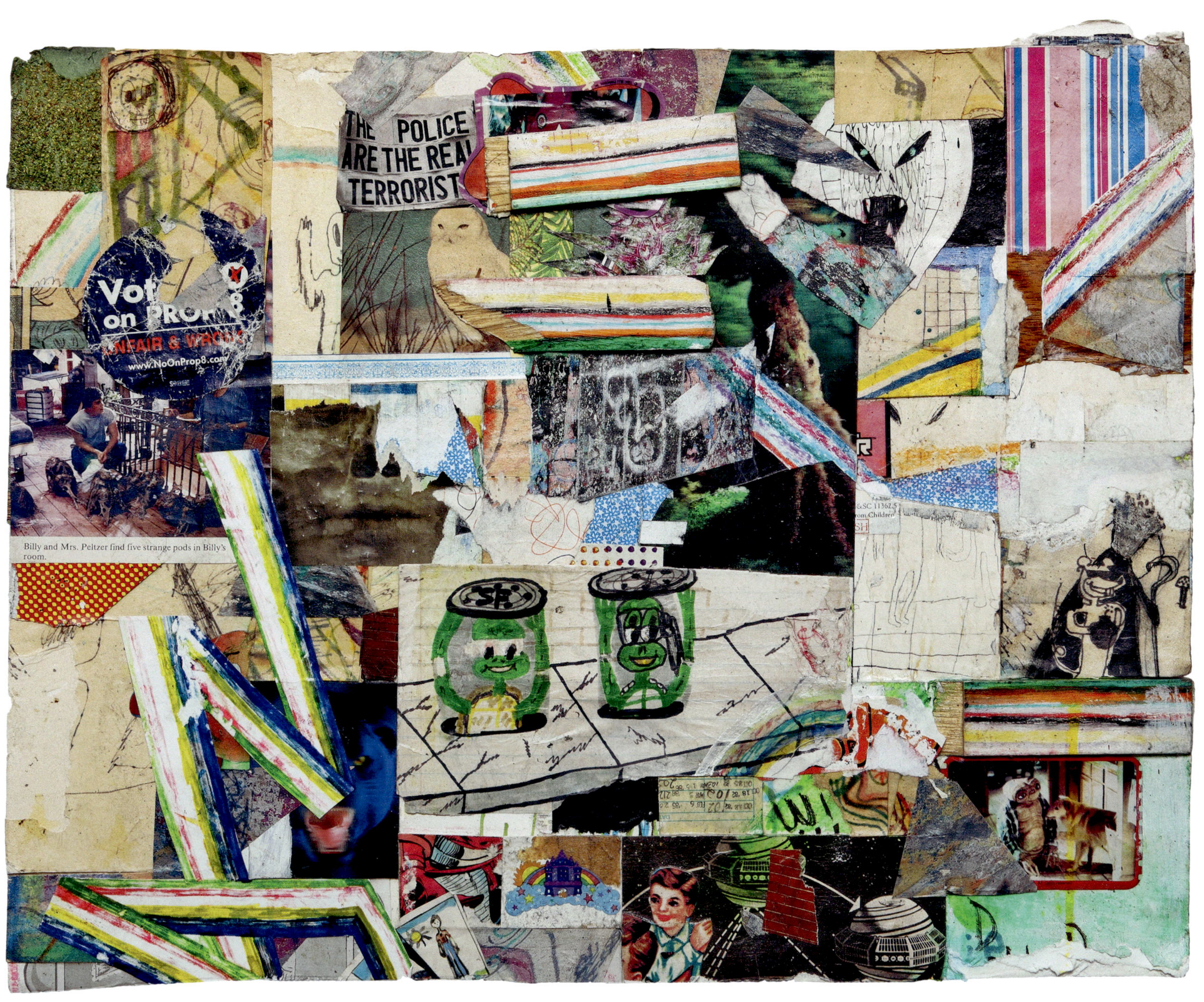

Yesterday Today Tomorrow, 2011

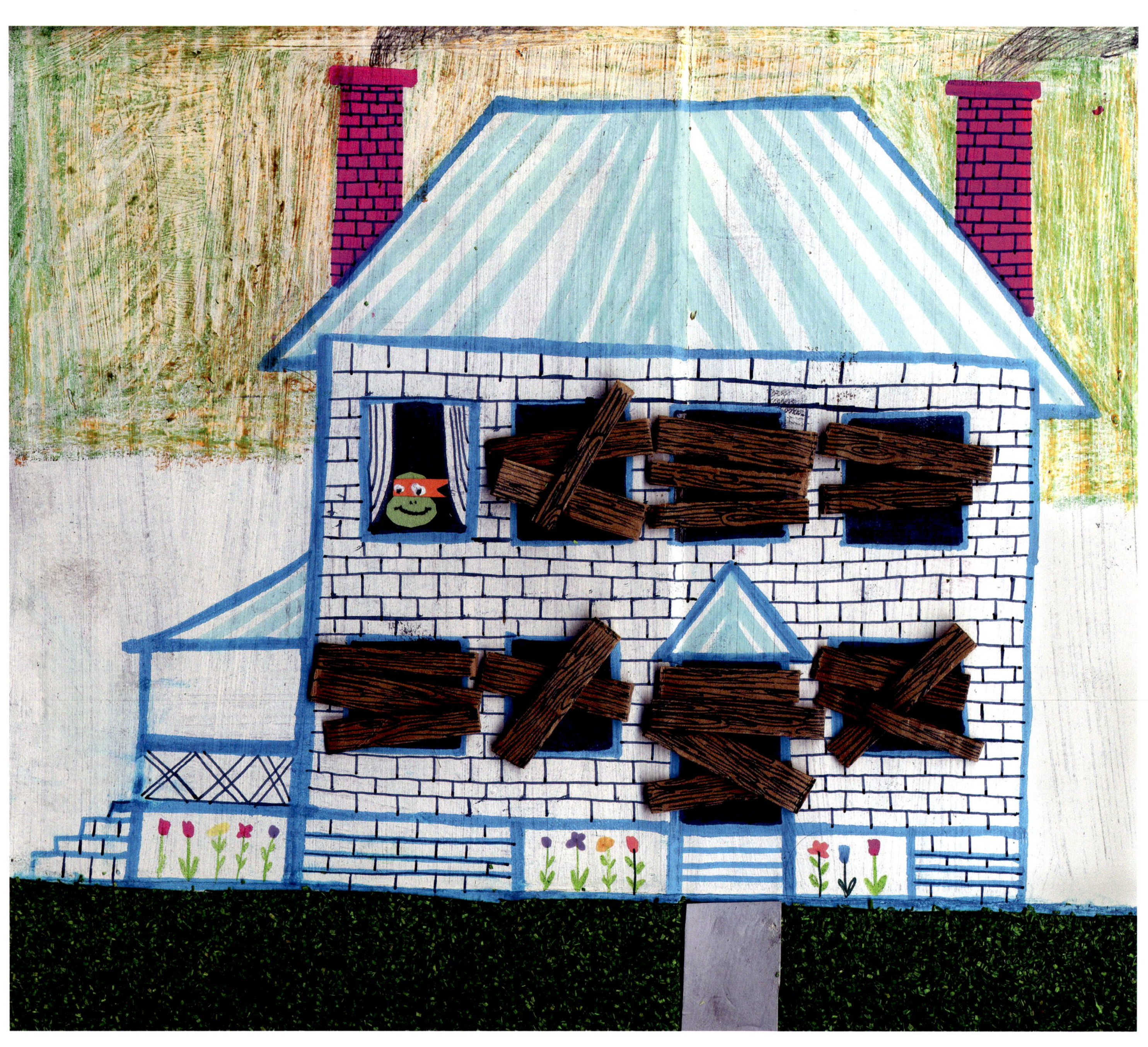

Safe House, 2009

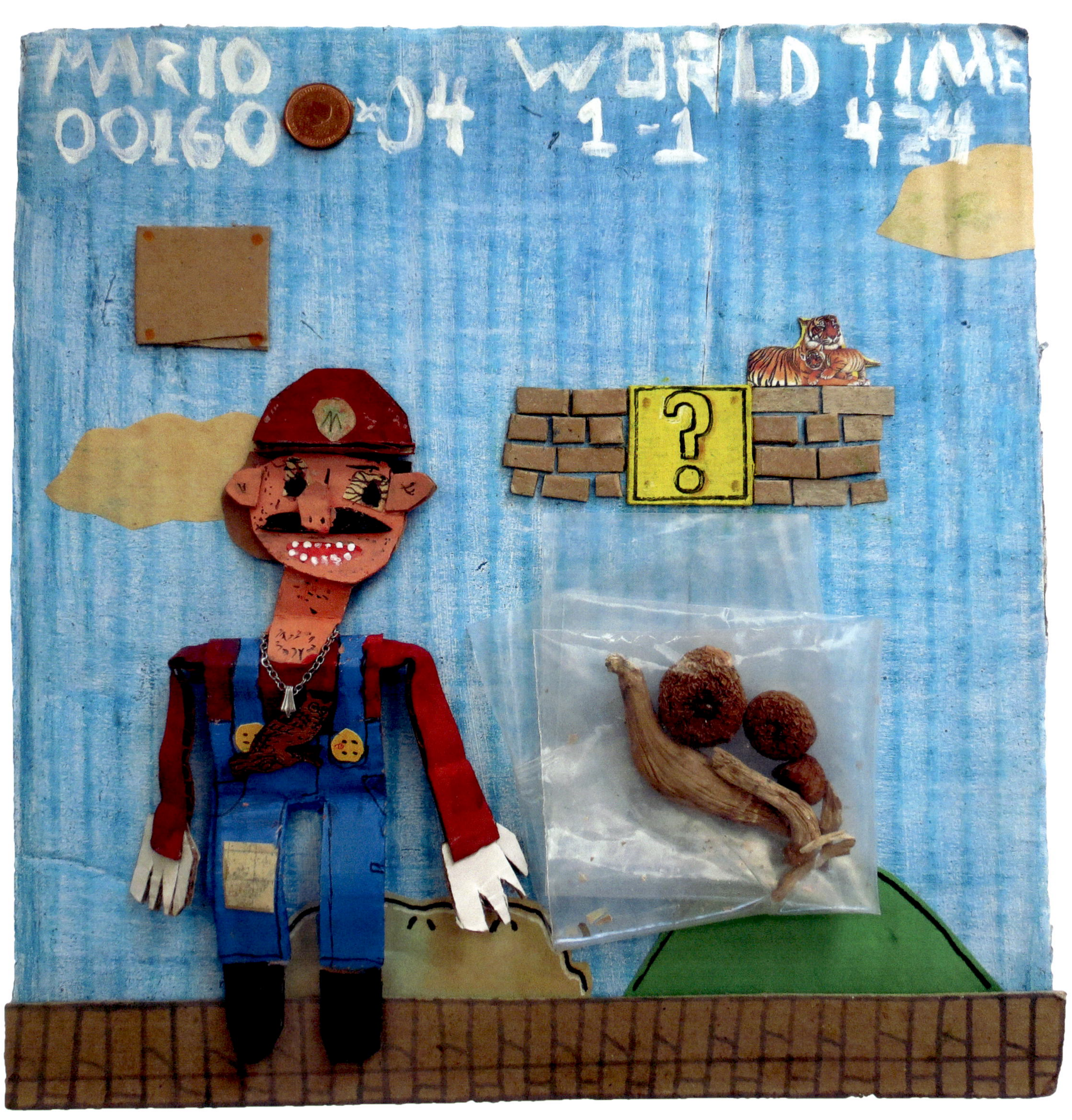

Mario, 2008

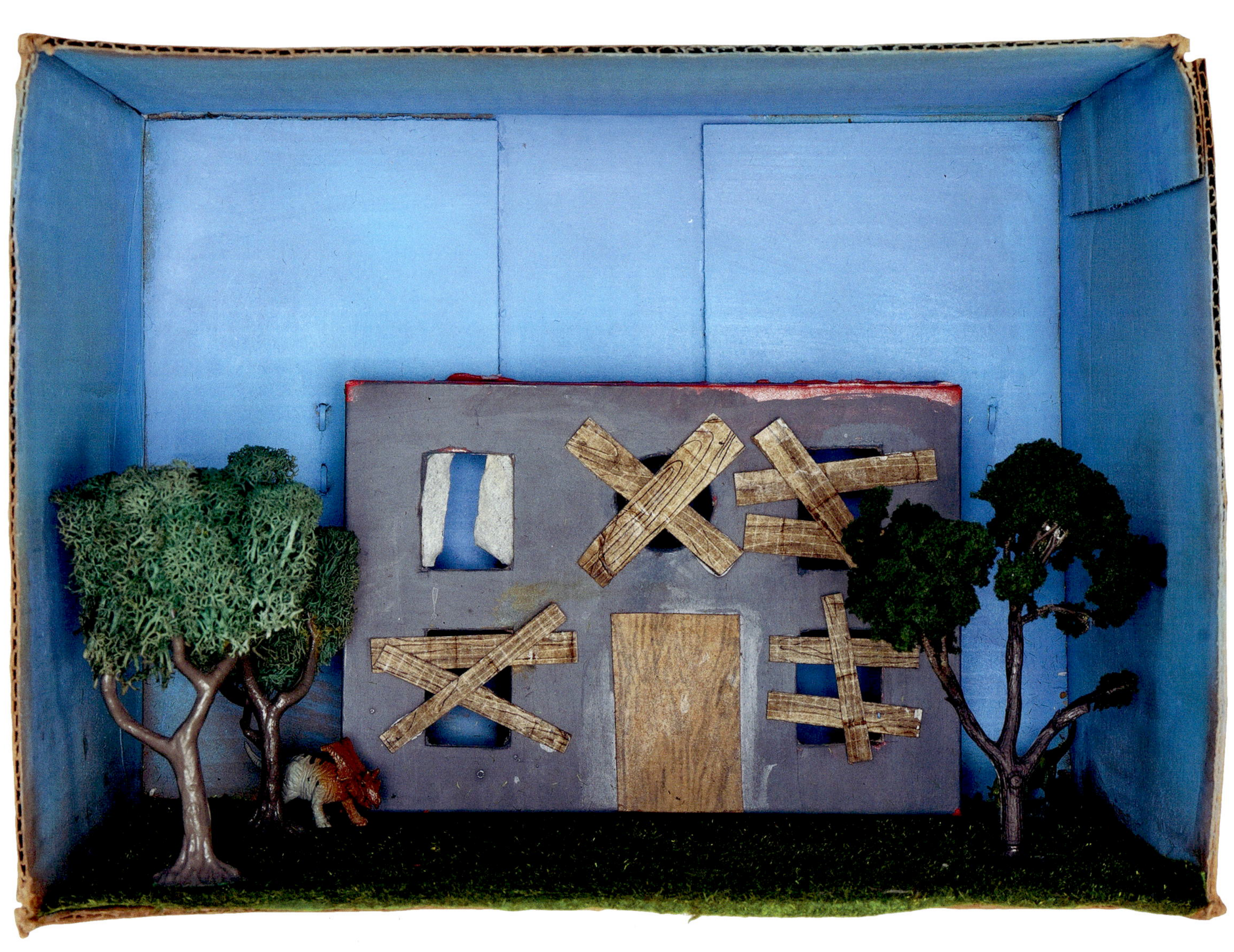

Summer School, 2009

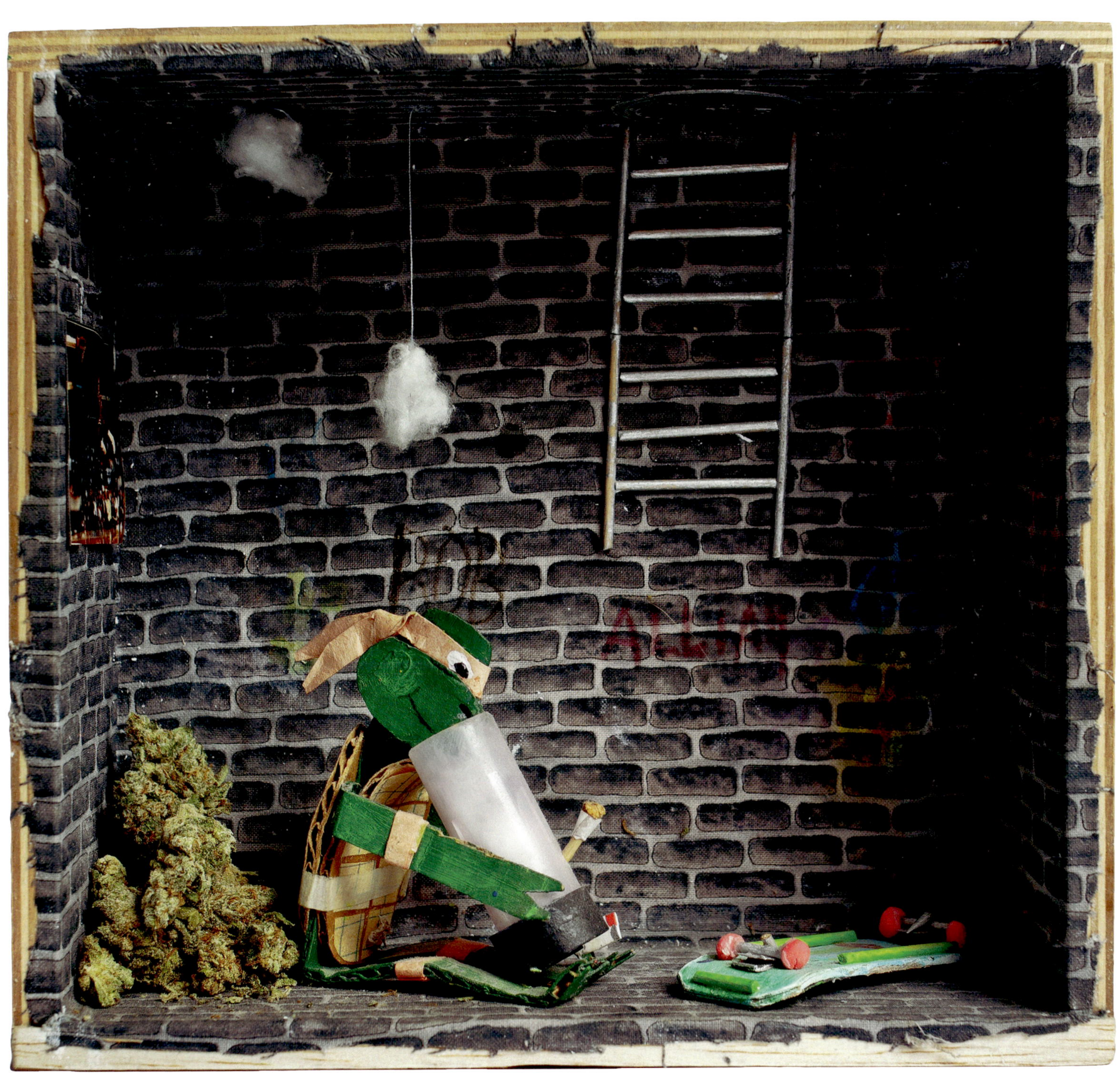

Home Sweet Home, 2009

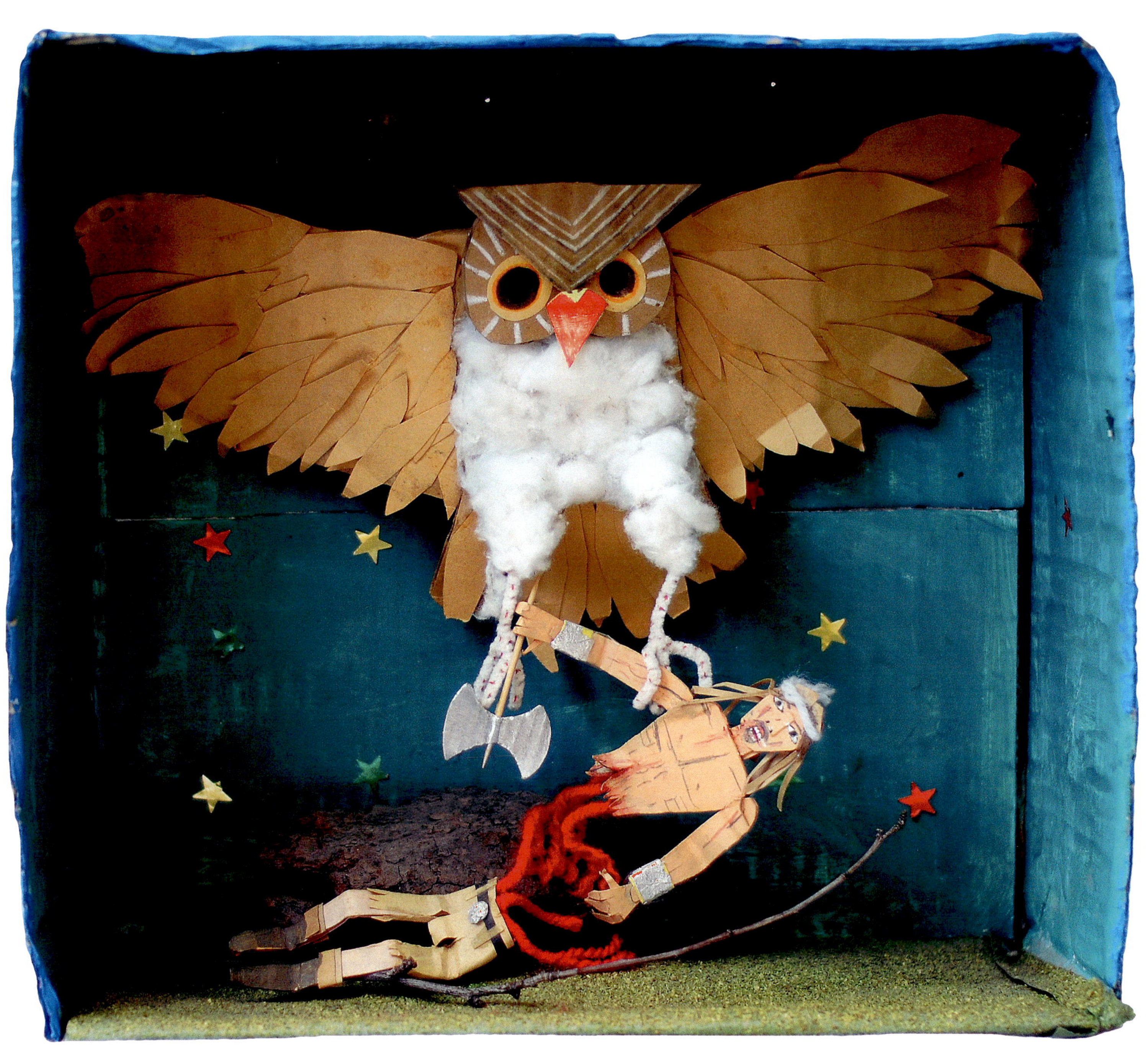

Owl vs. Barbarian, 2009

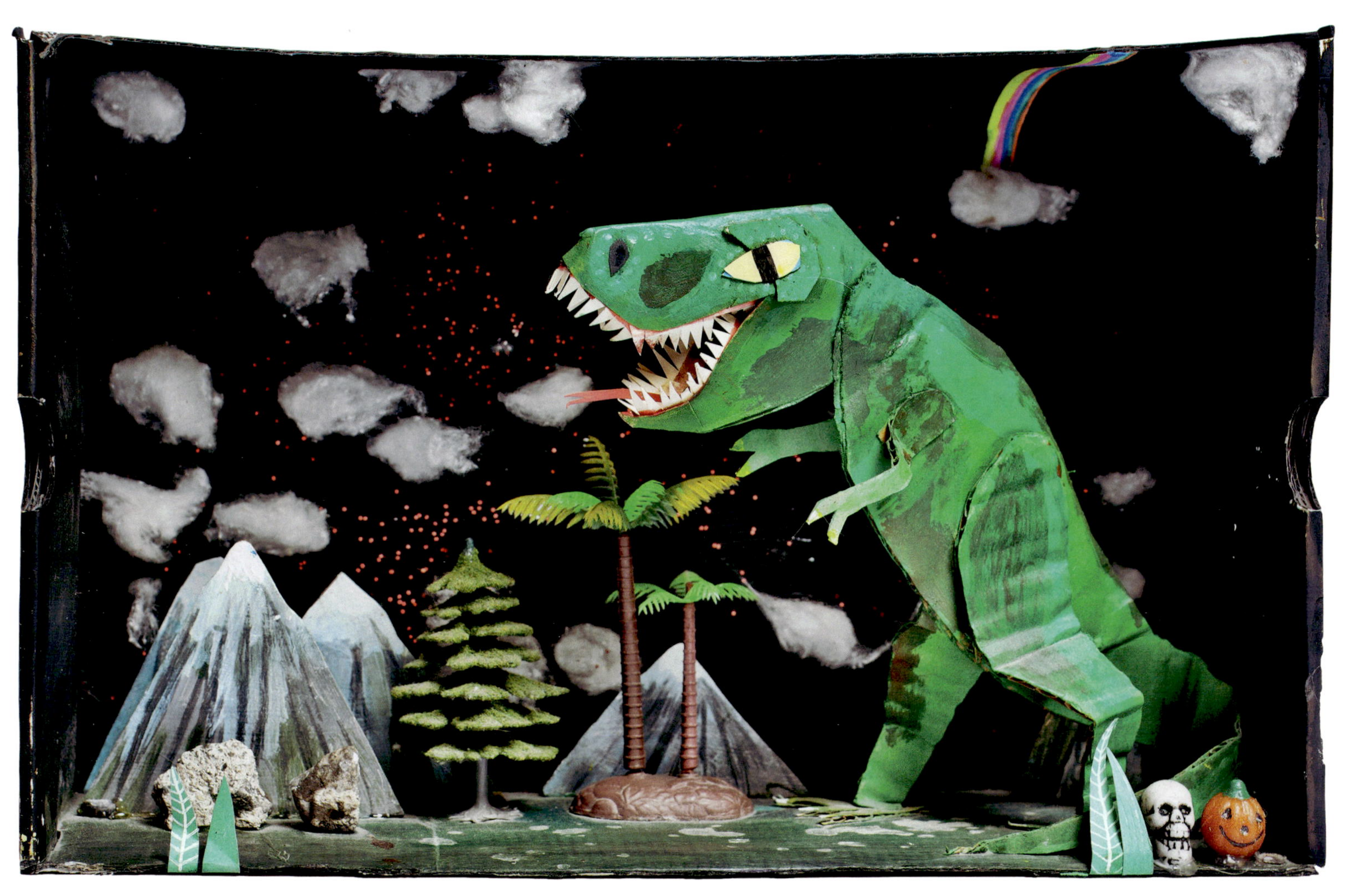

Lost World, 2008

YoUng
GRUFFY
#27
3 29
Total Price
$2.29
PAY & SAVE
R.I.P.
2PAC
BIC
Tanqueray
IMPORTED
DRY GIN
NOW LATER

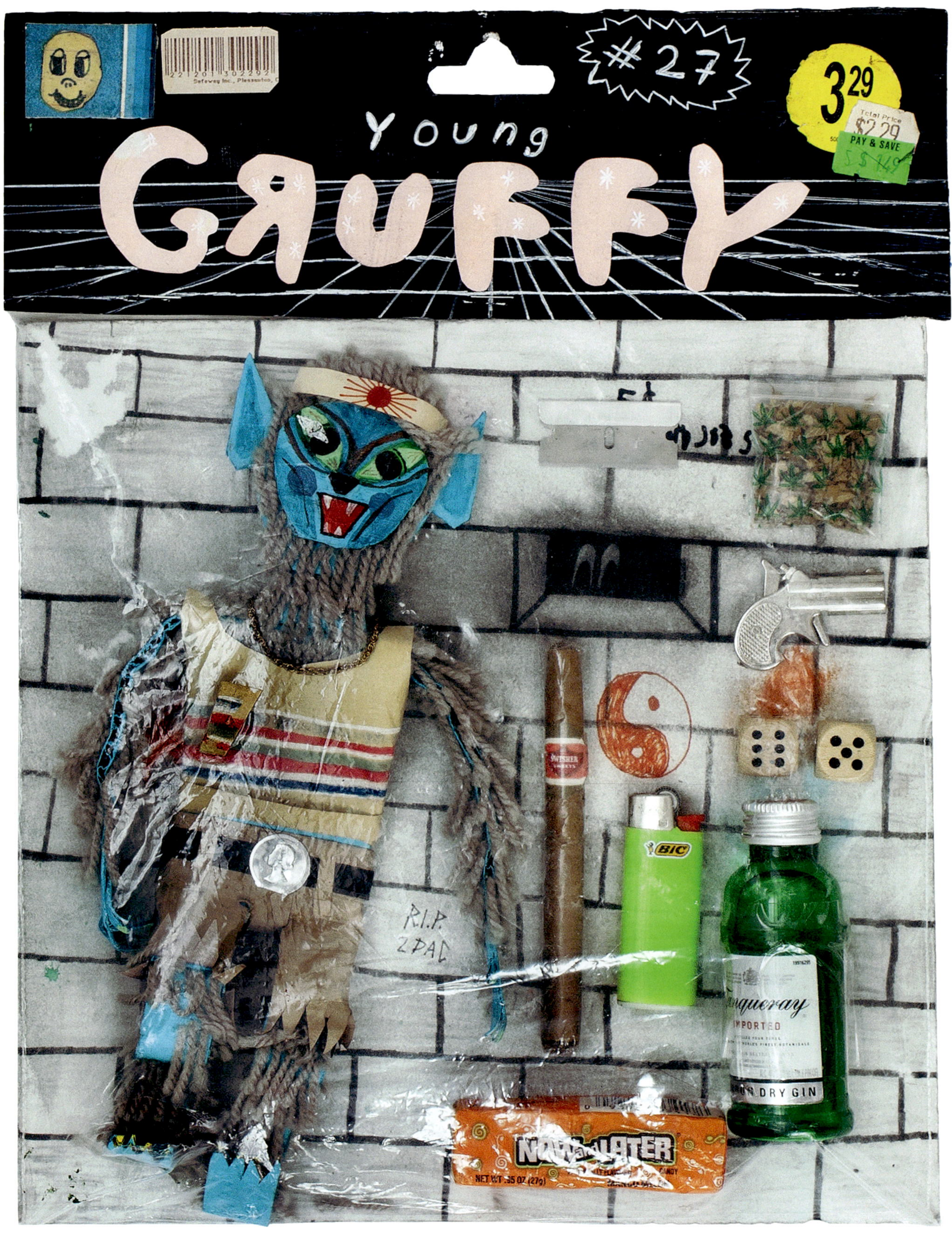

Gruffy, 2010

SAM
$ 3.99
7 36249 03005 7
JACK DANIEL'S
OLD TIME
Old
No 7
BRAND
Tennessee
SOUR MASH
WHISKEY
BOB
WUZ
HERE

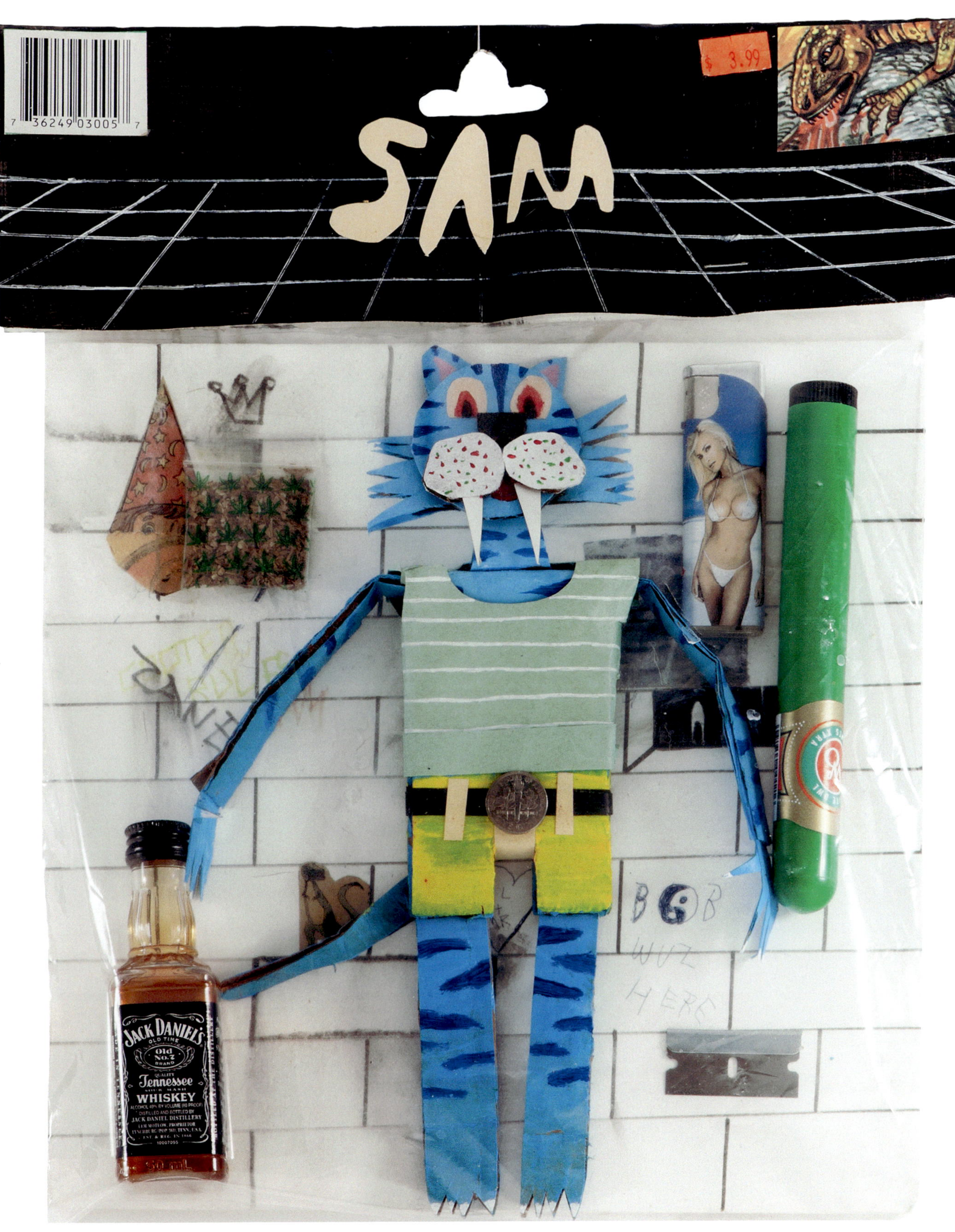

Sam, 2010

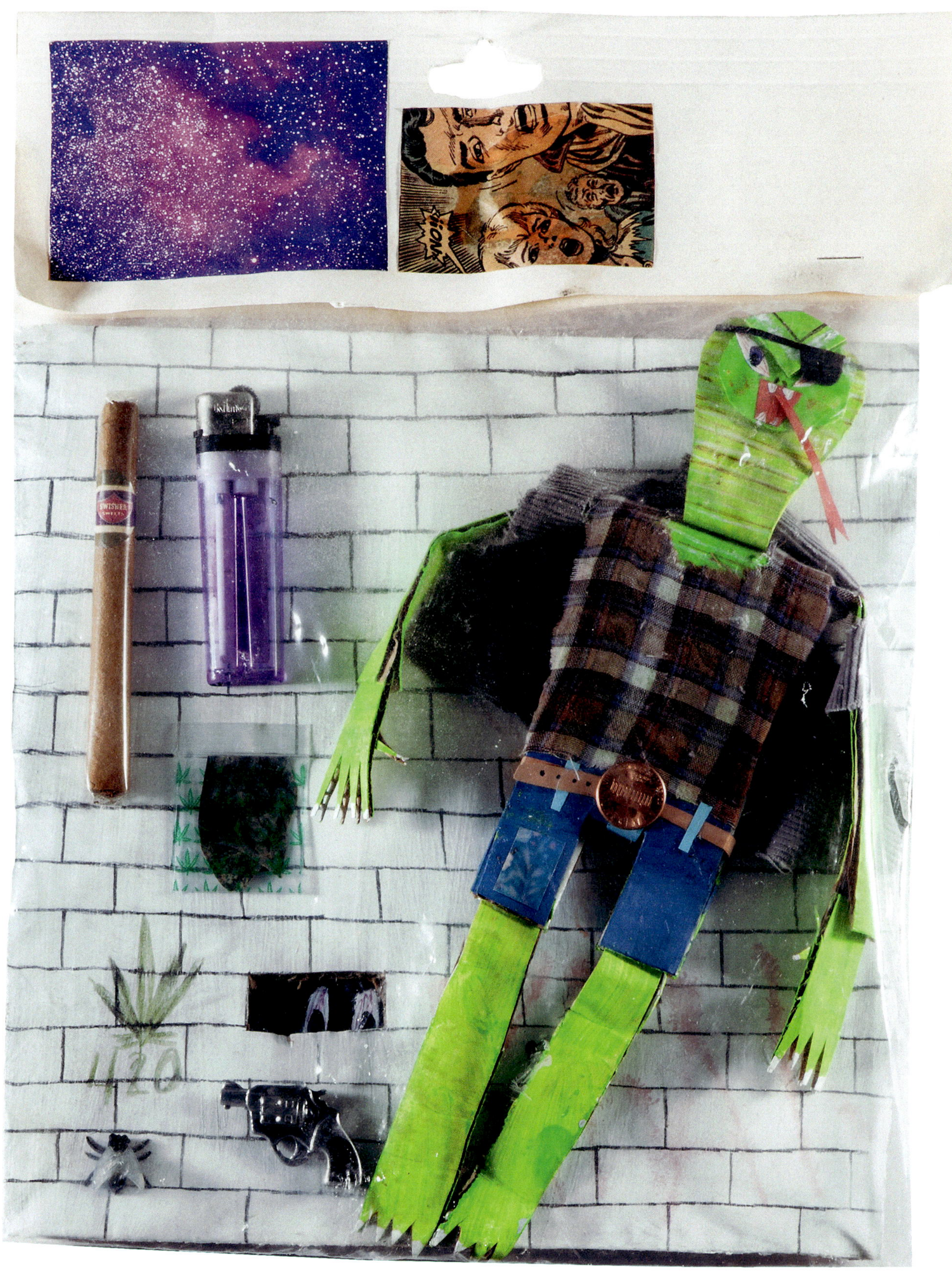

Valencia, 2010

94

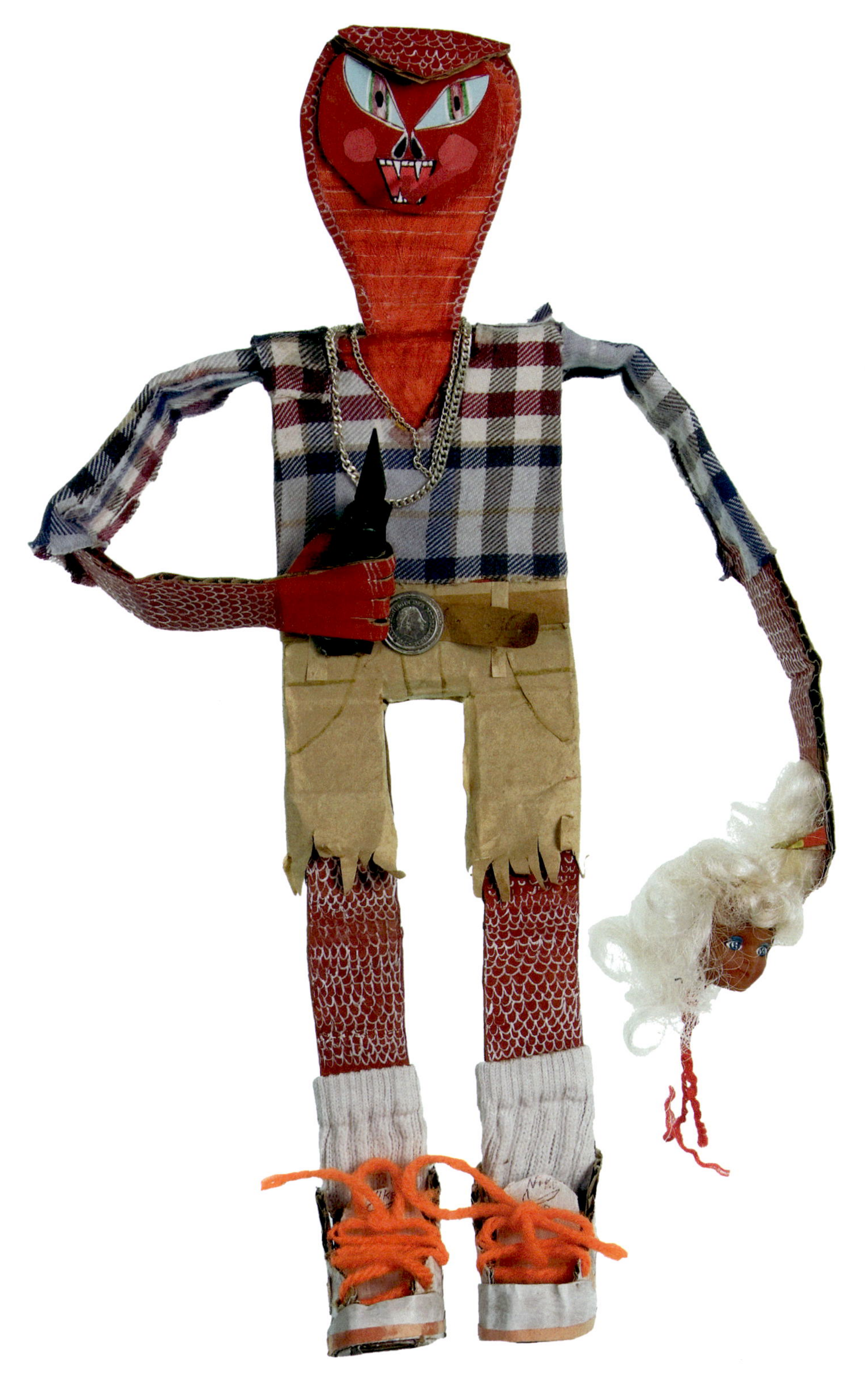

Karl, 2009

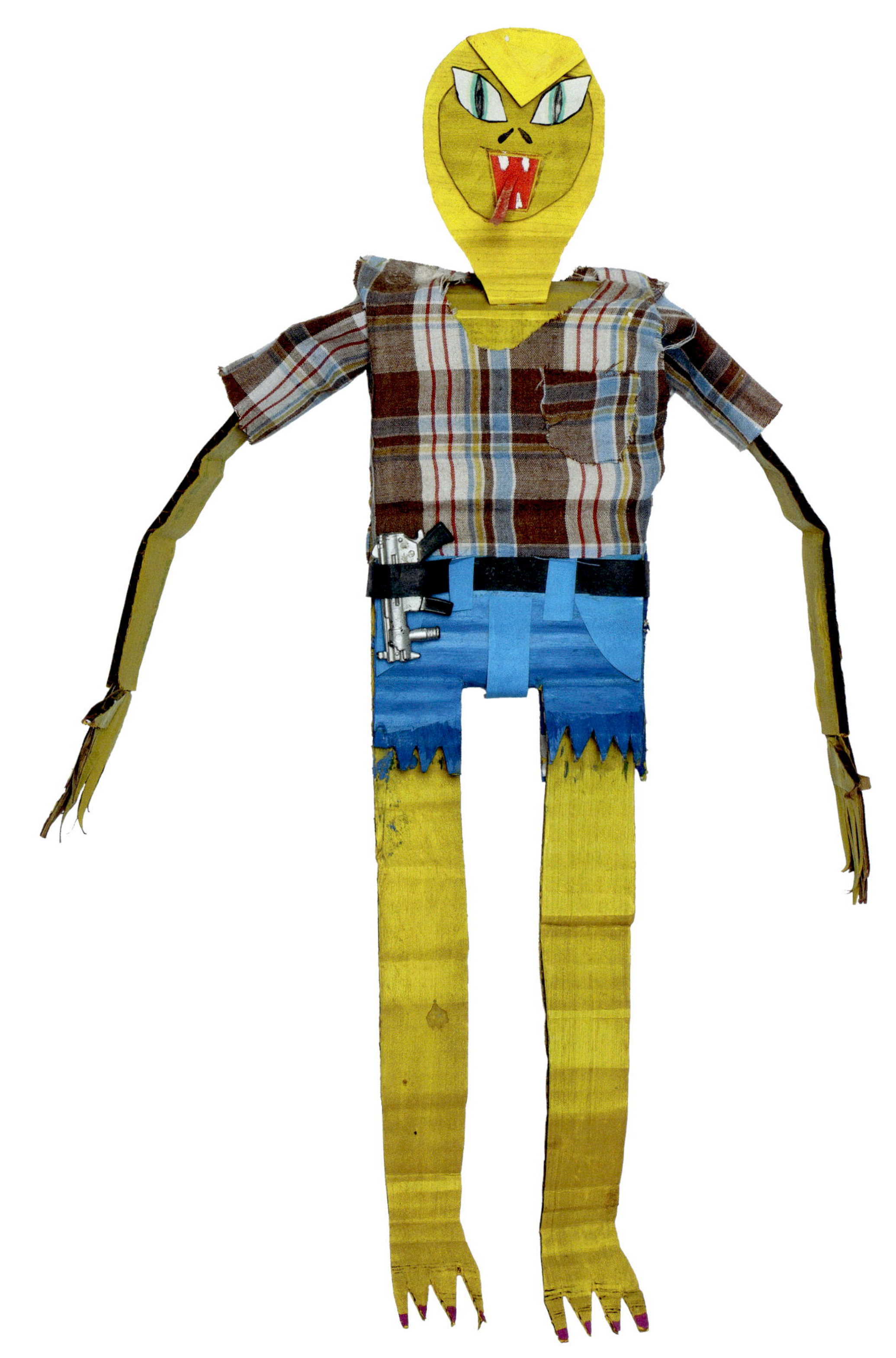

Brad, 2009

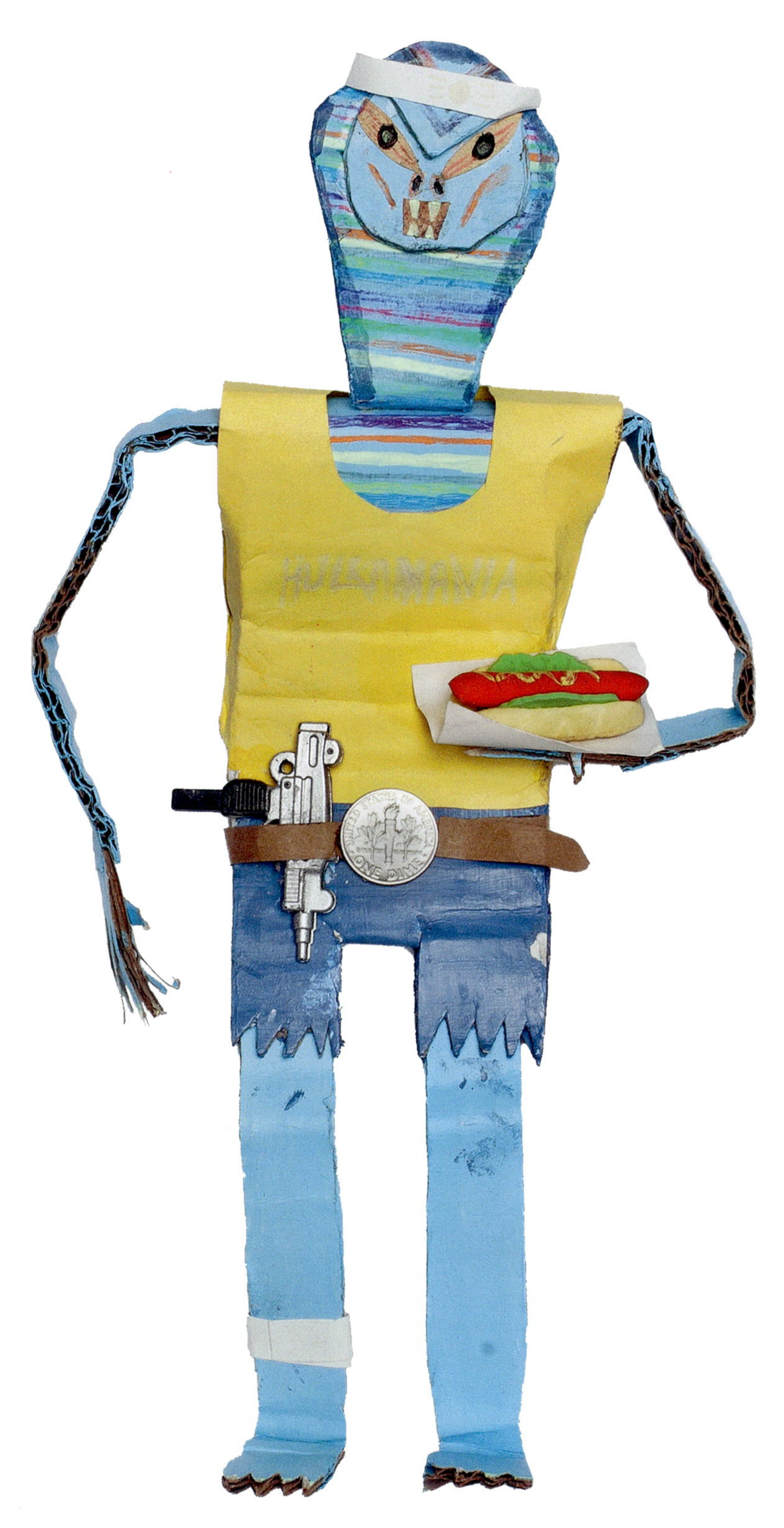

Howard, 2009

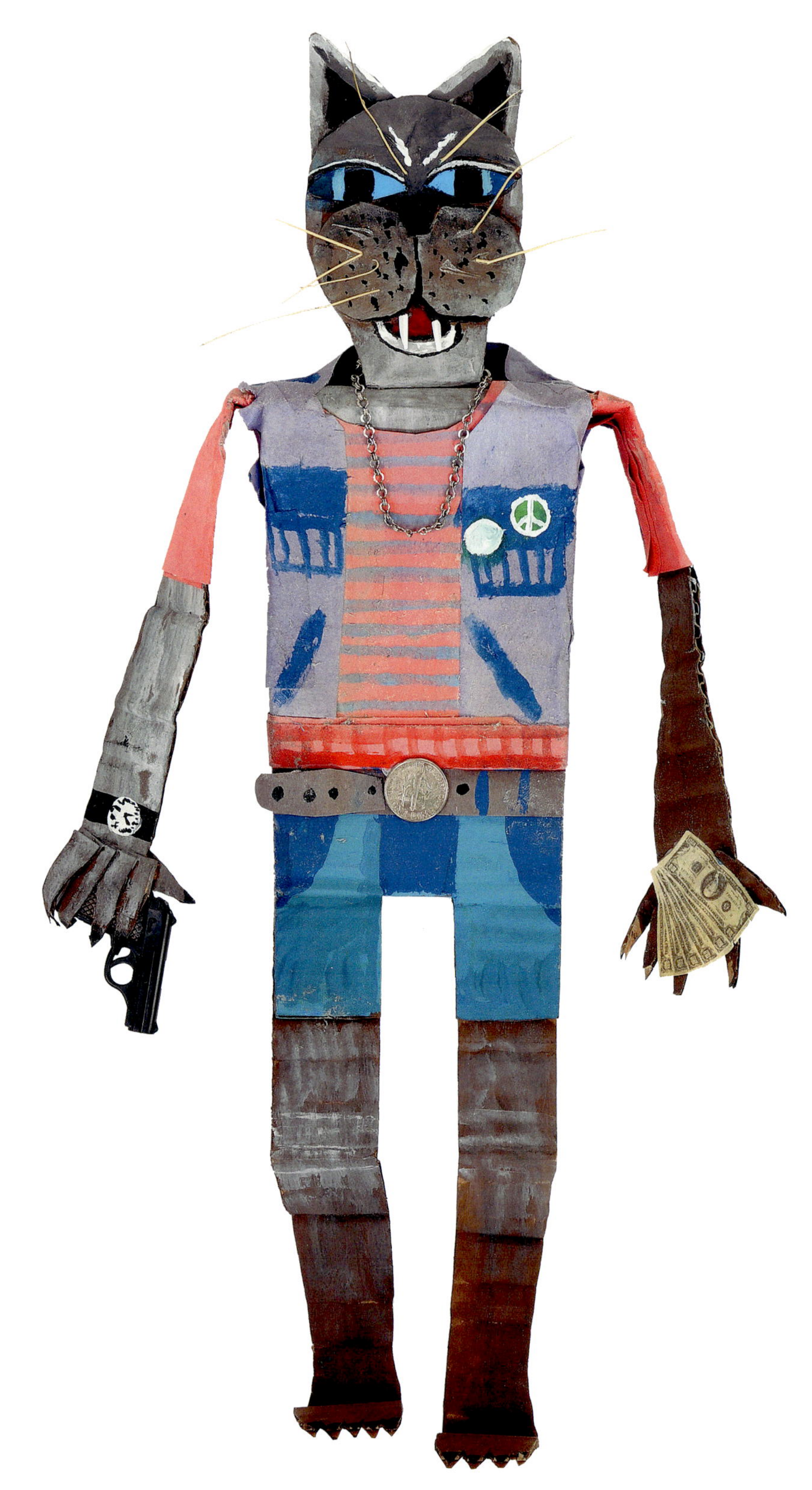

Mr. Pizzaman, 2013

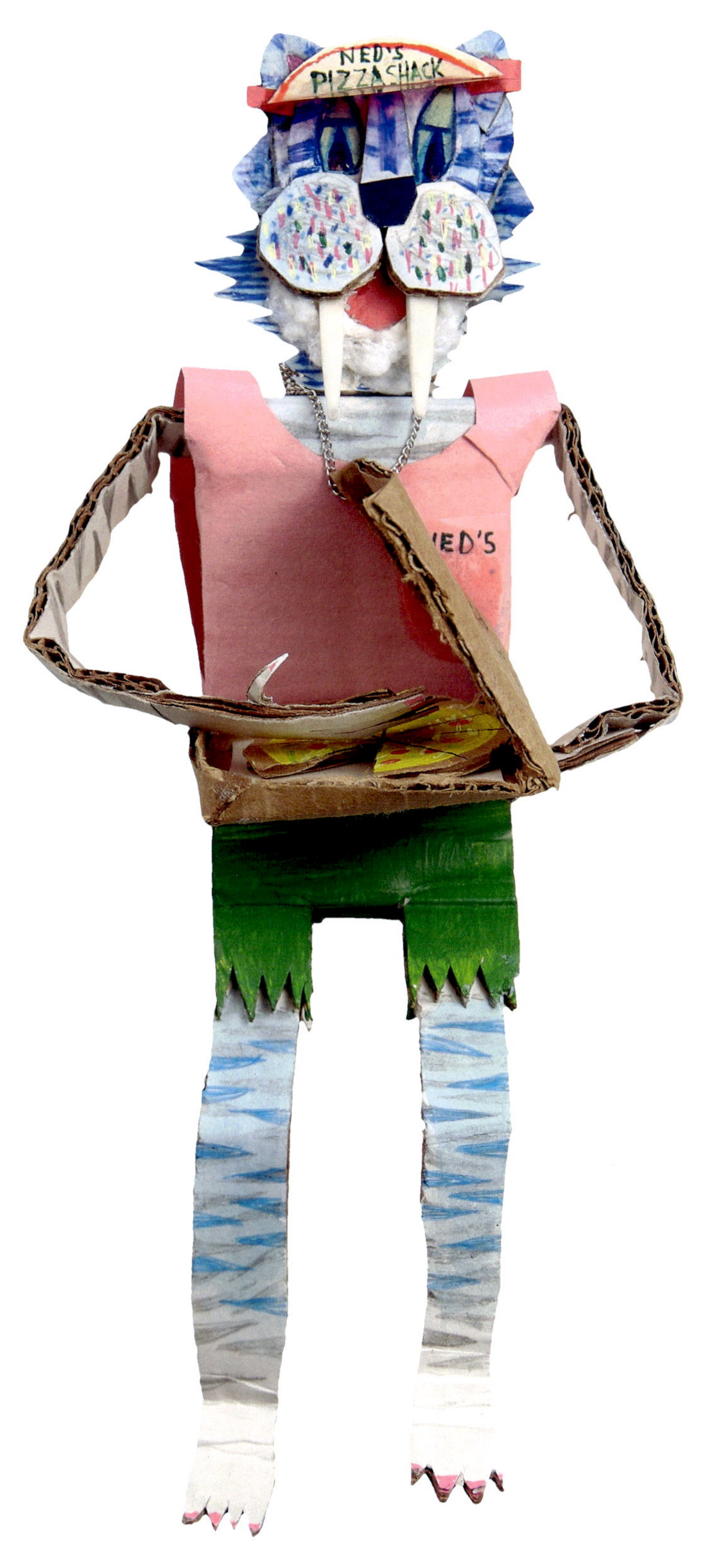

Louie, 2010

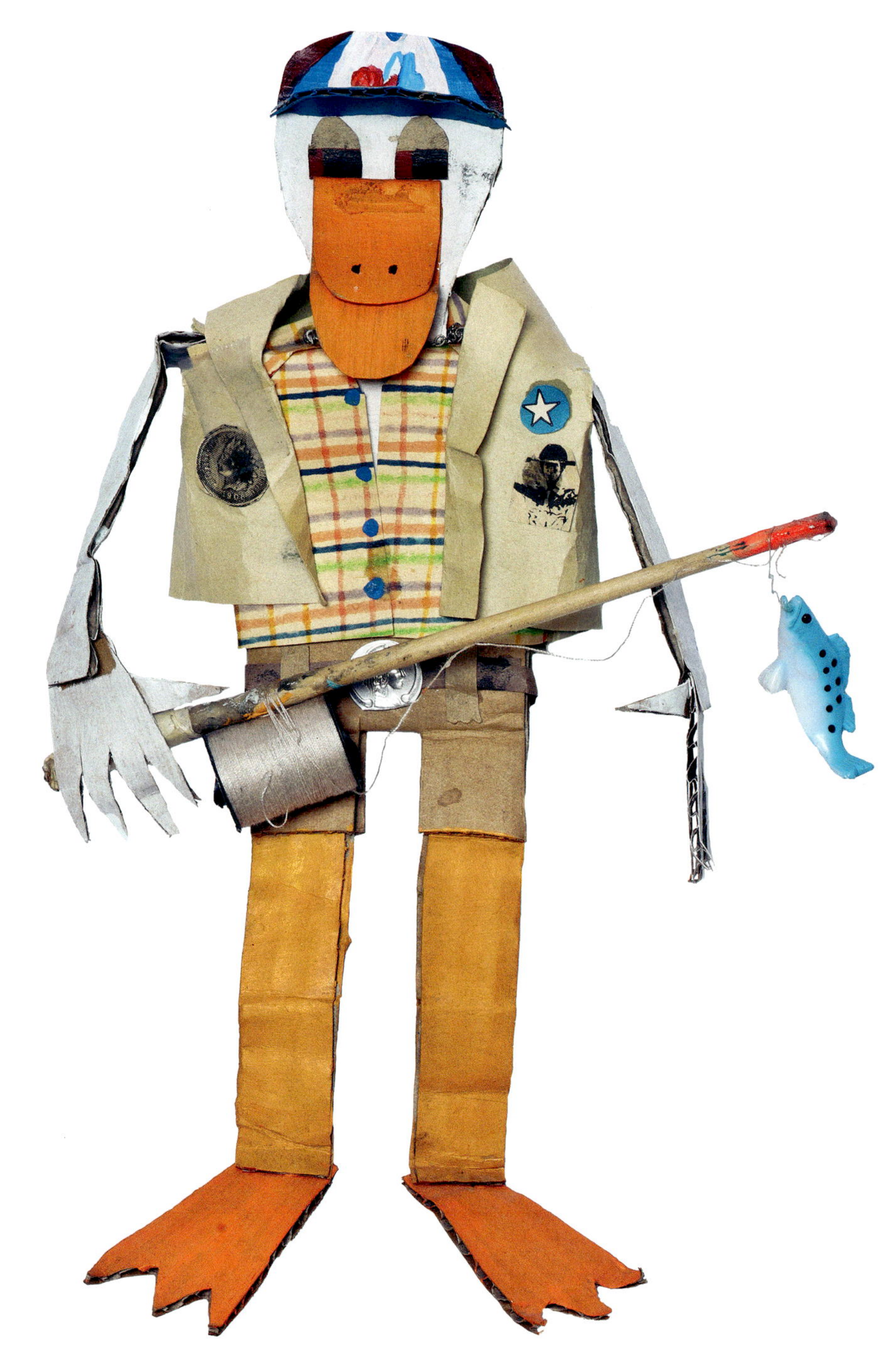

Duck, 2010

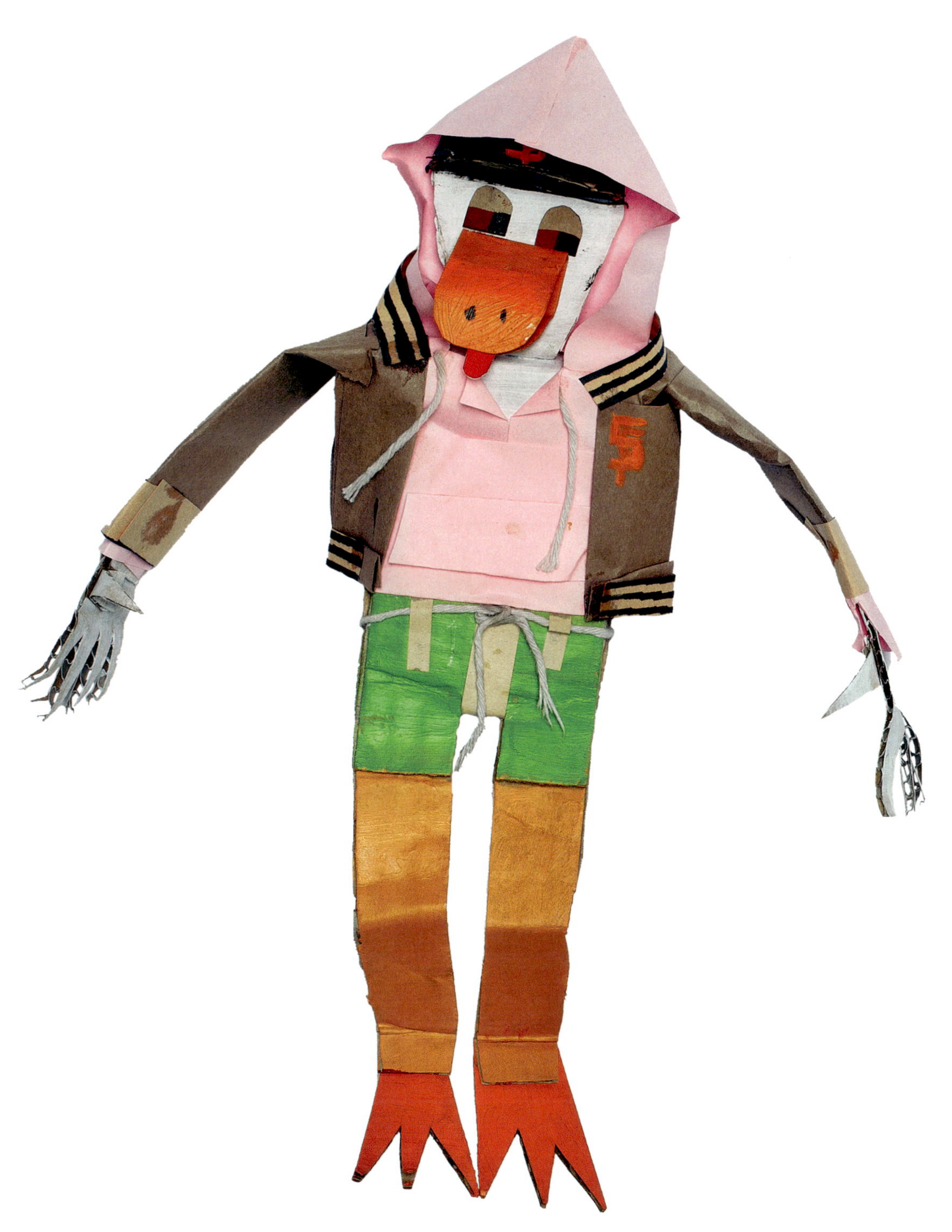

Duck 2, 2010

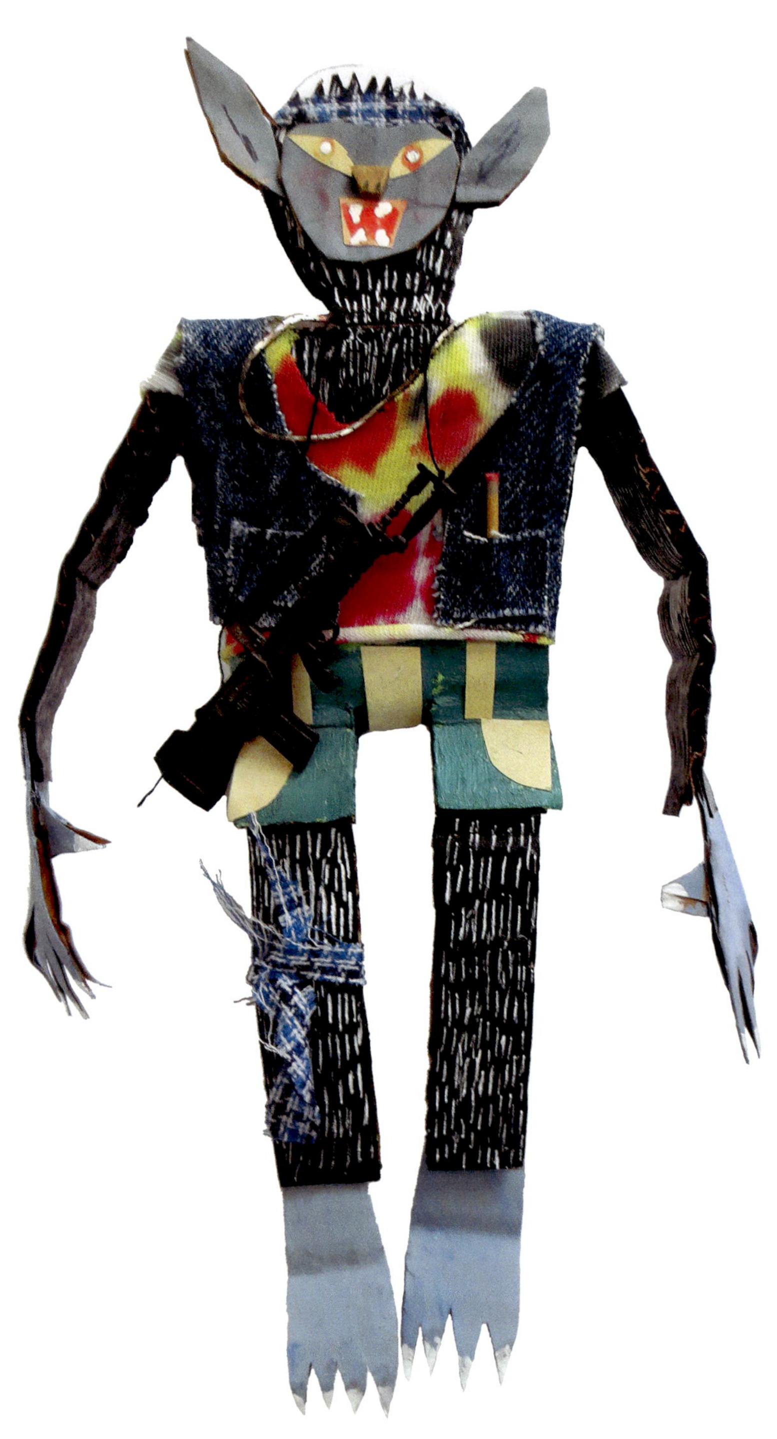

Bat Boy Tell Em, 2008

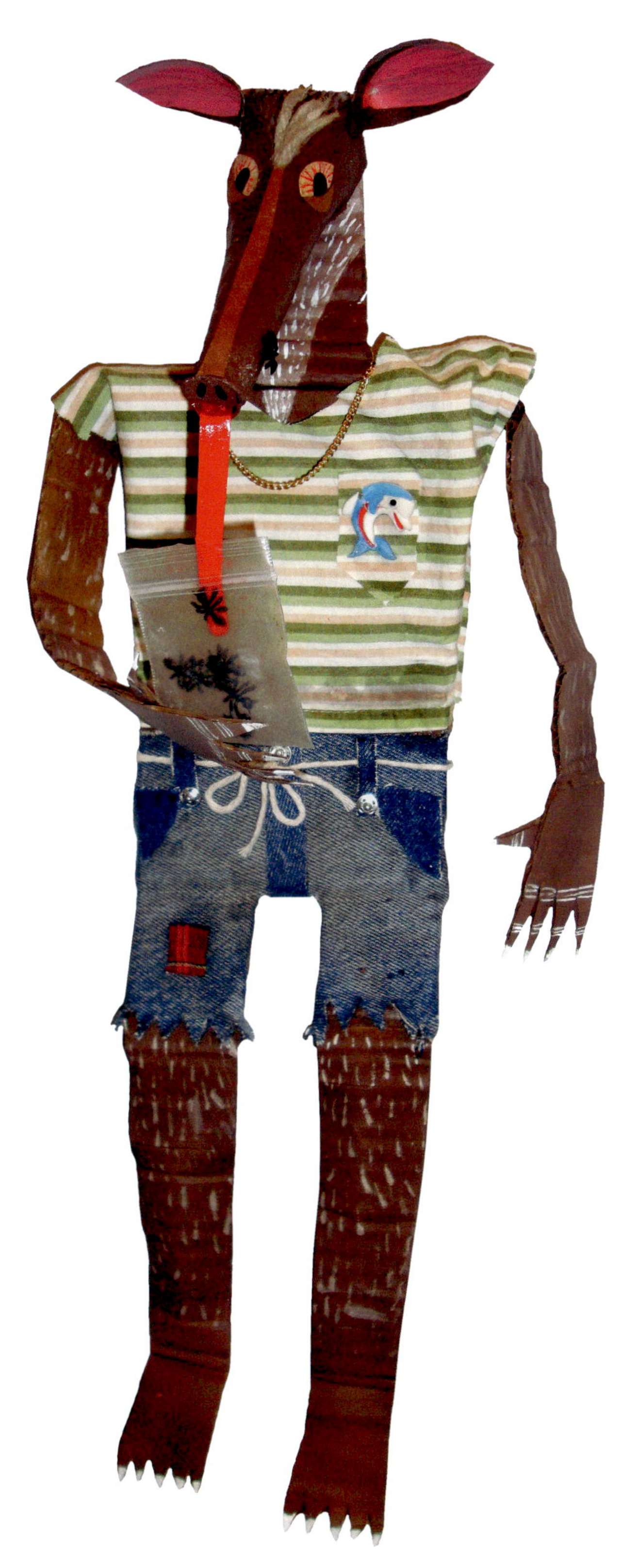

Anteater, 2010

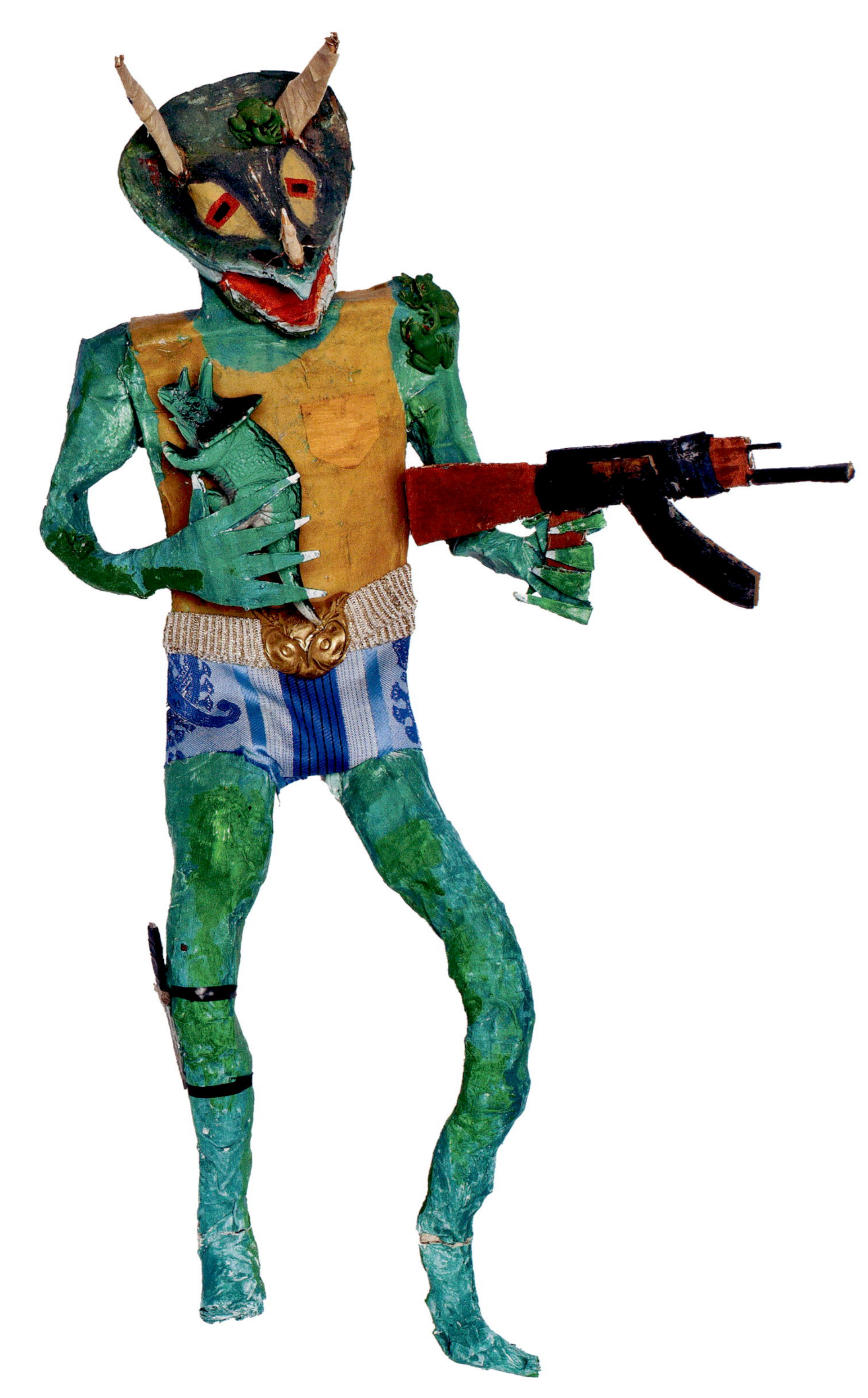

Tricepticon, 2011

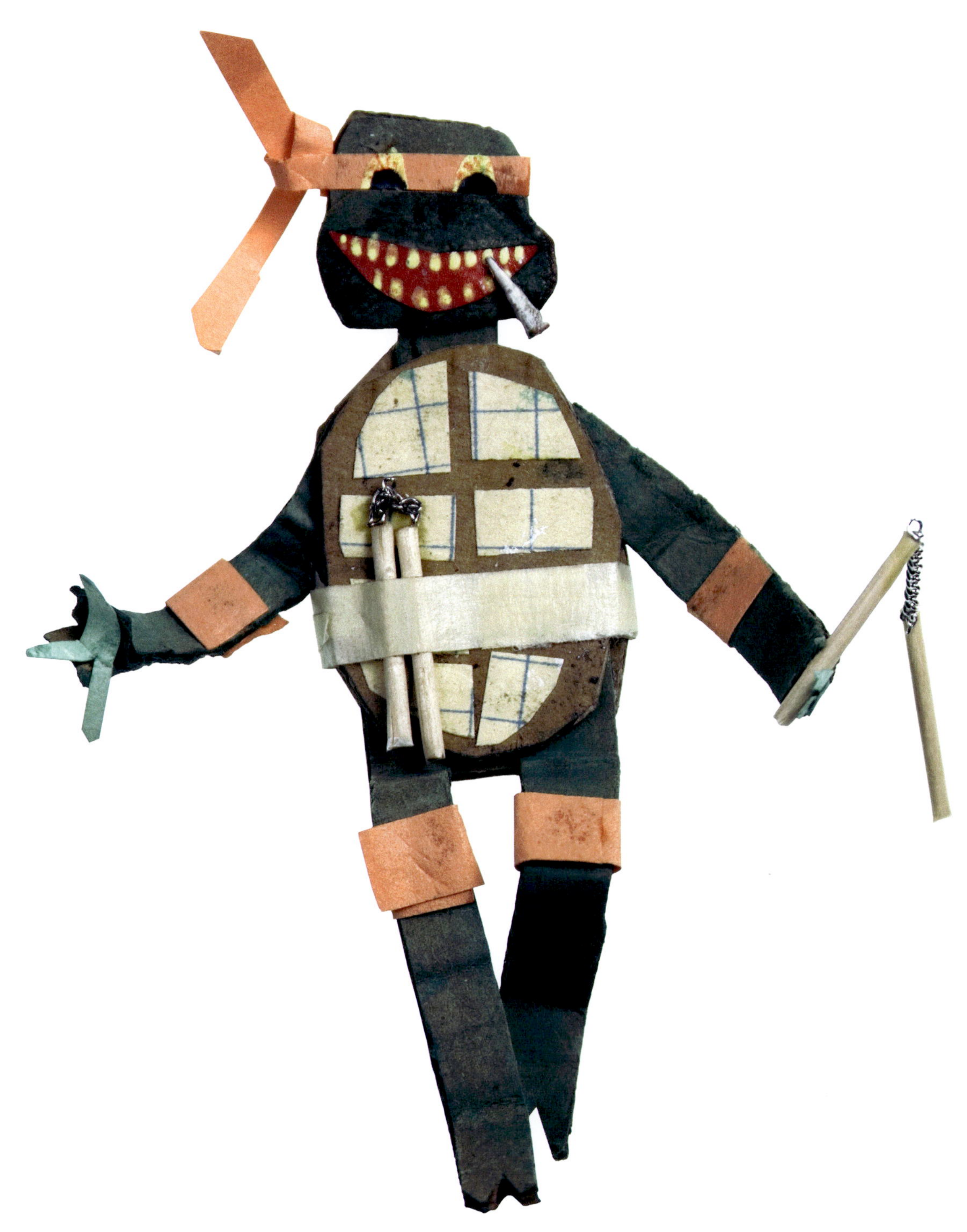

Mike, 2010

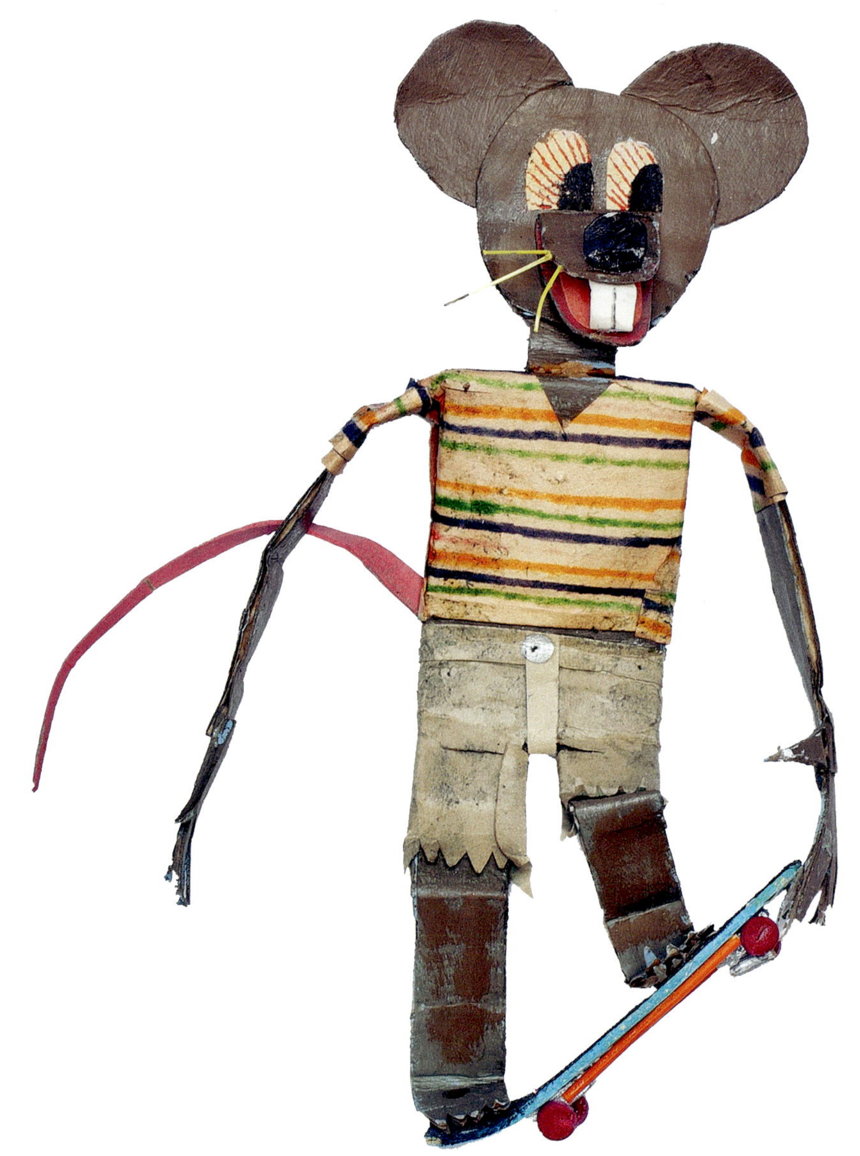

Skate Rat, 2010

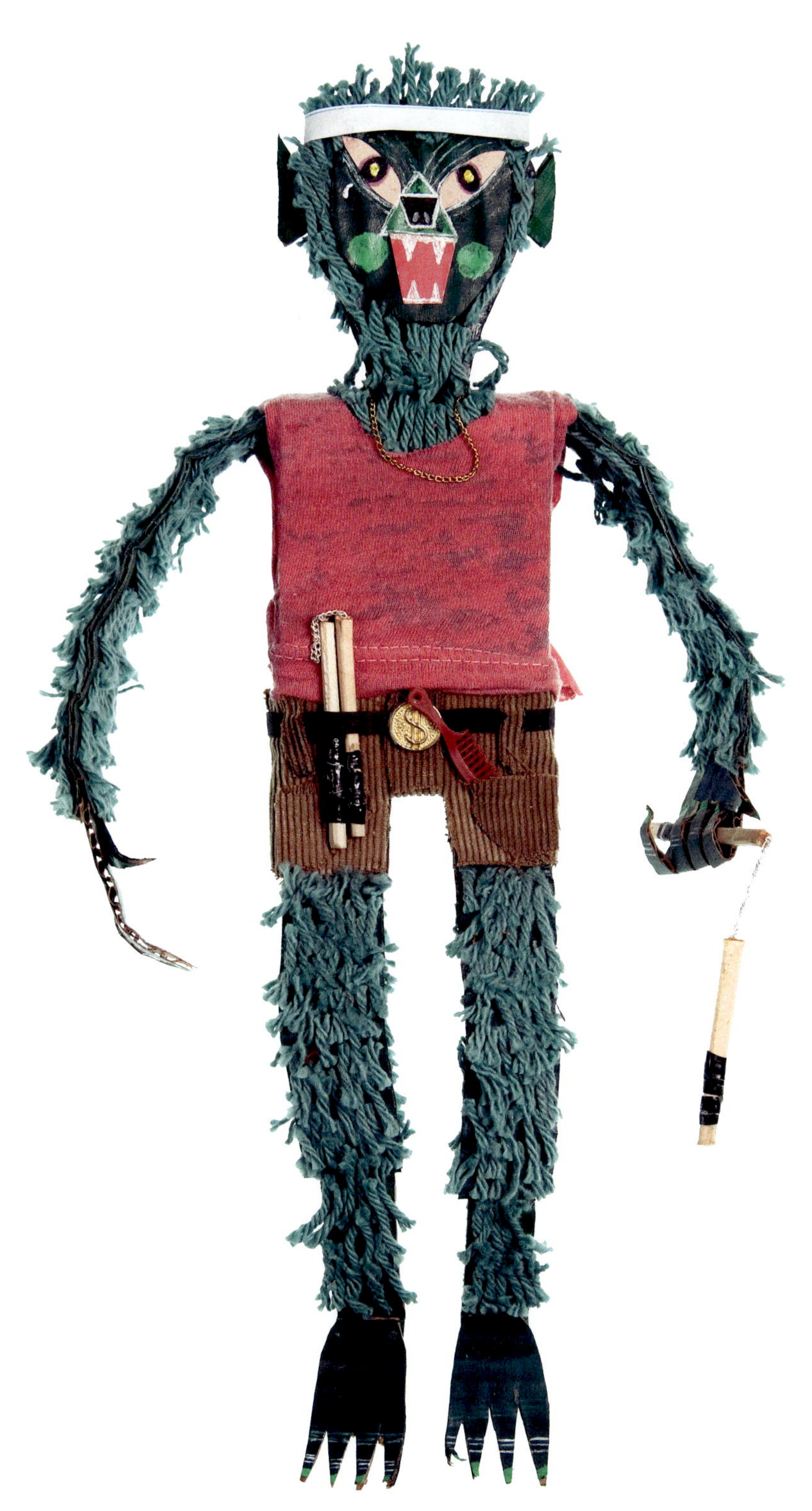

Doug, 2009

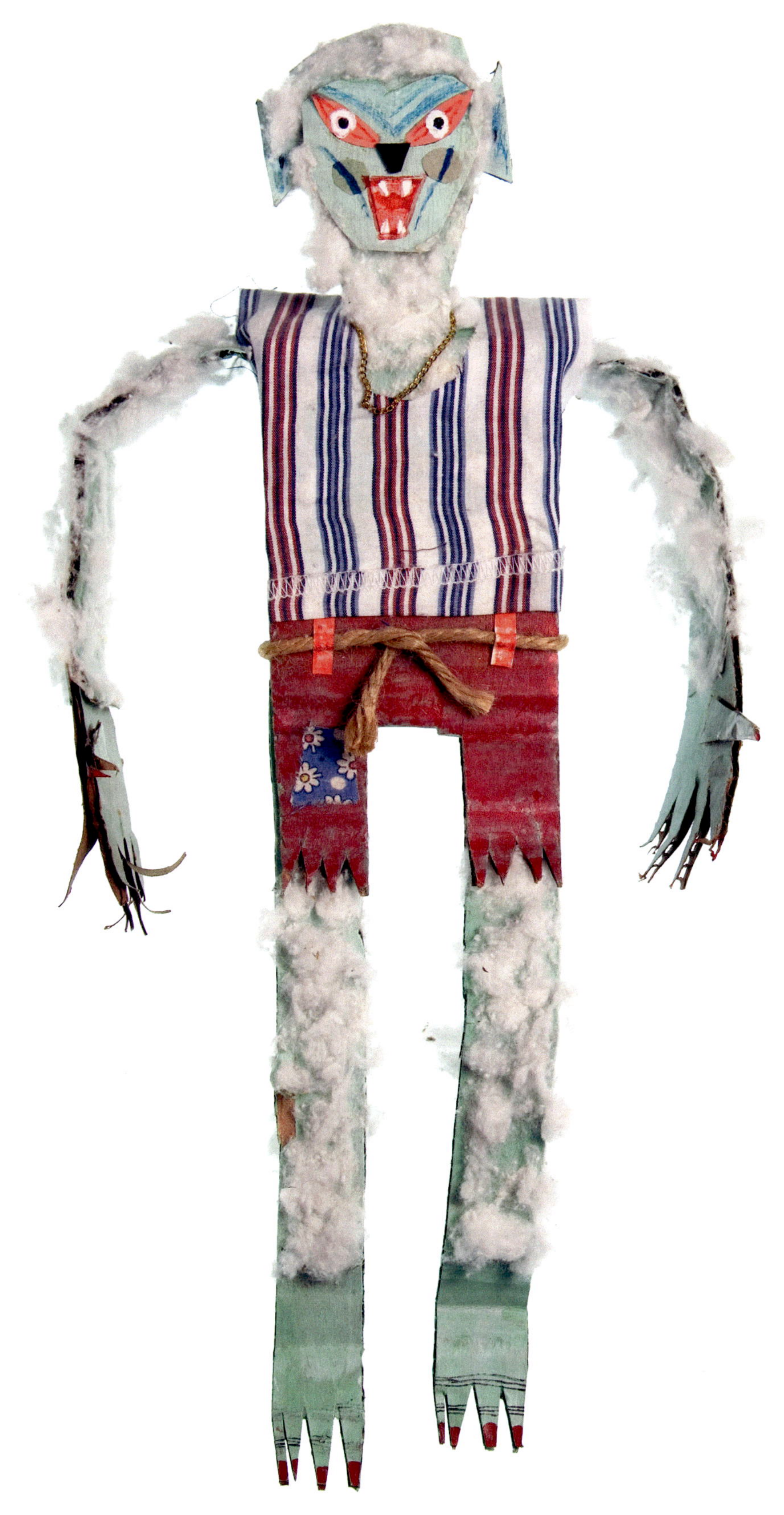

Ron, 2009

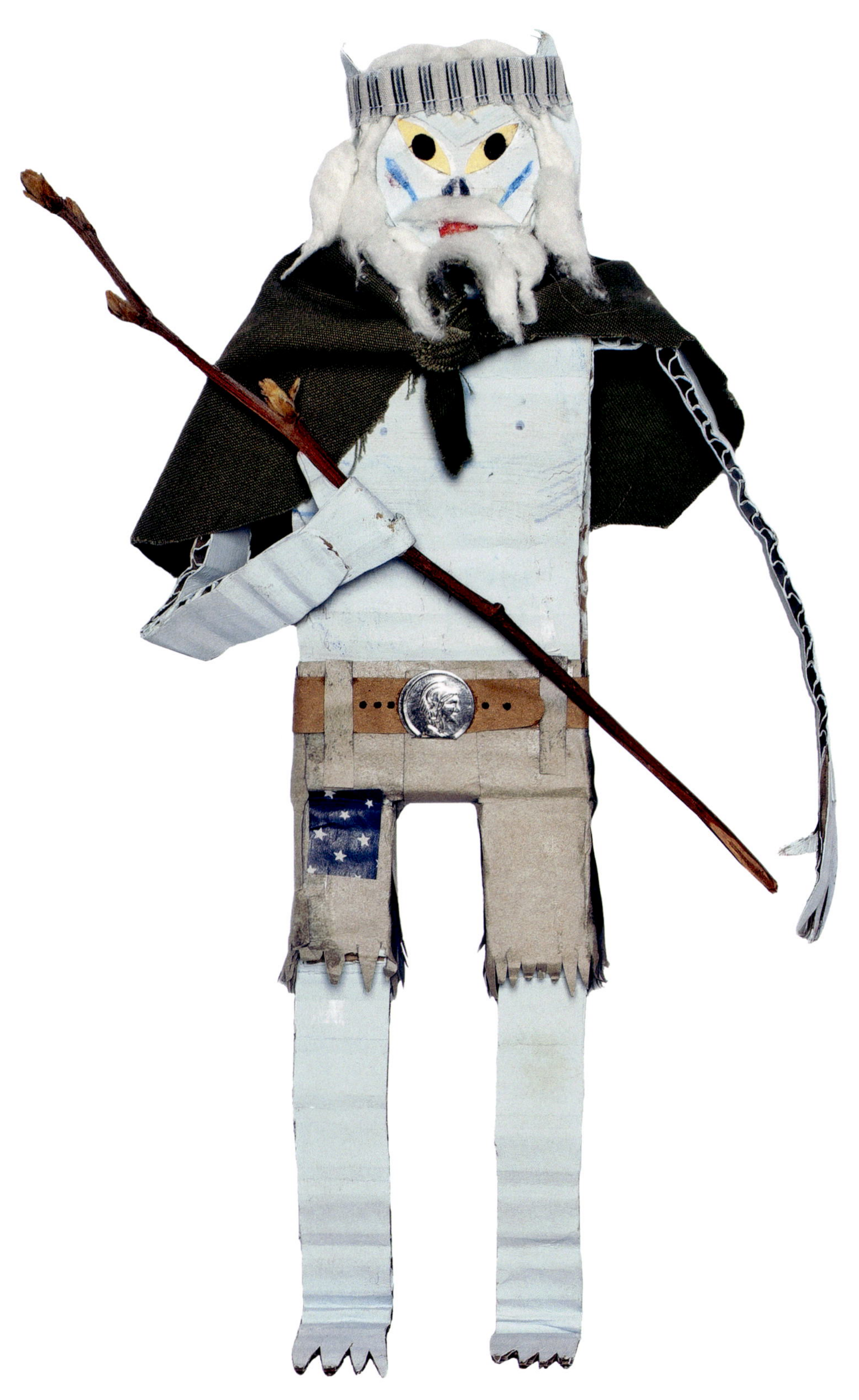

Matt, 2010

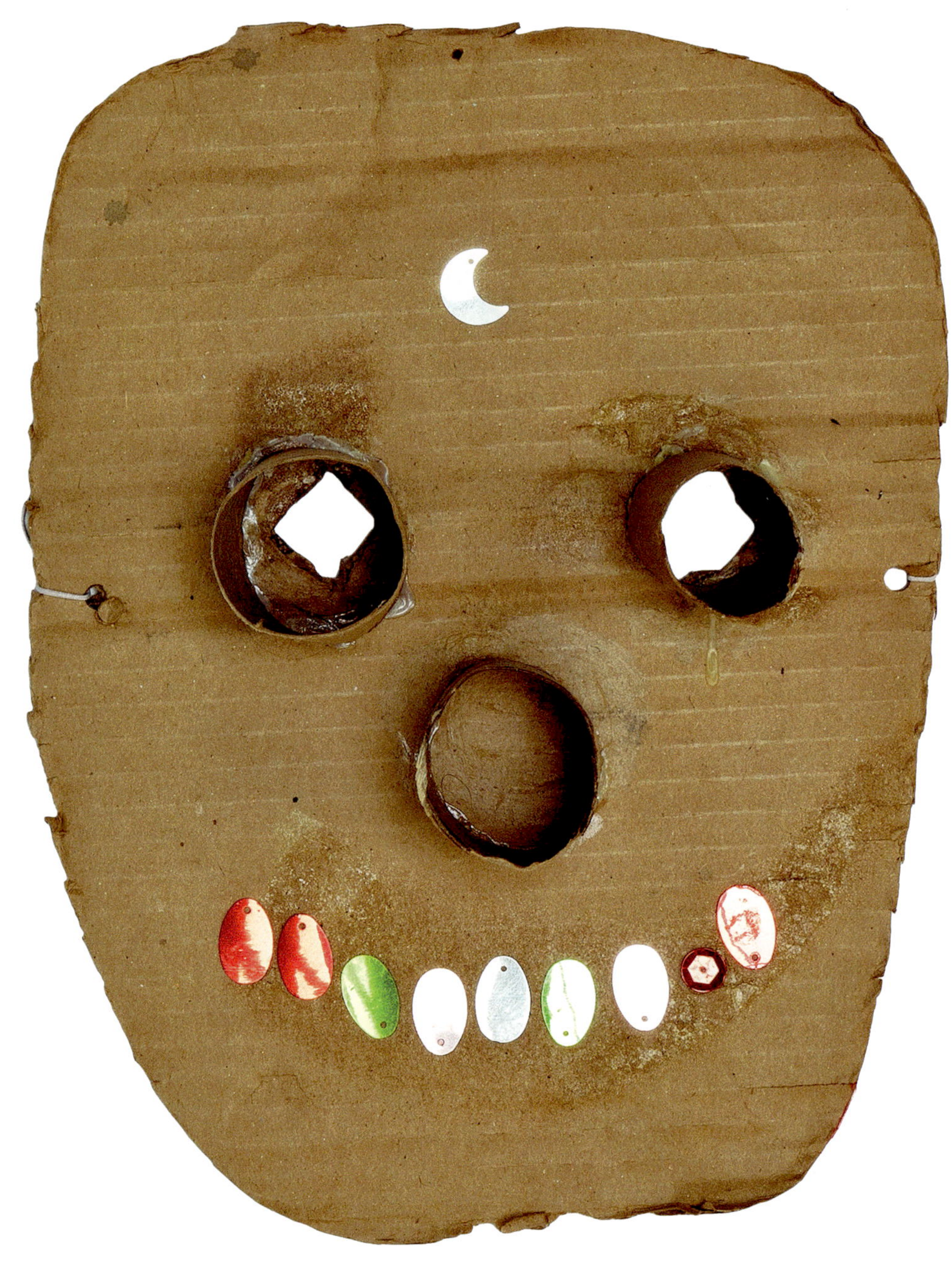

Mask 1, 2008

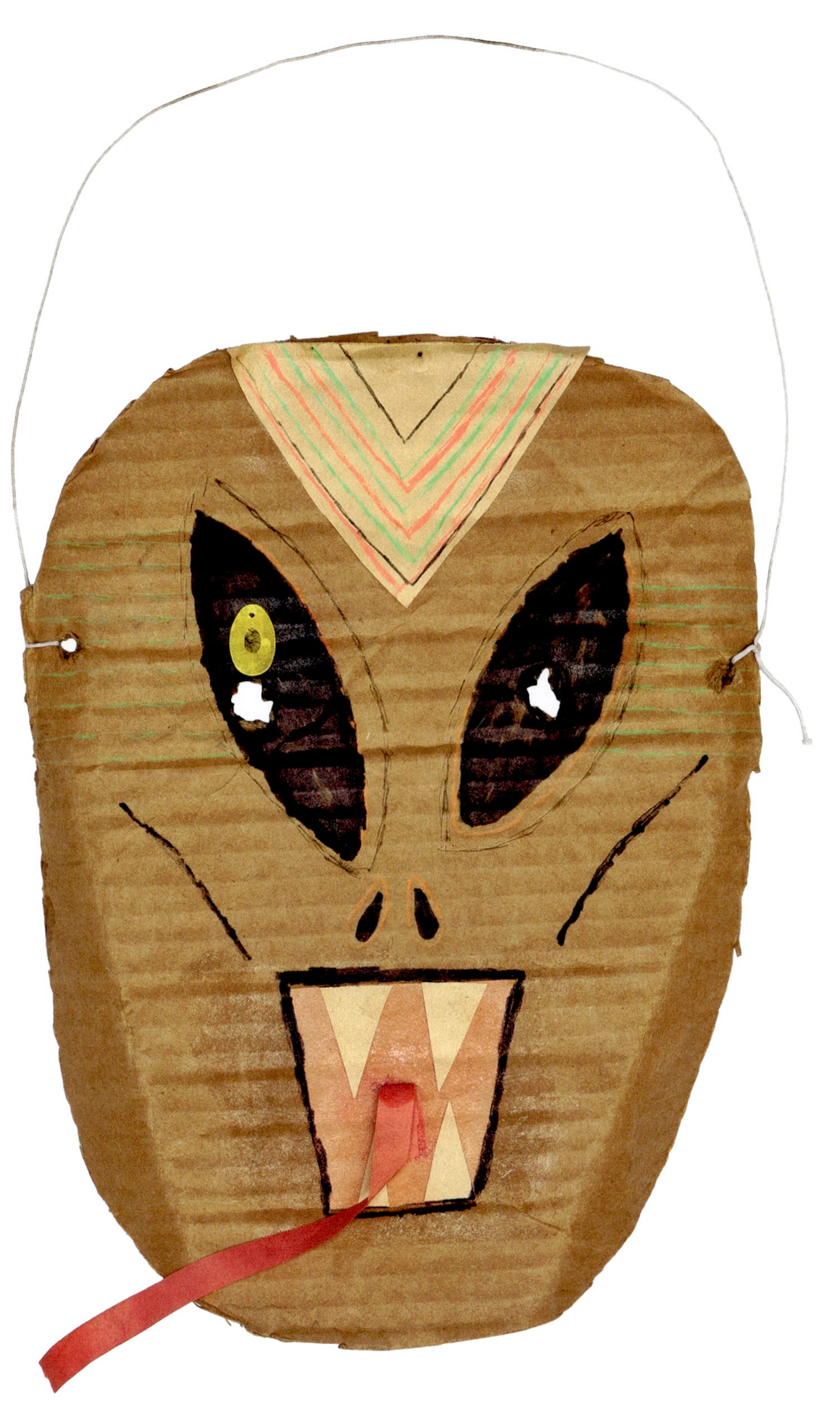

Mask 2, 2008

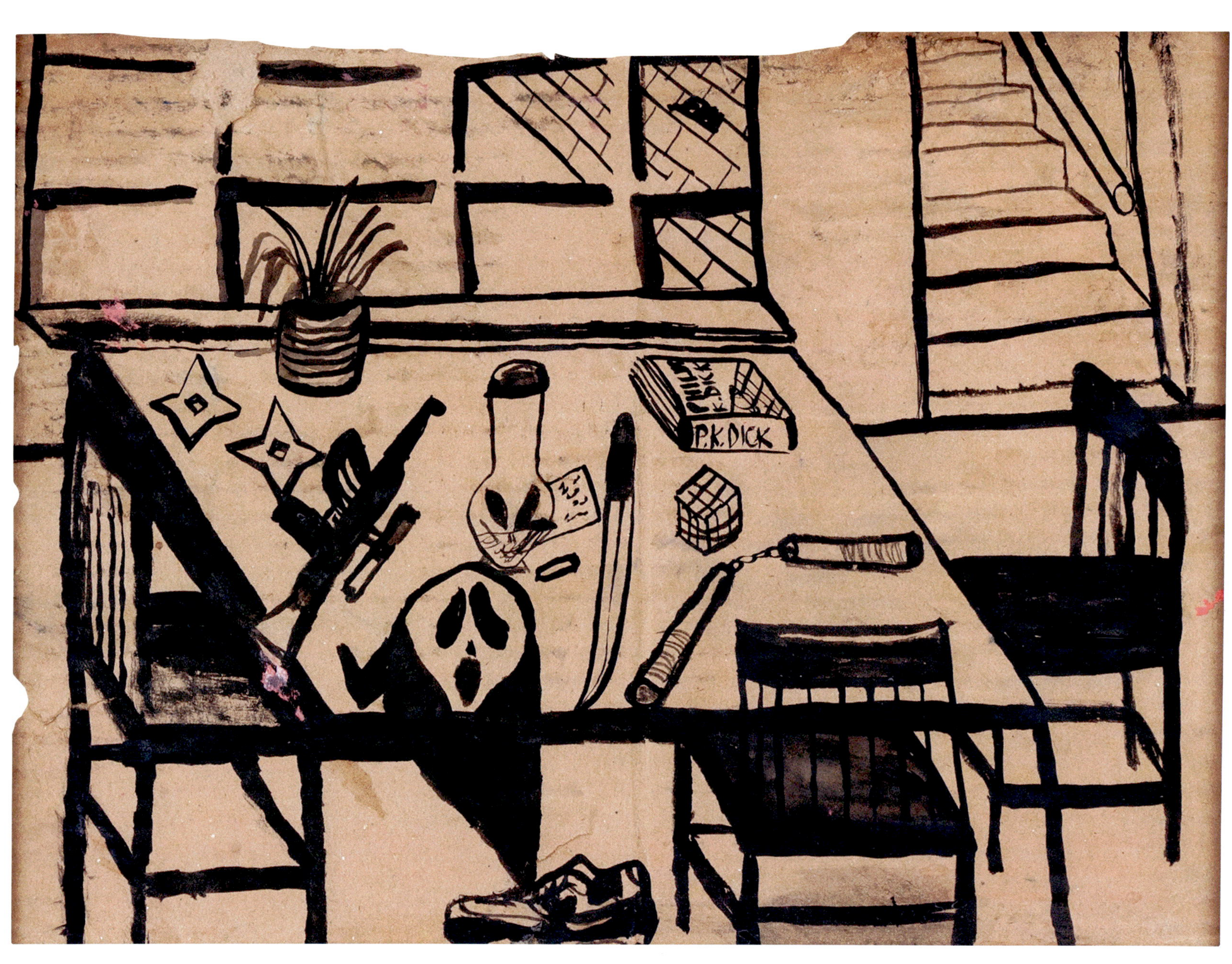

Still Life 5, 2012

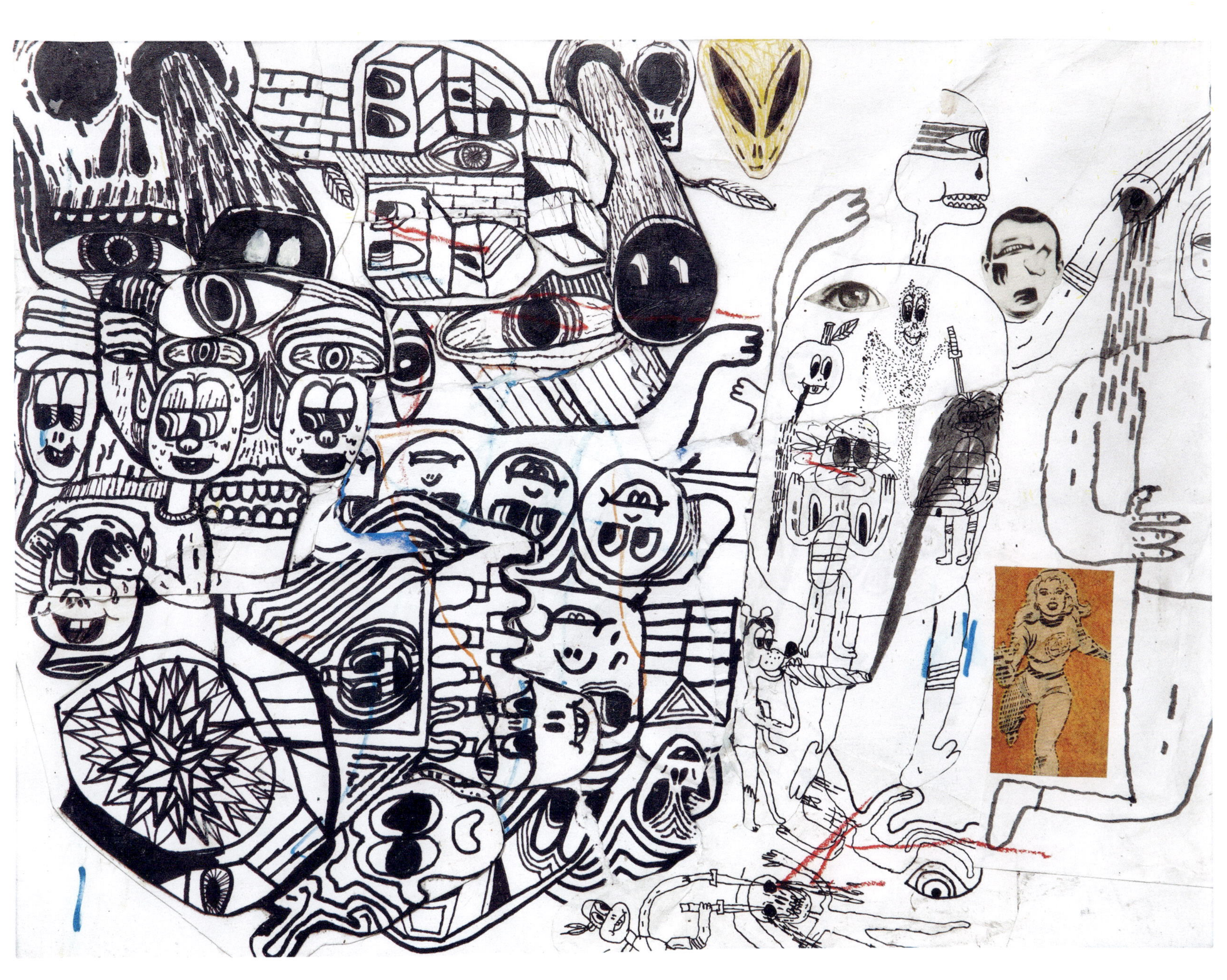

The Life of the Invisible Women, 2011

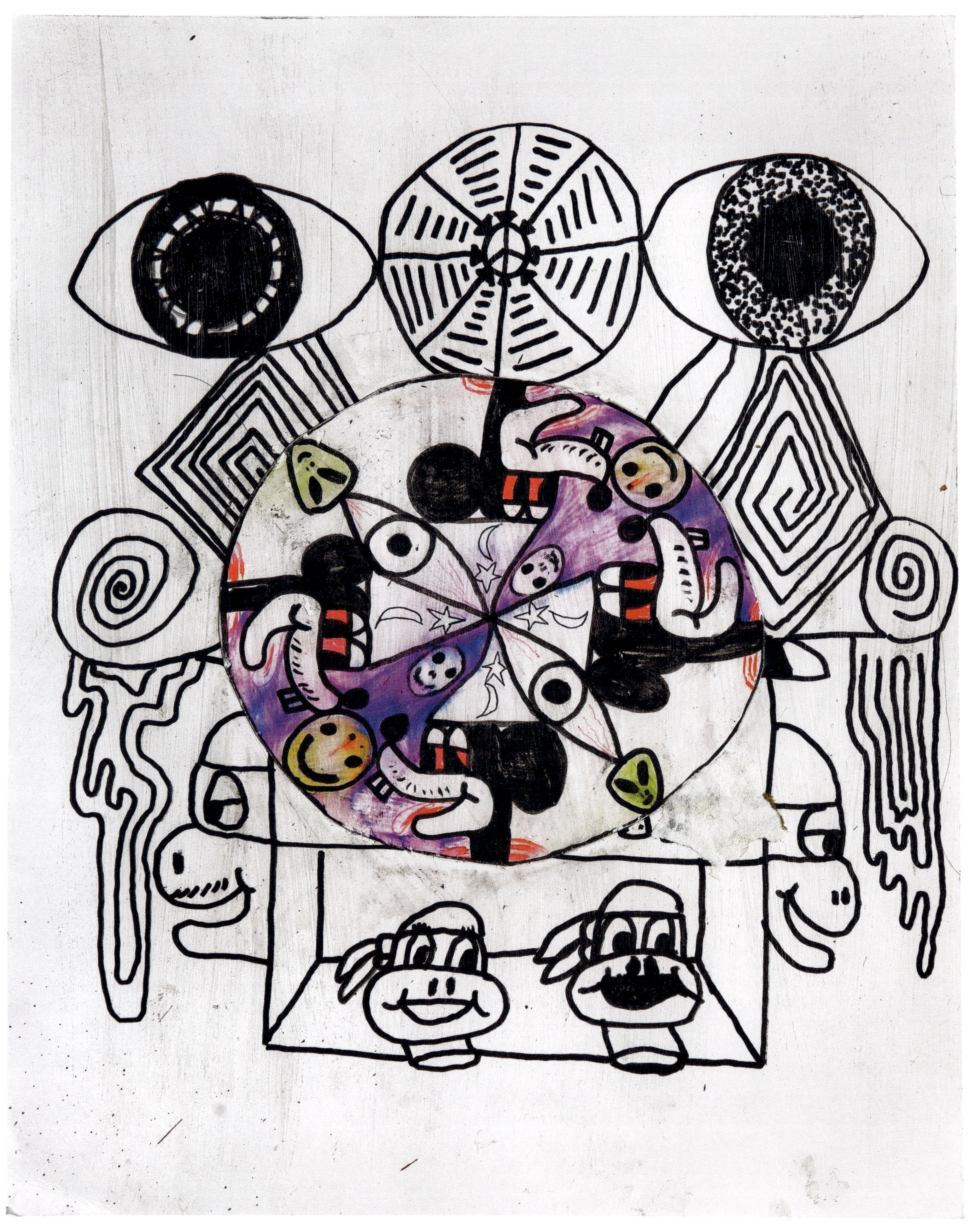

The Shift, 2013

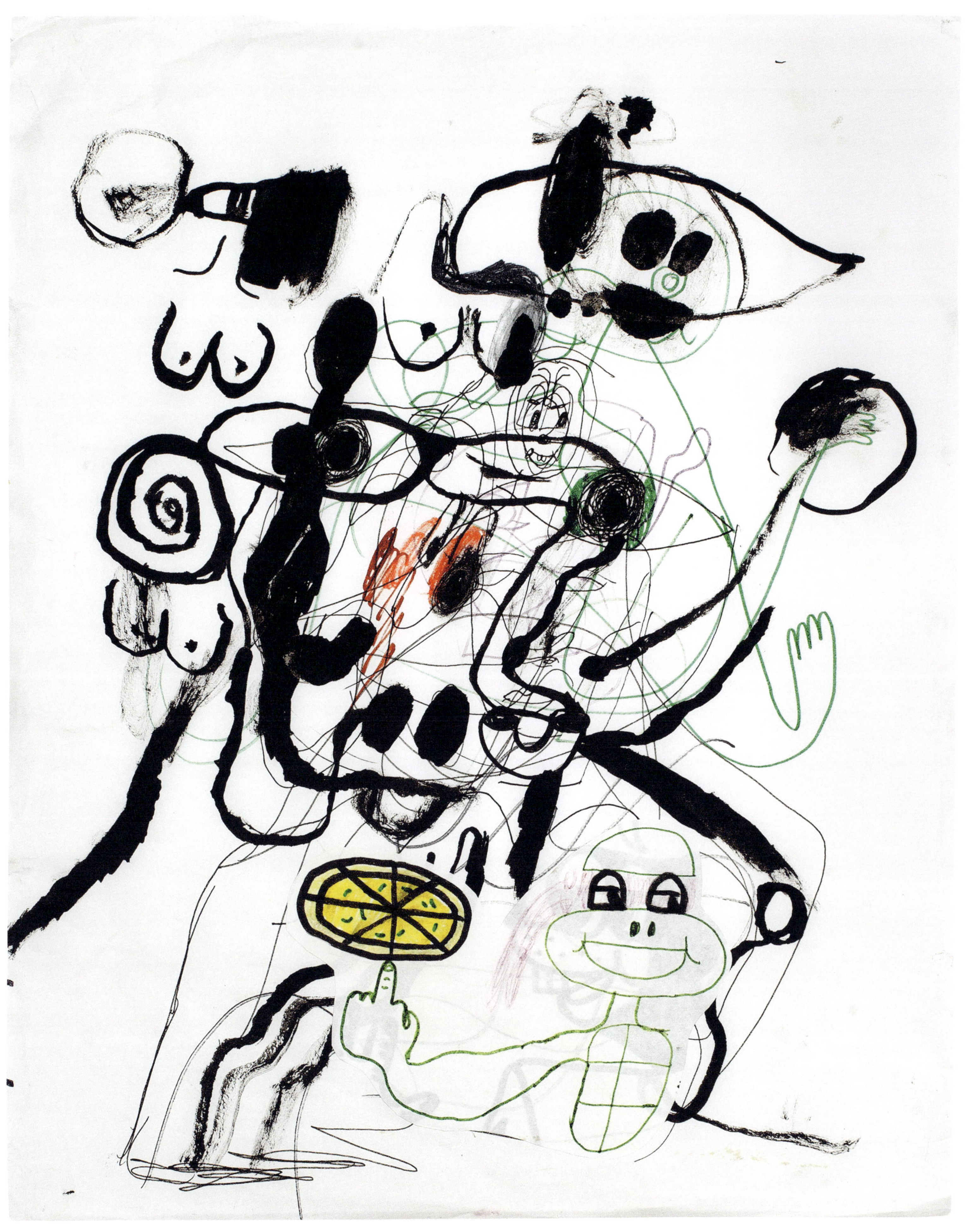

Saturday Night, 2012

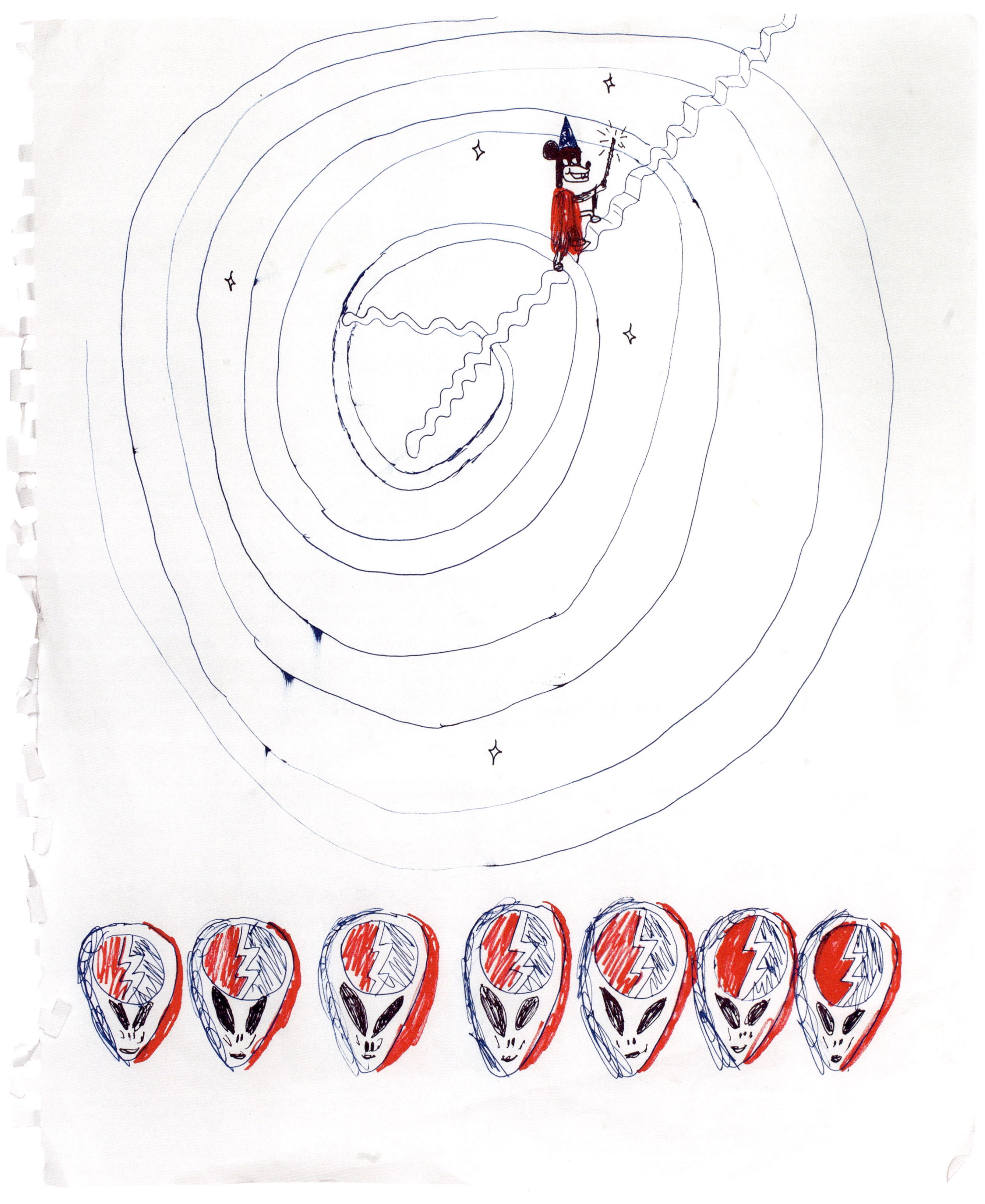

Untitled, 2014

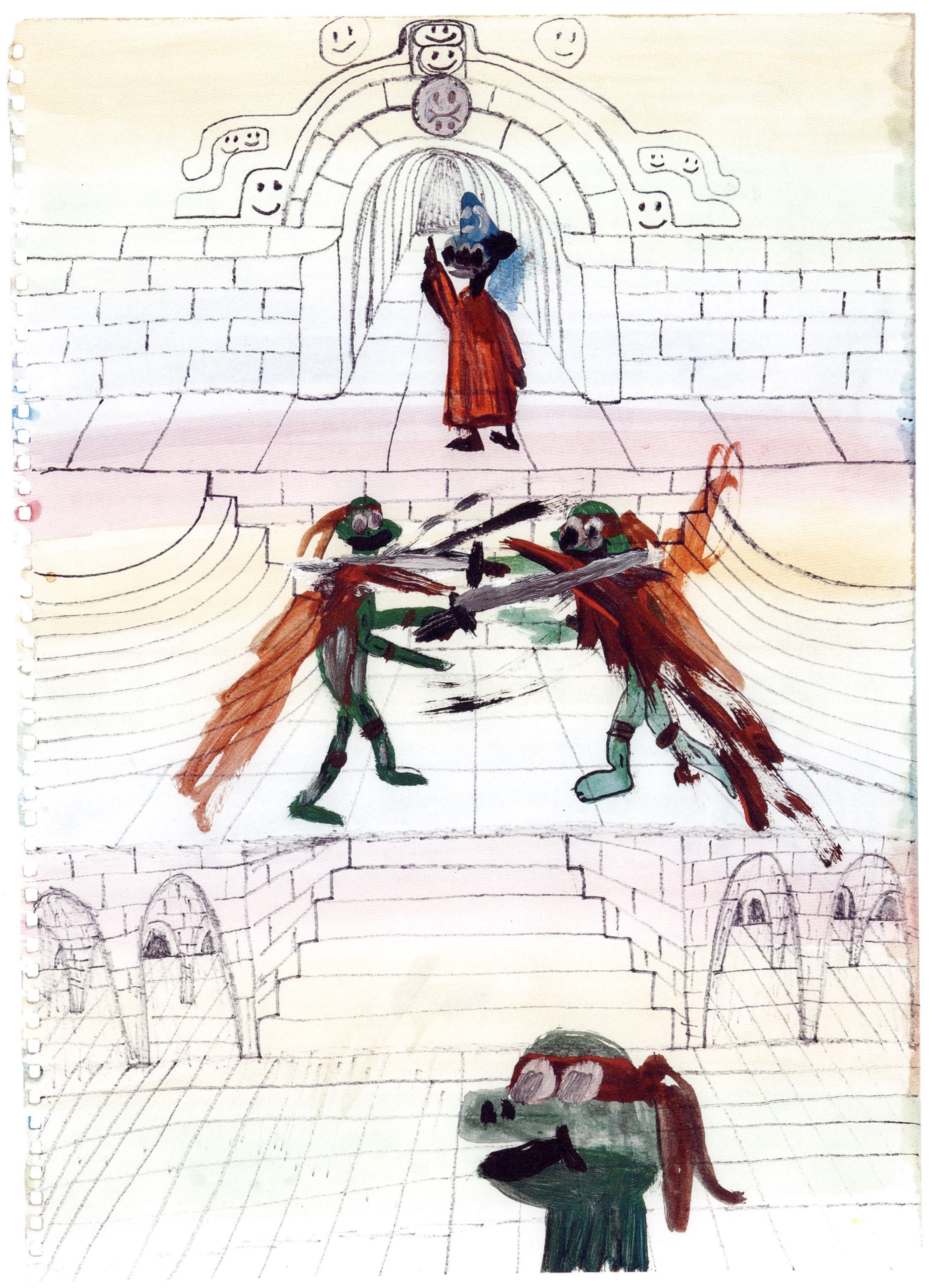

Meet the Buddha Kill the Buddha, 2014

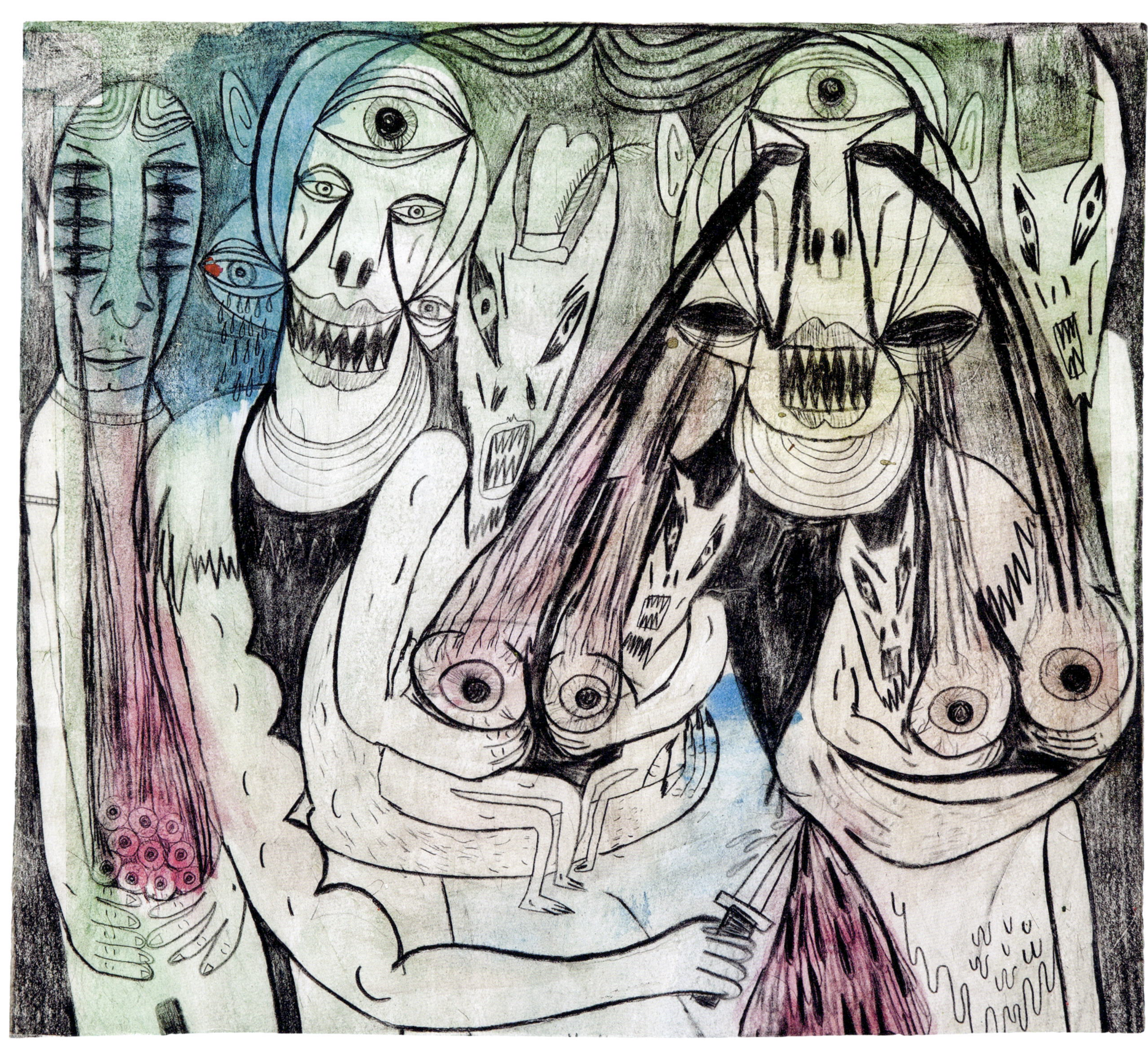

Untitled, 2007

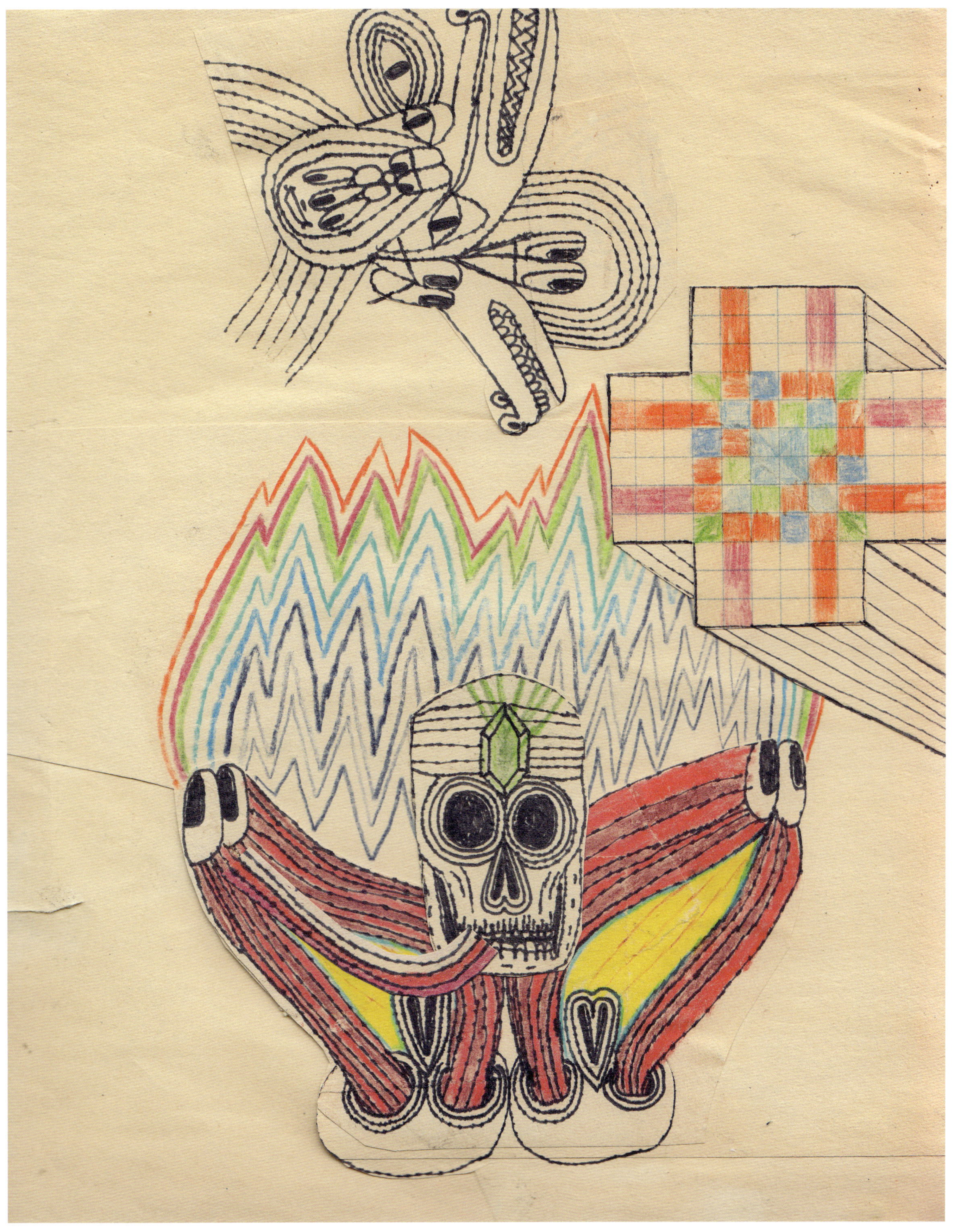

Untitled, 2007

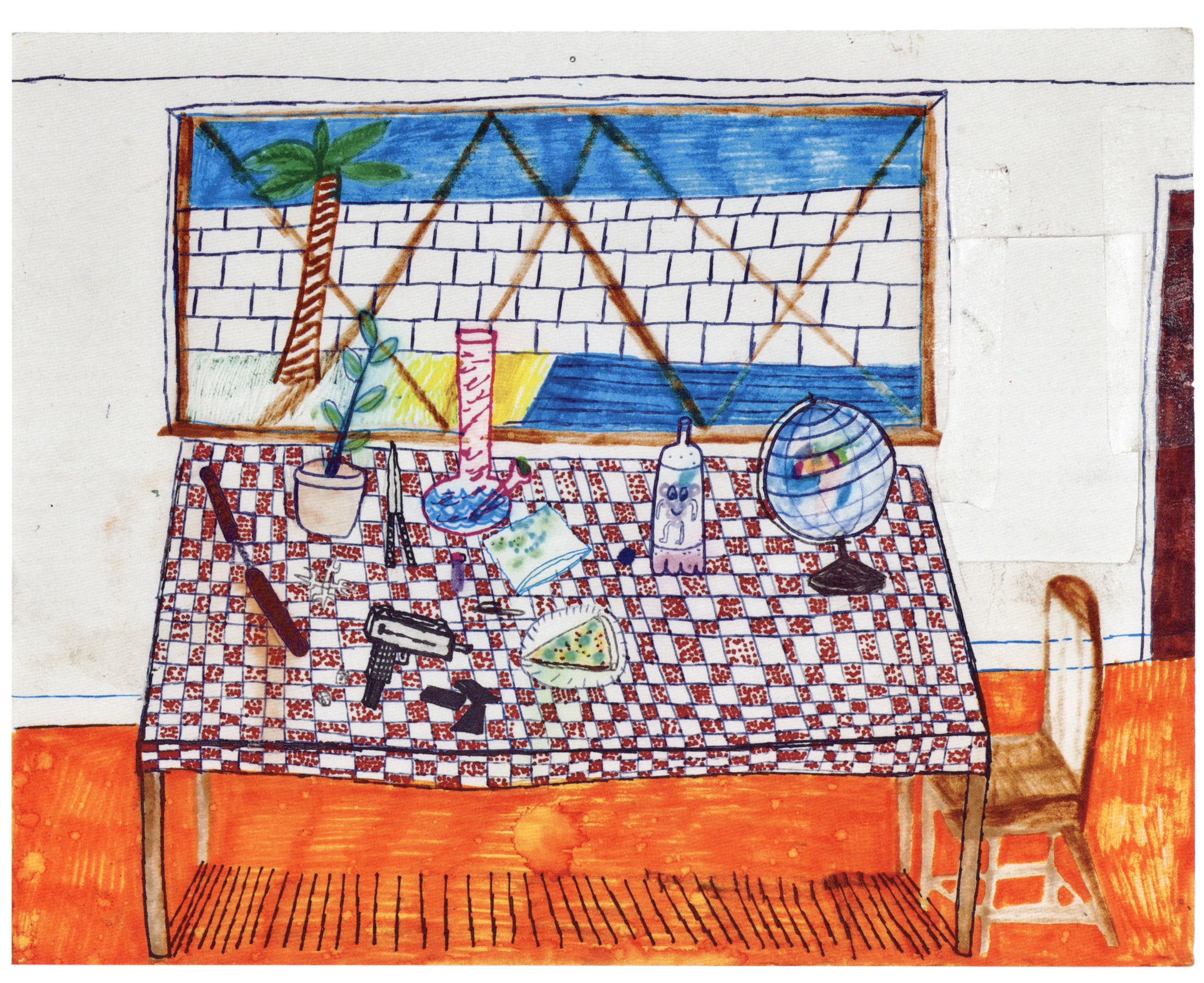

Still Life 4, 2010

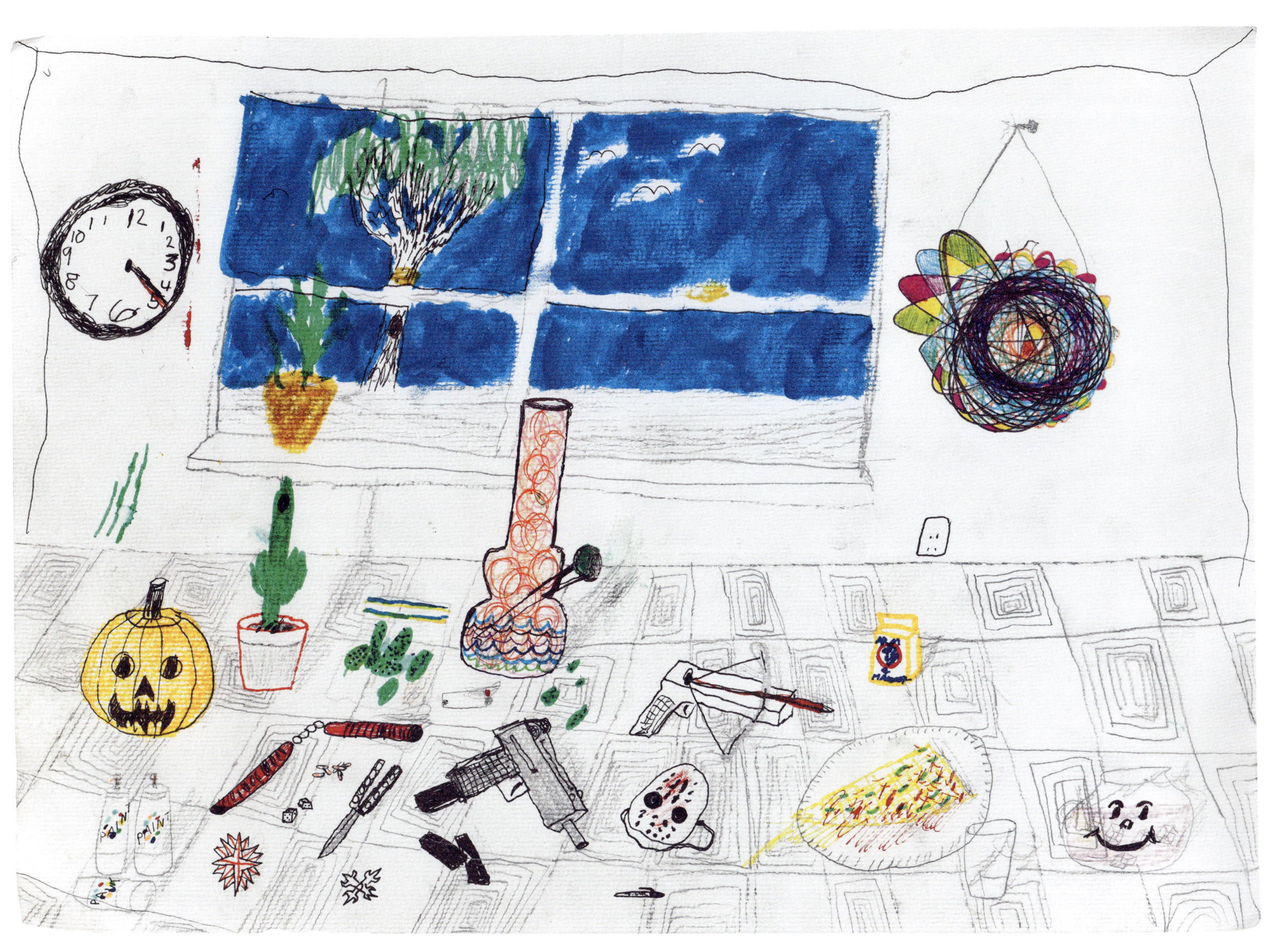

Still Life 6, 2010

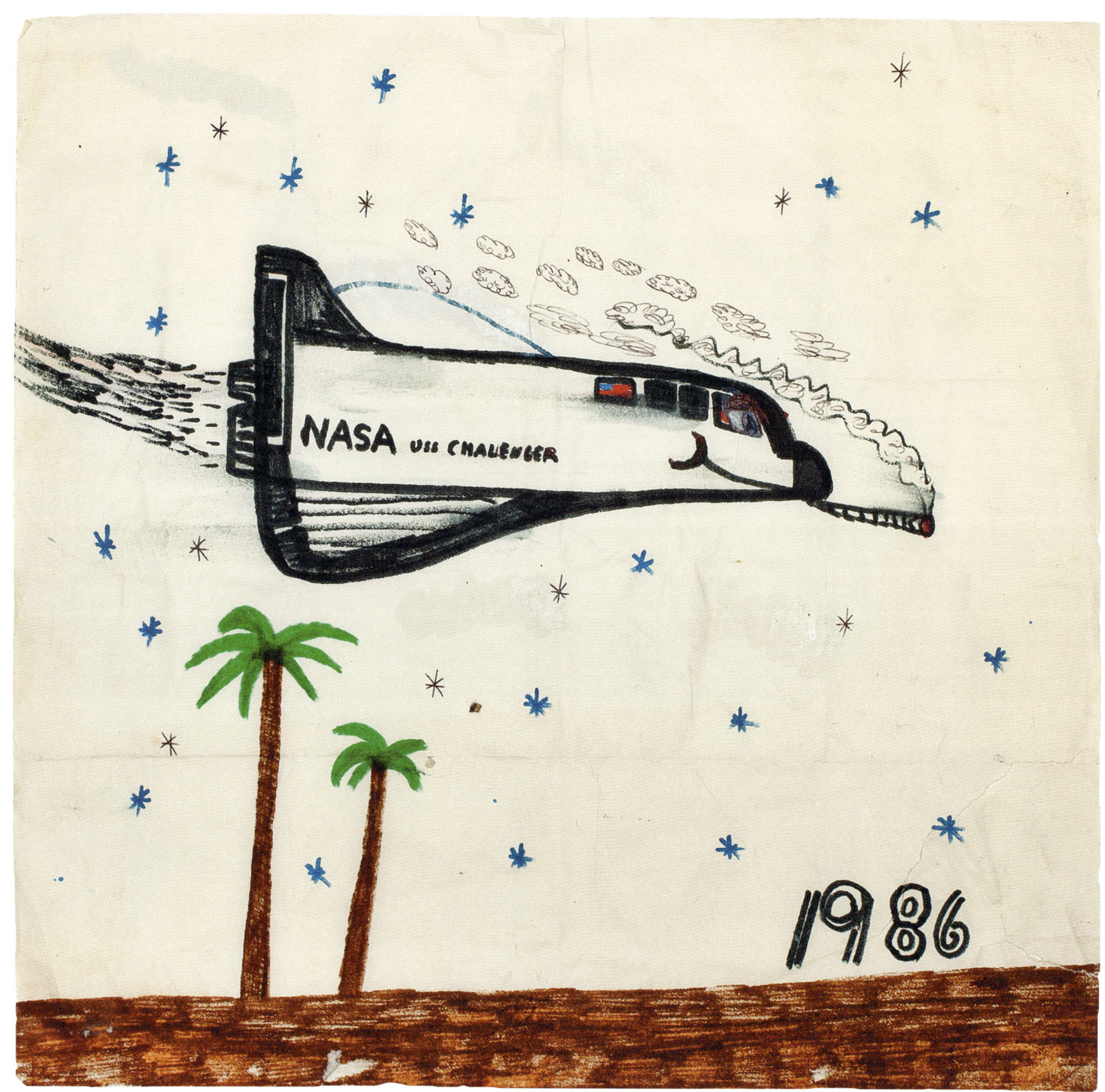

1986, 2007

122

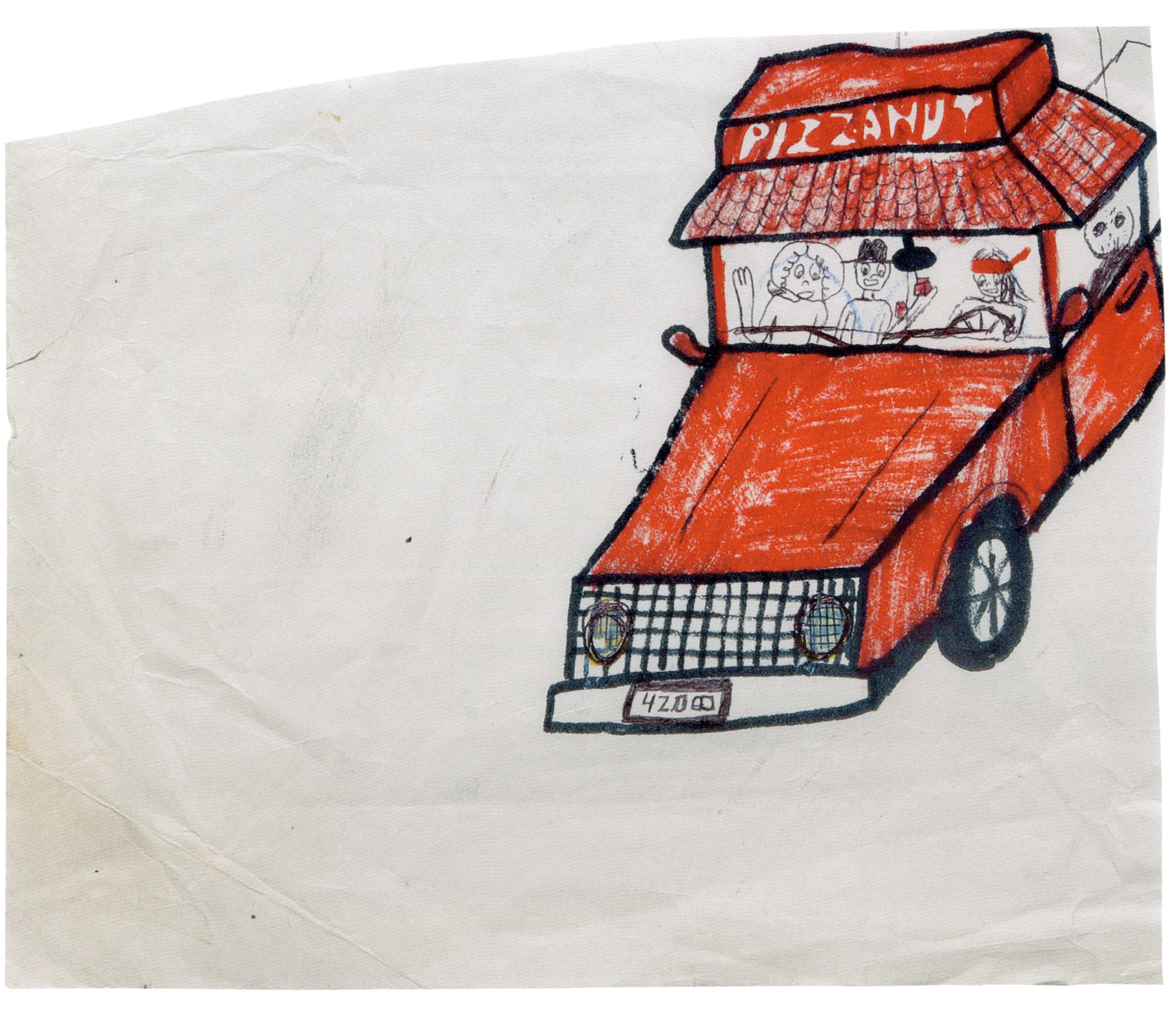

Tony Hawk's Whip, 2007

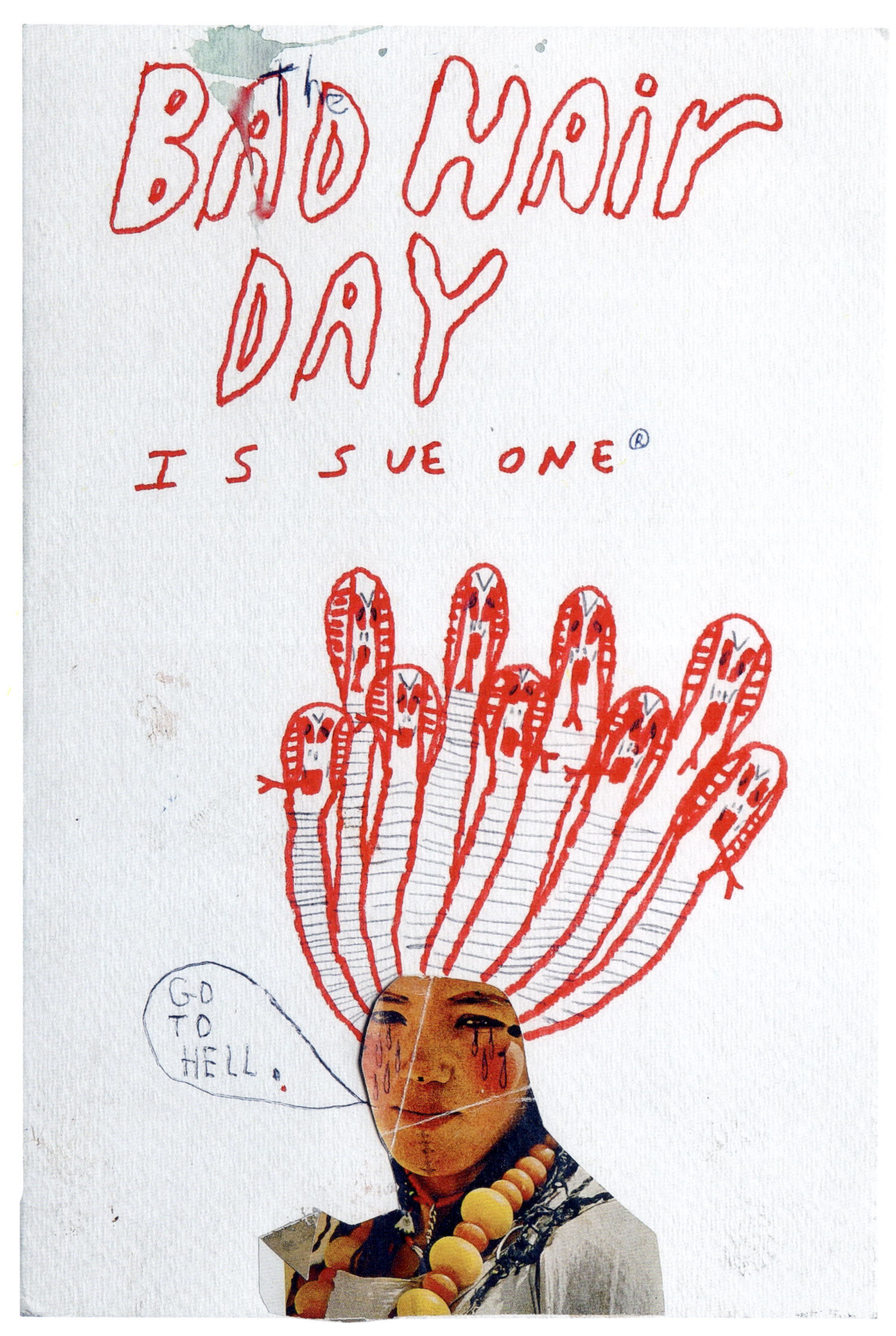

Bad Hair Day, 2010

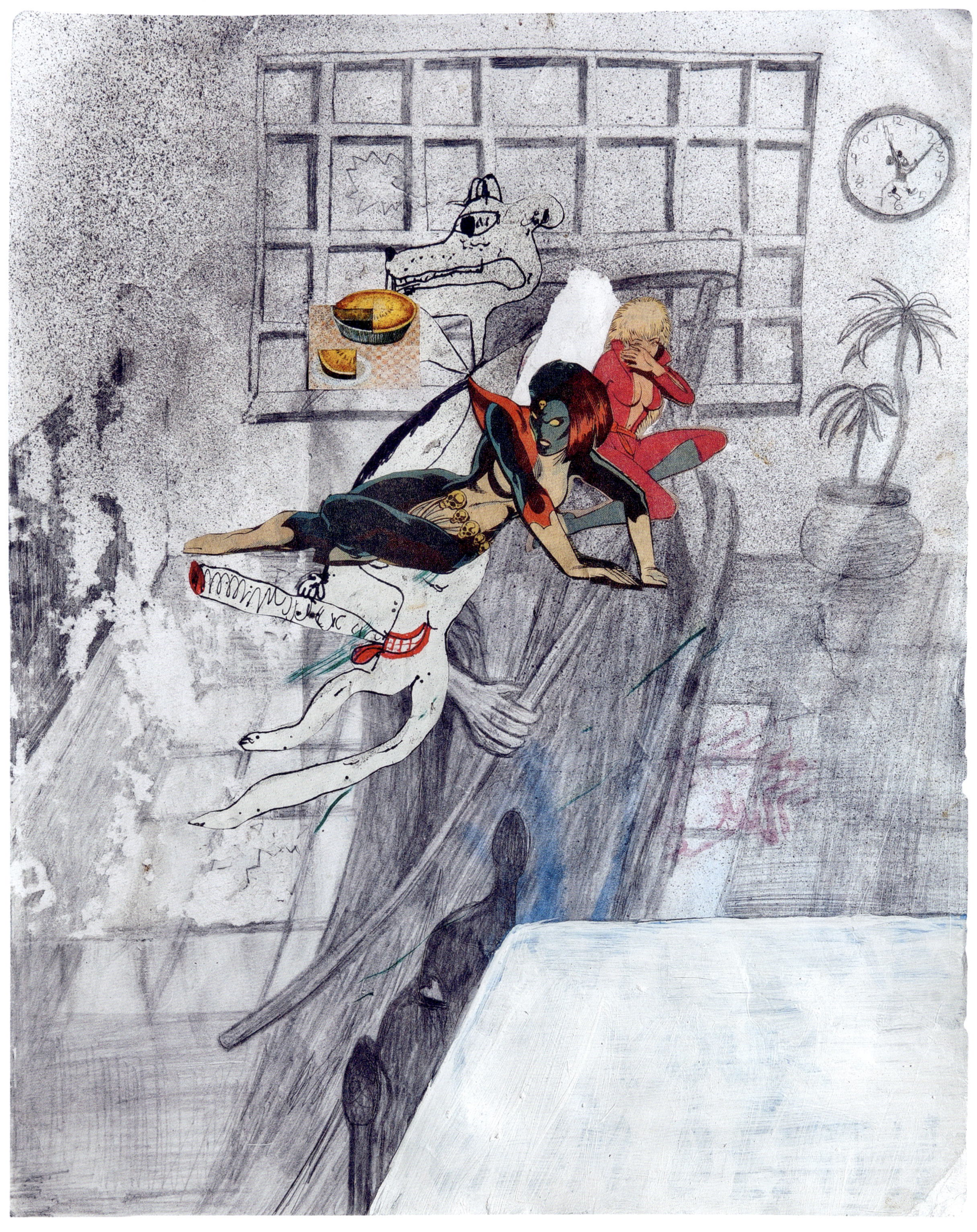

Fifth Dimension, 2012

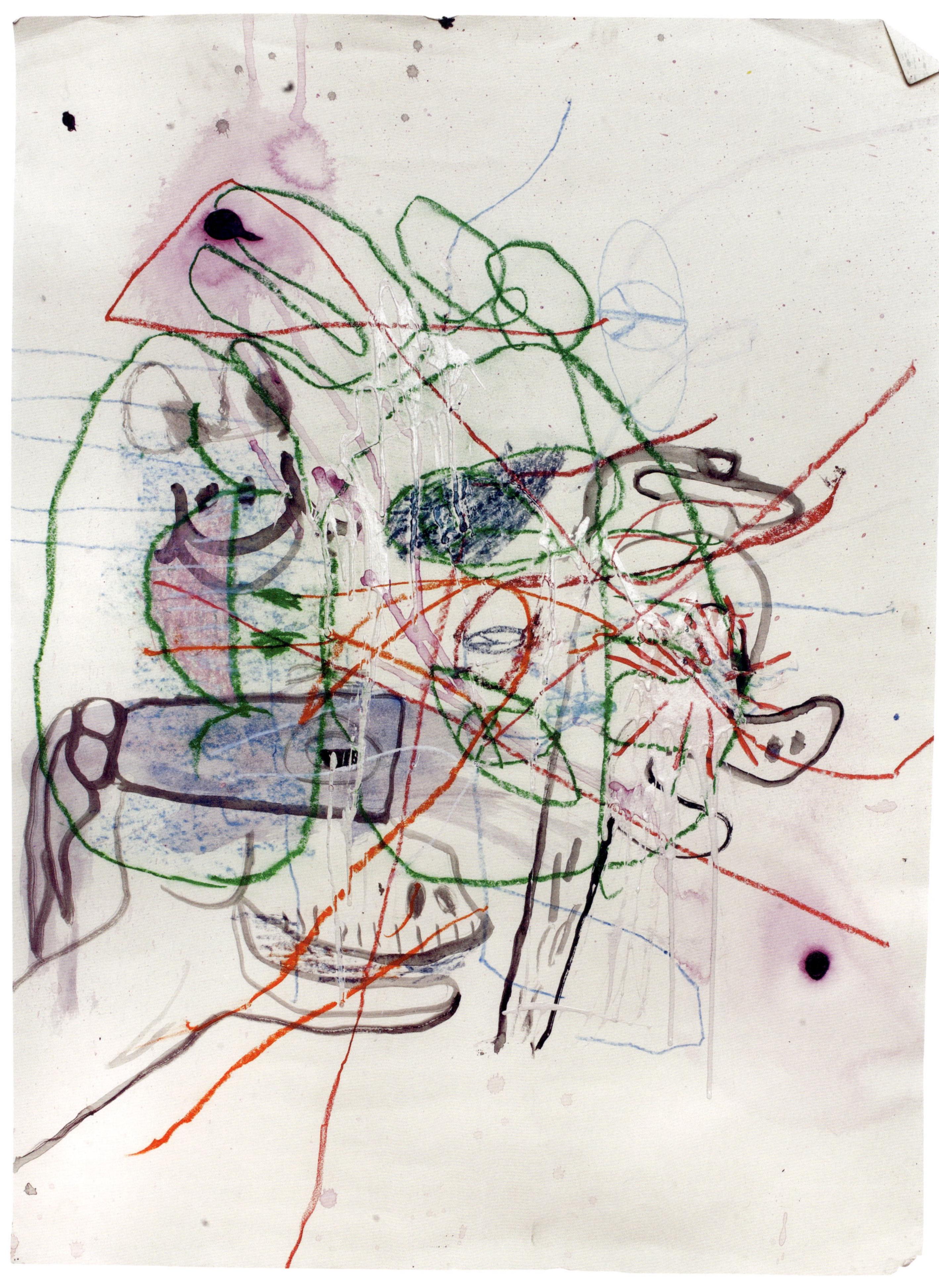

Center Street, 2013

126

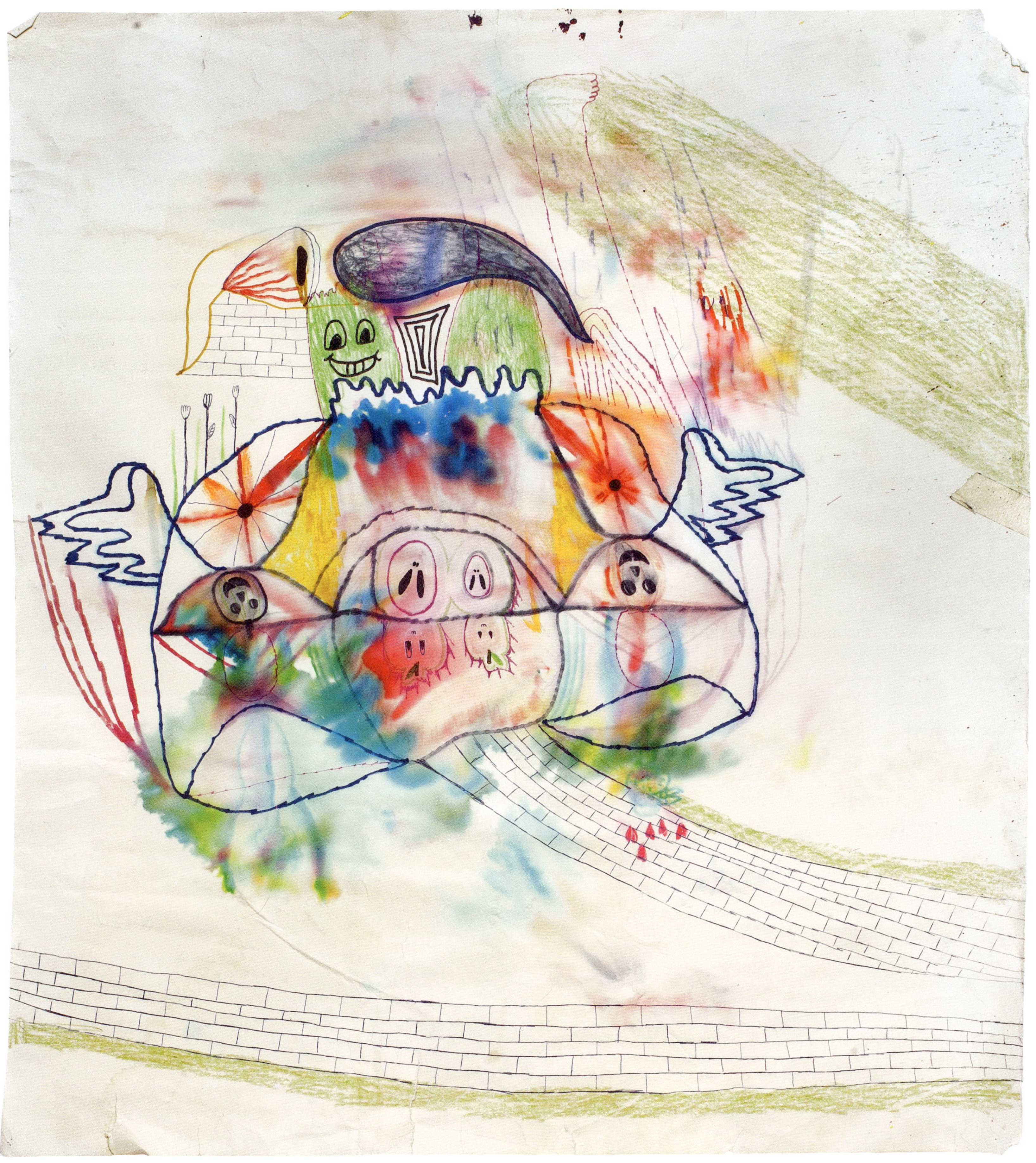

Dragon, 2010

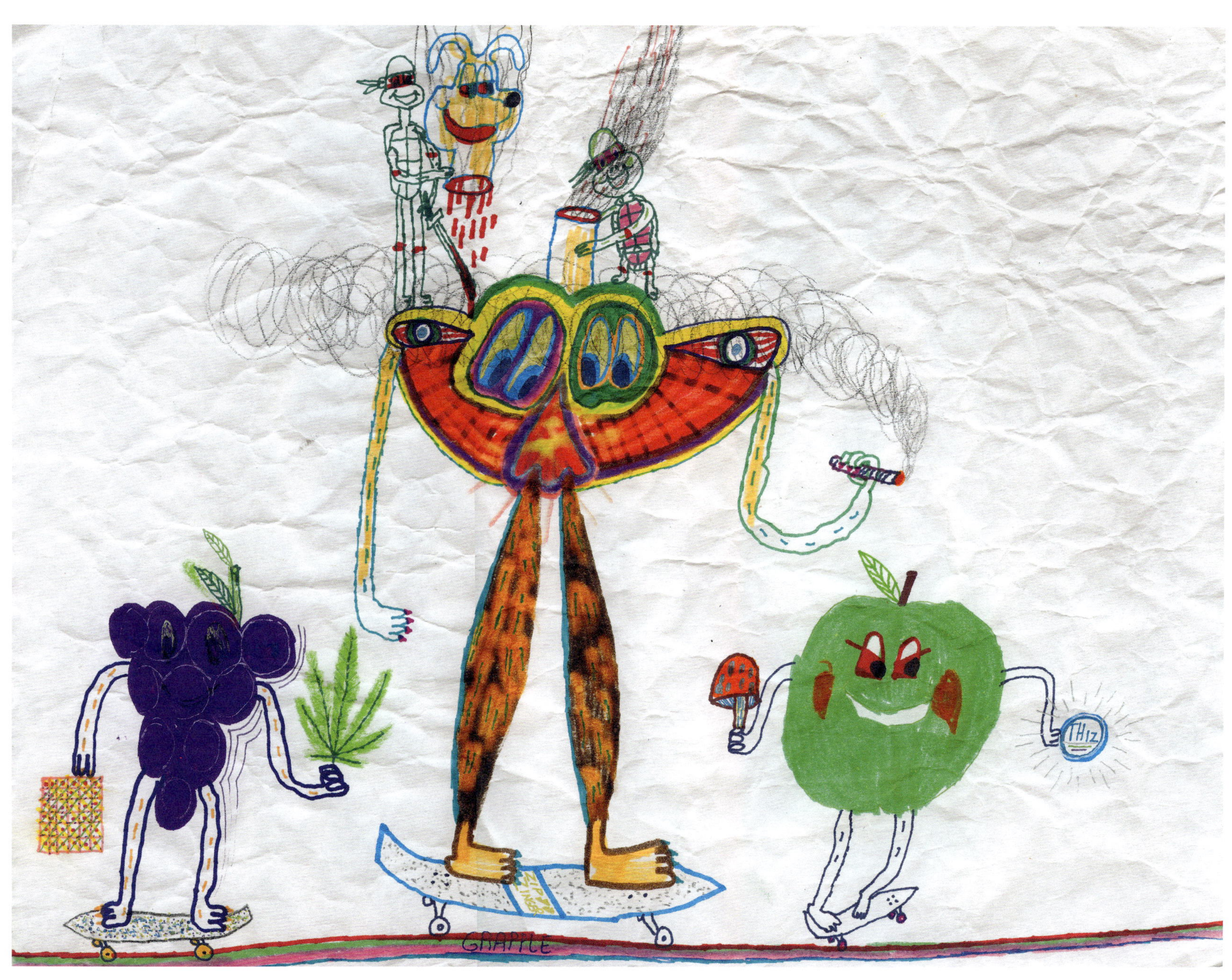

Grapple, 2005

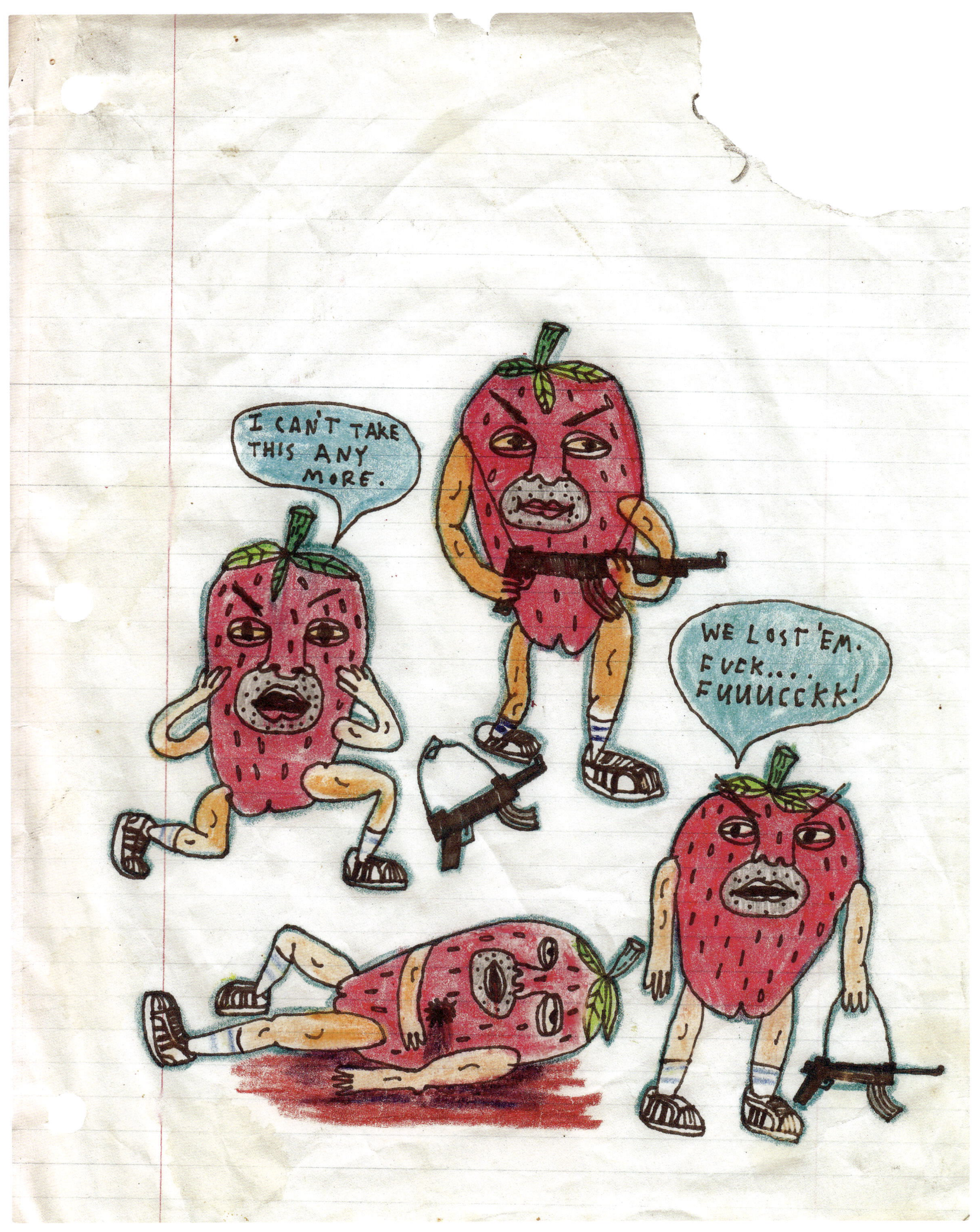

I Can't Take This, 2005

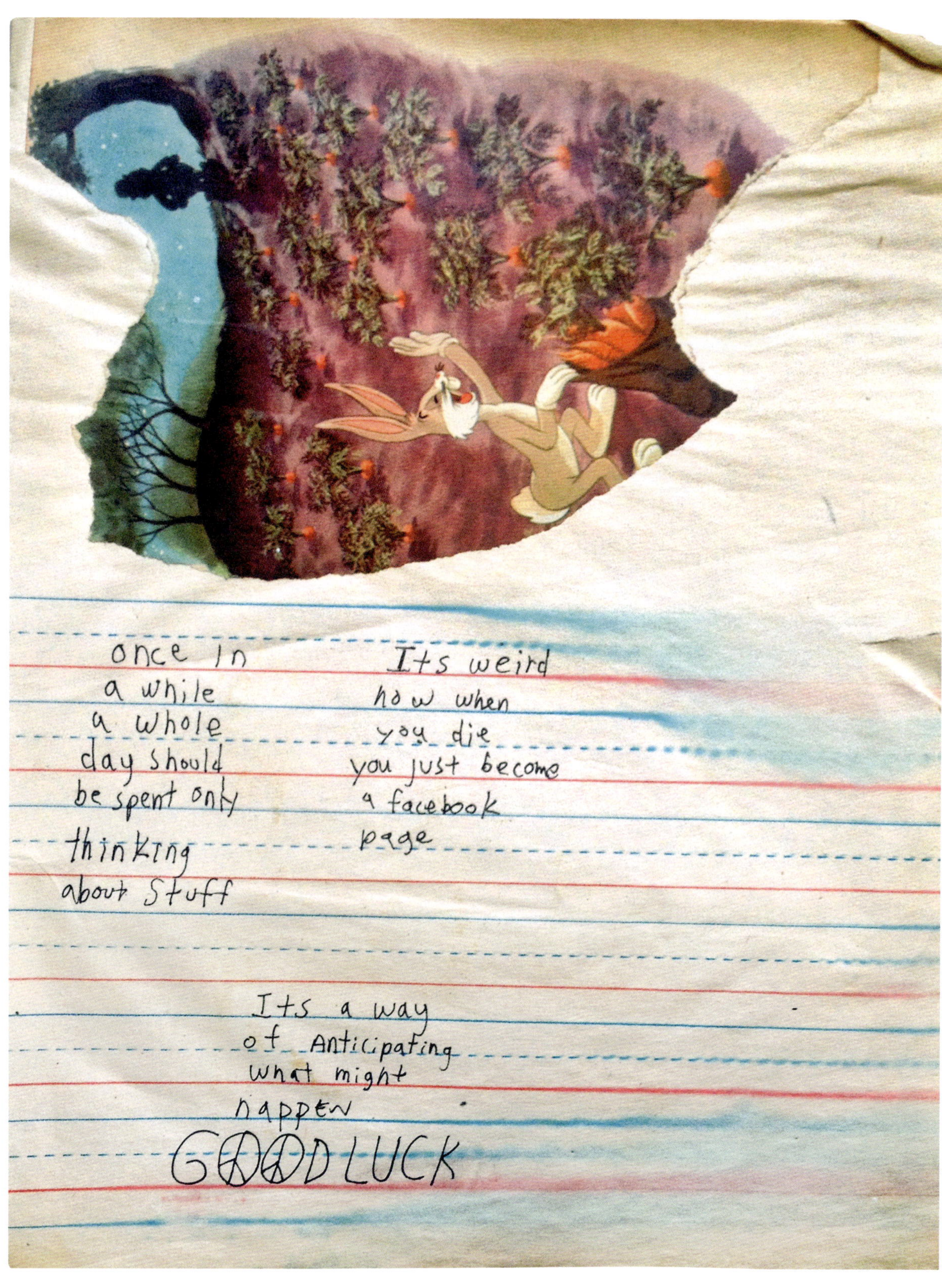

Good Luck, 2012

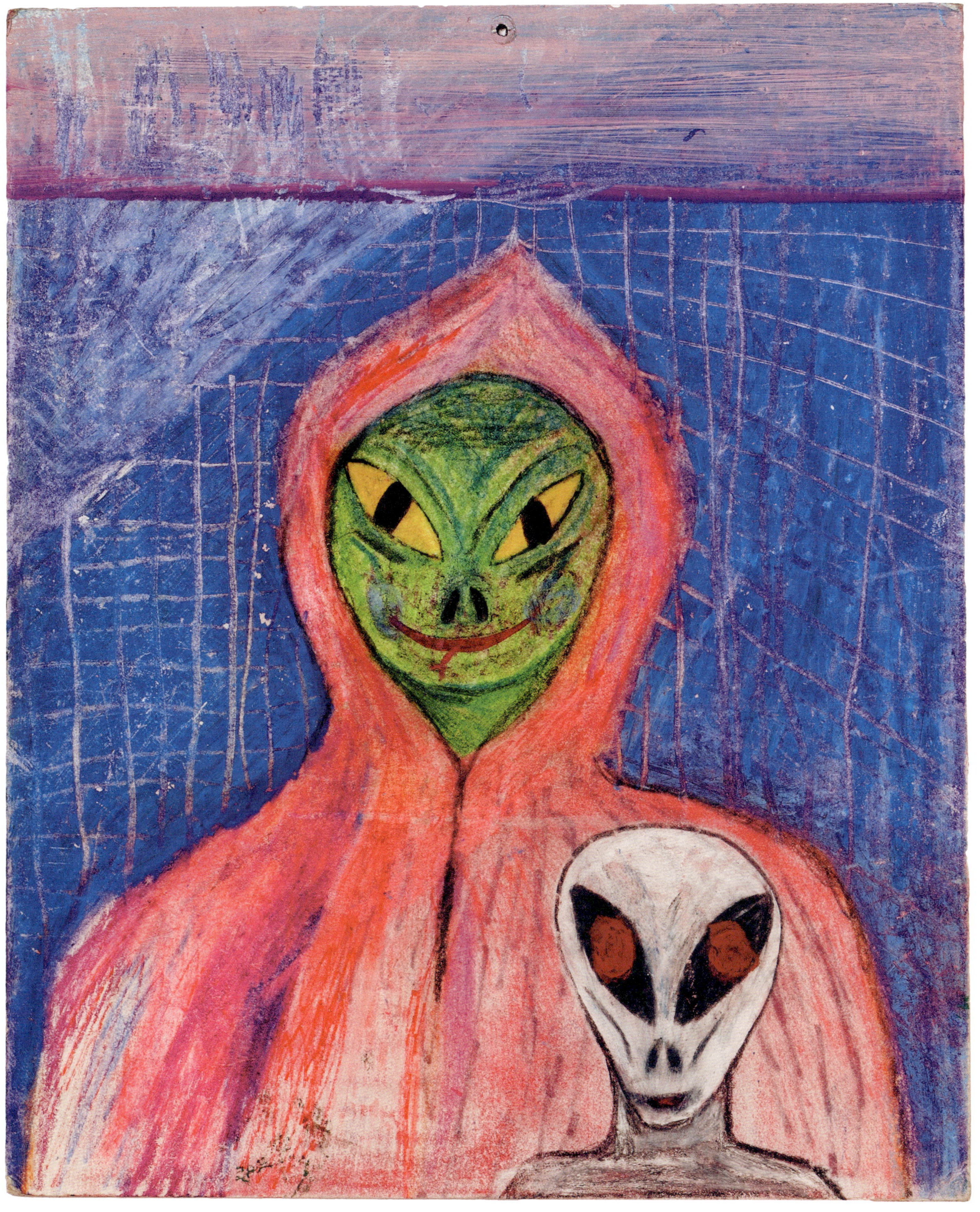

Reptillian and Grey, 2006

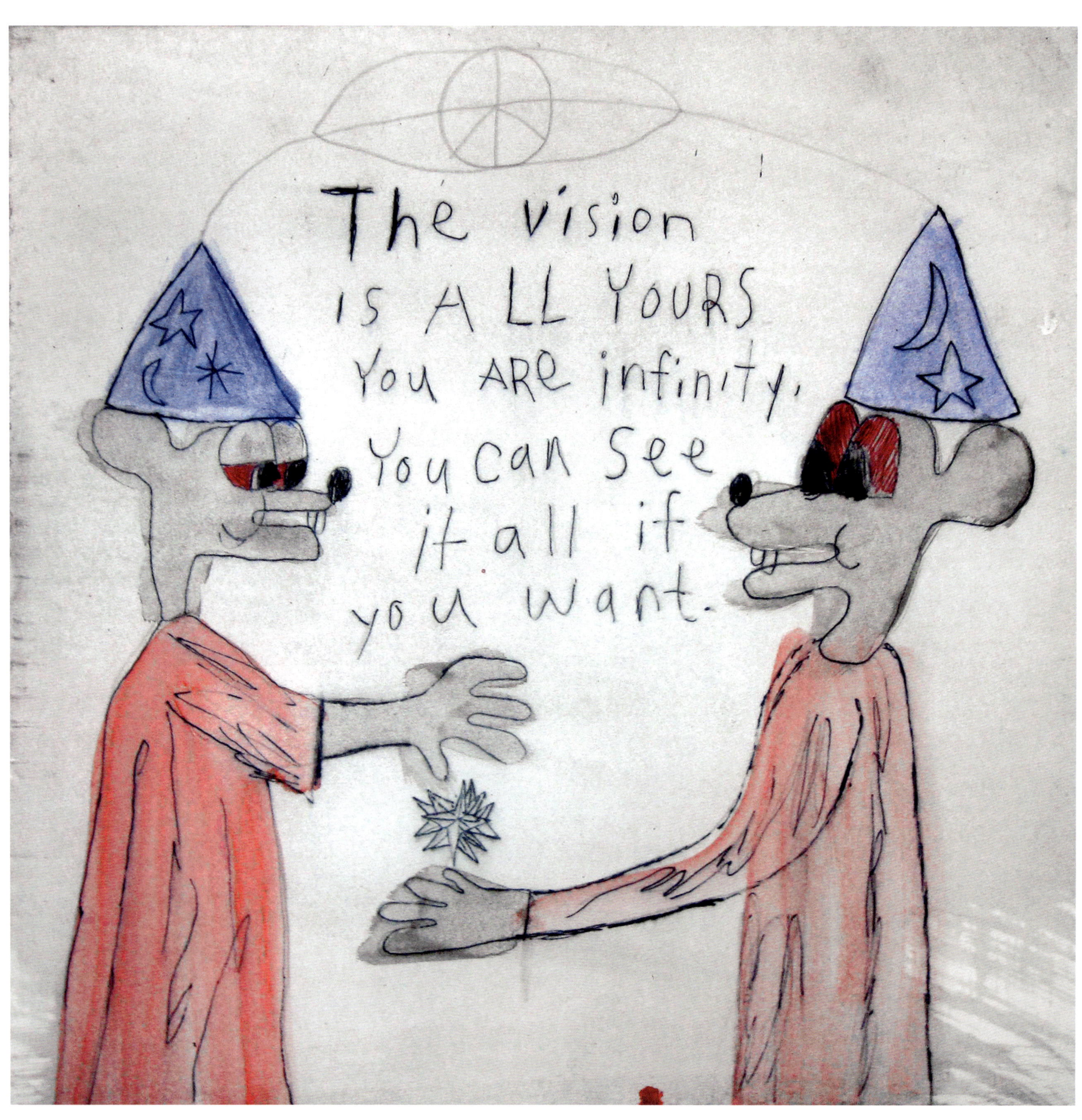

Vision Quest, 2013

WISH MACHINE

clock

$$\frac{1440}{2} = 720$$

1440 = minutes in a day

= 4:20's 11:11's a day

So 1 of clocks will say 11:11 or 4:20 but it will change witch clock every minute.

720 digital clock's make one wish every minute as I set clocks

If you set 720 clocks each one minute appart one will always say 11:11 so you can always wish.

3: shes work? HELL YEAH THEY DO!

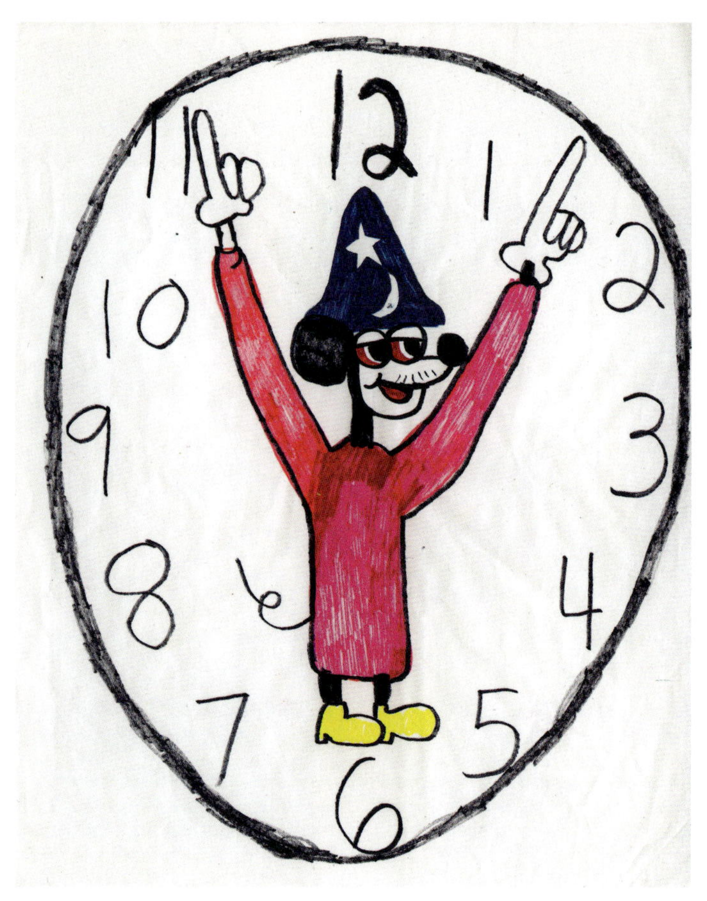

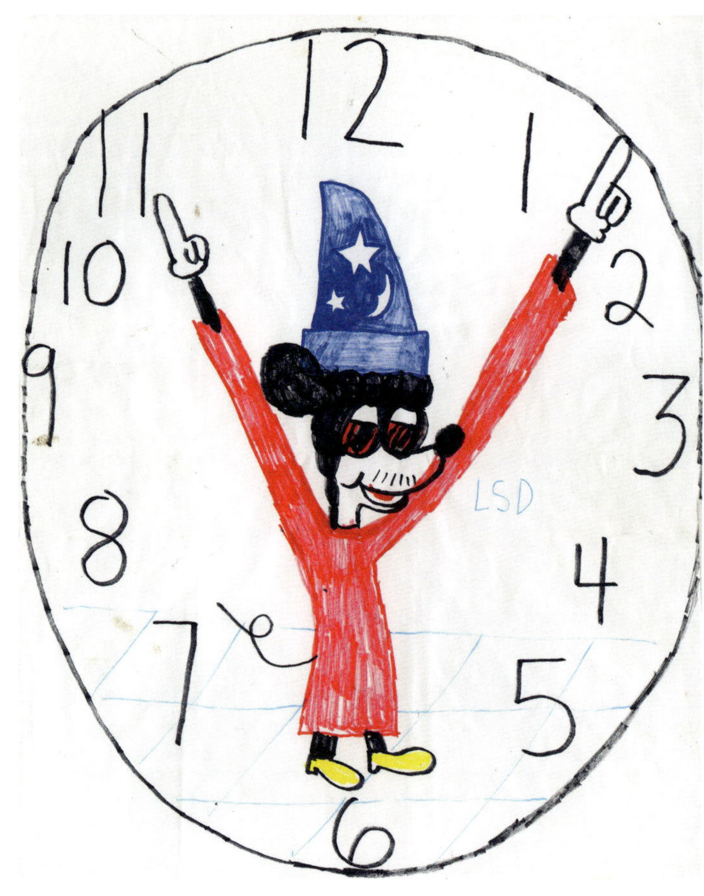

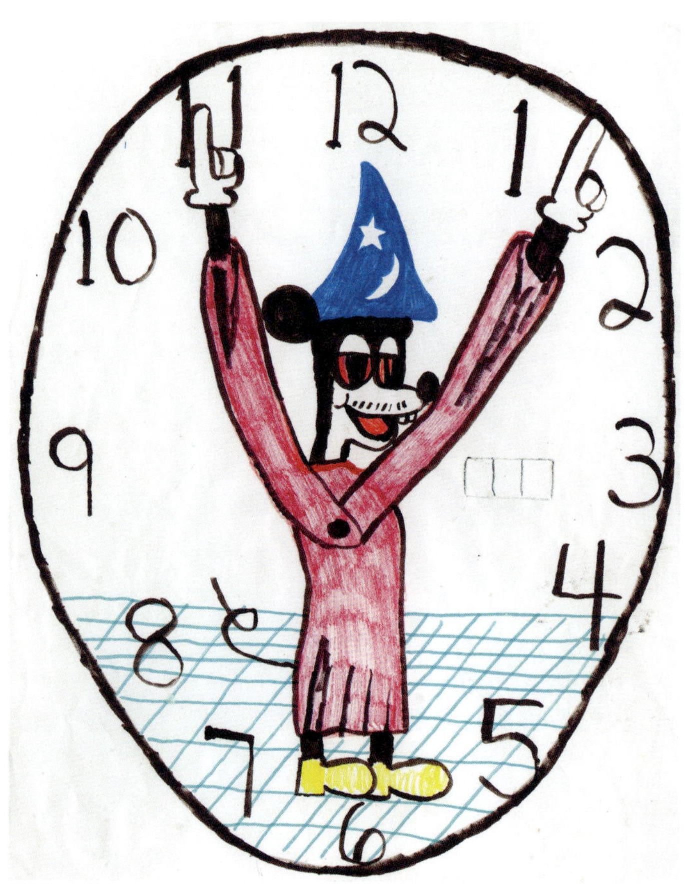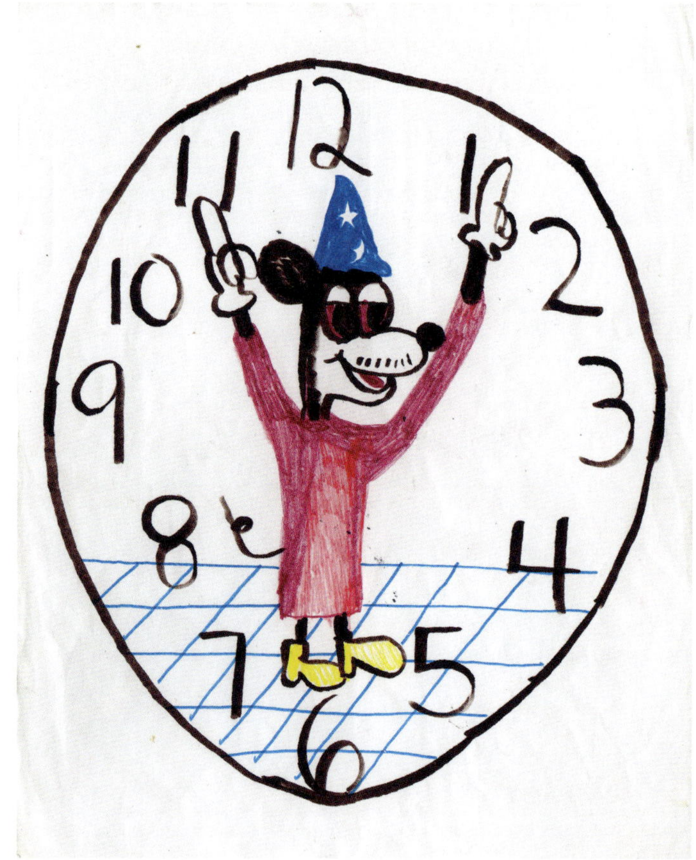

Clocks, 2012

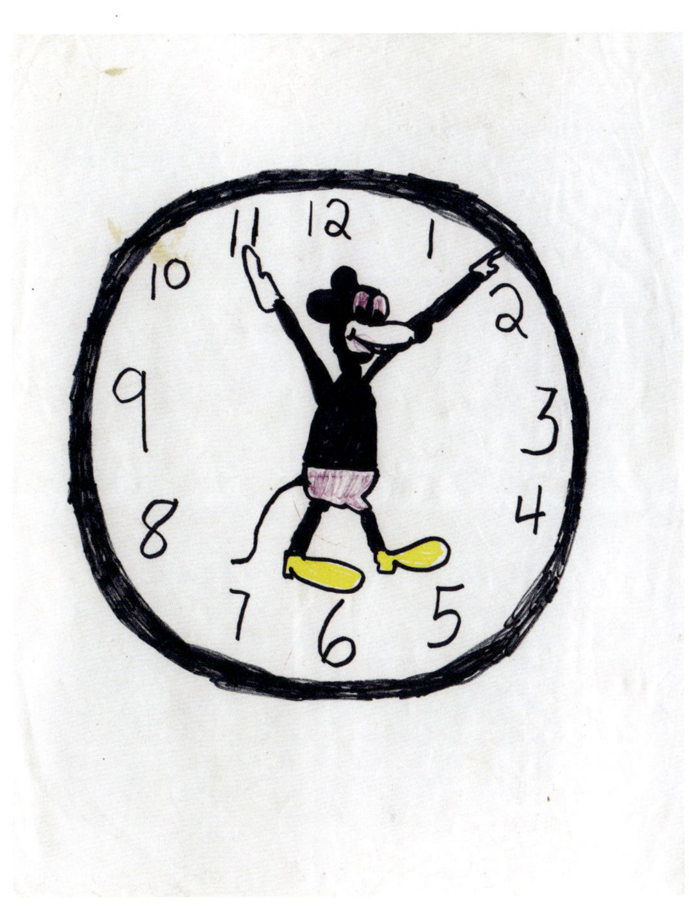
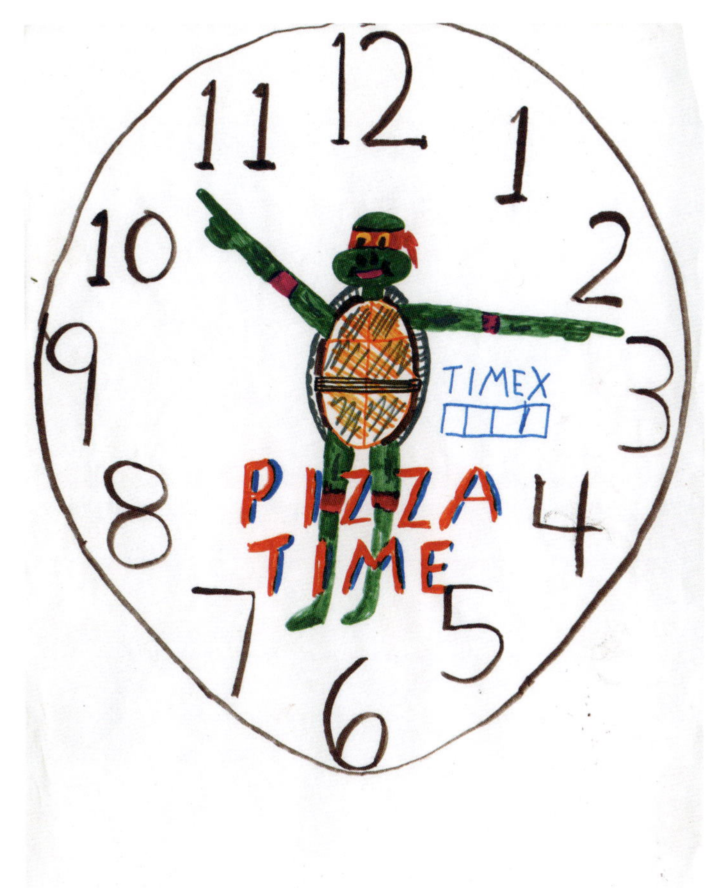

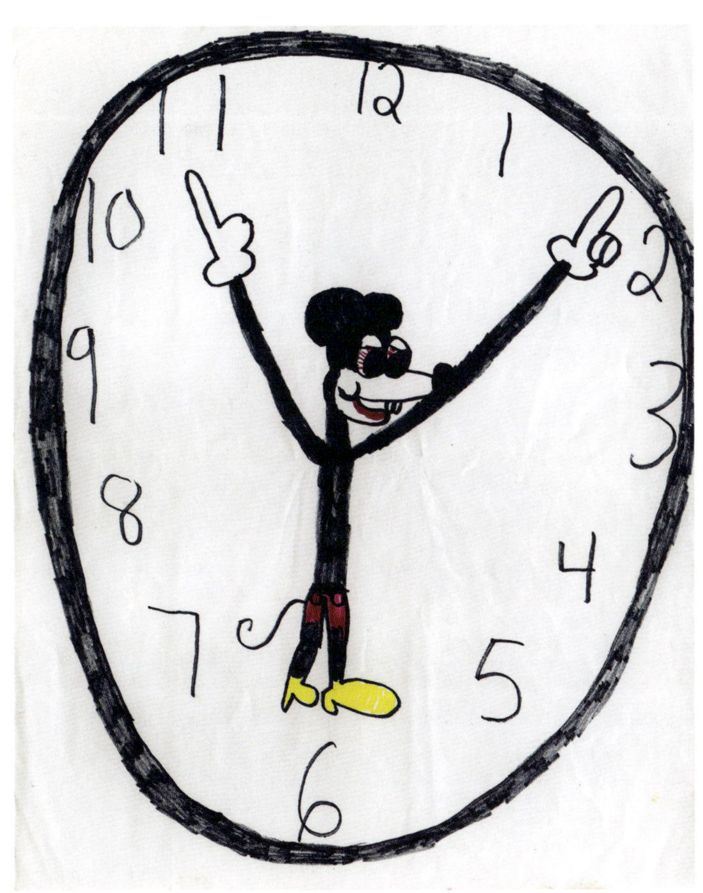
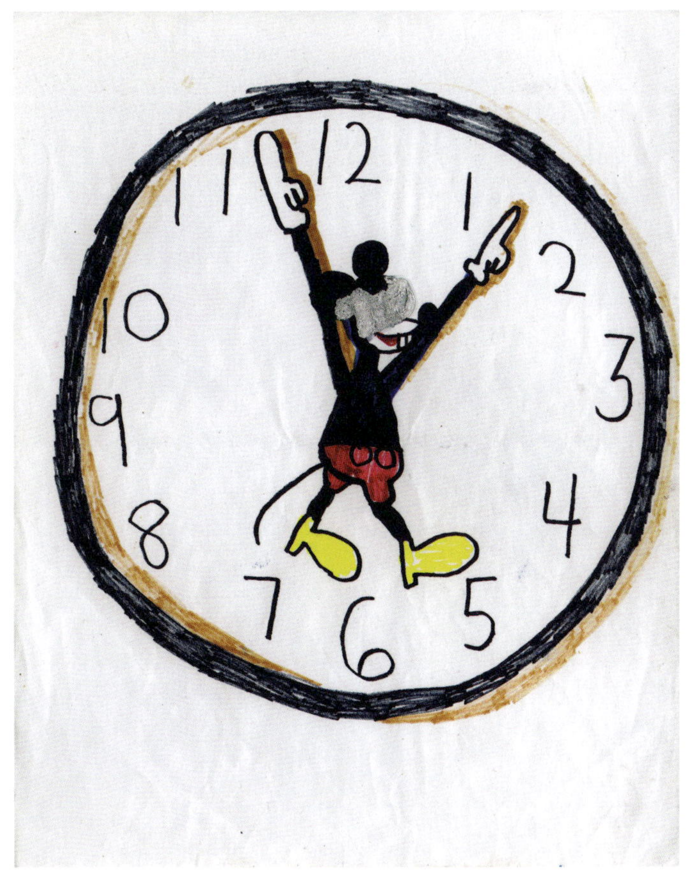

Clocks, 2012

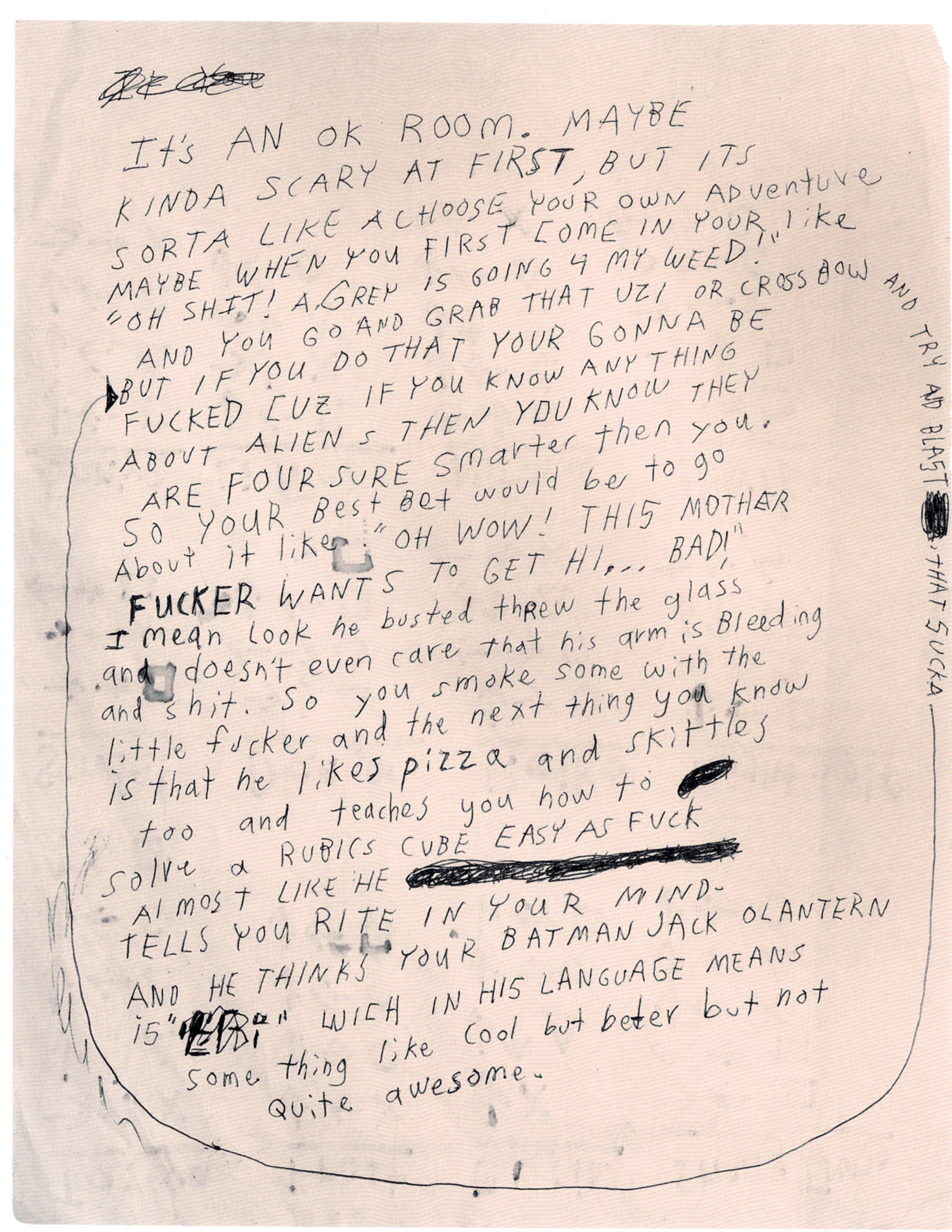

Description of Staba's Room, 2009

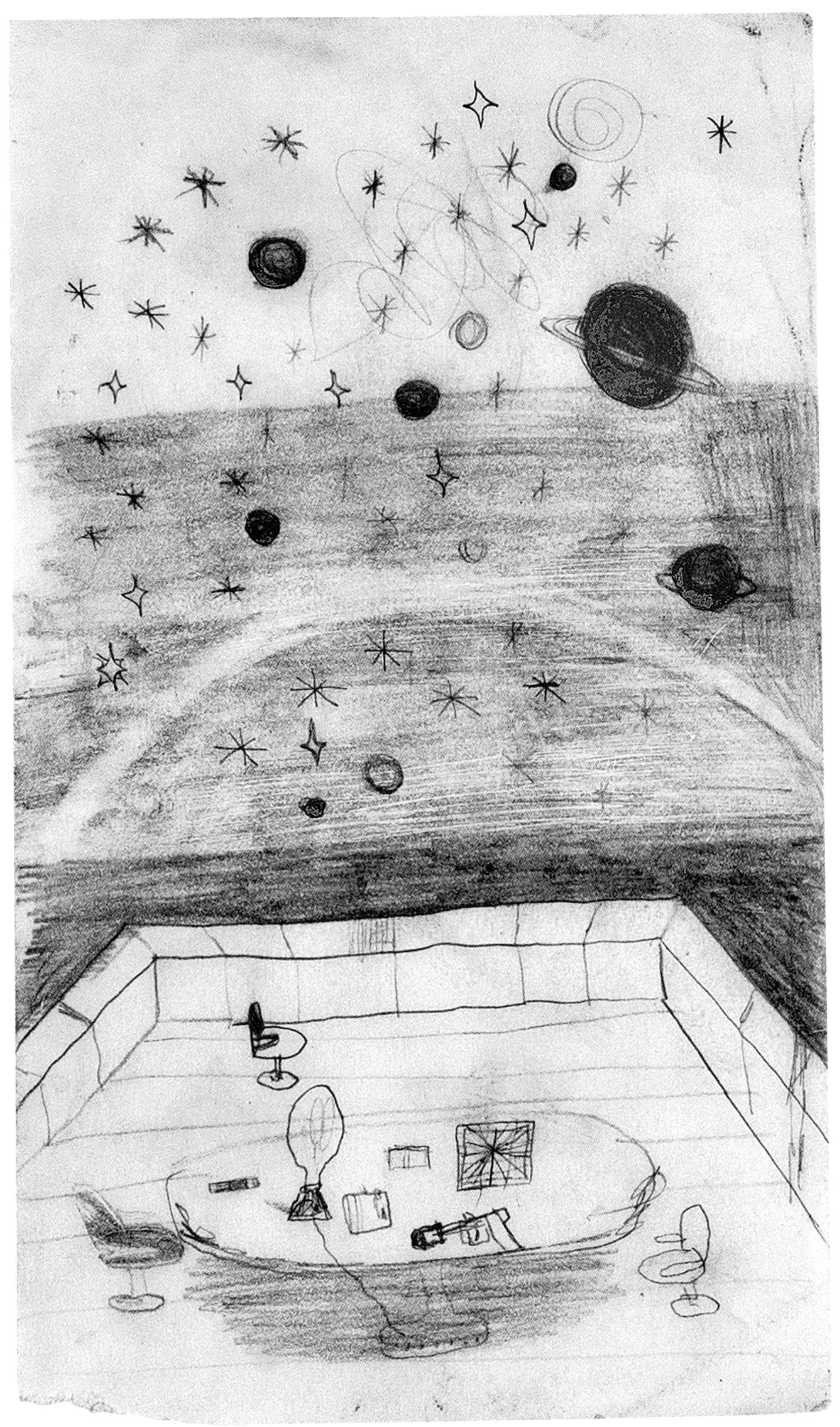

Moon Base Beta, 2009

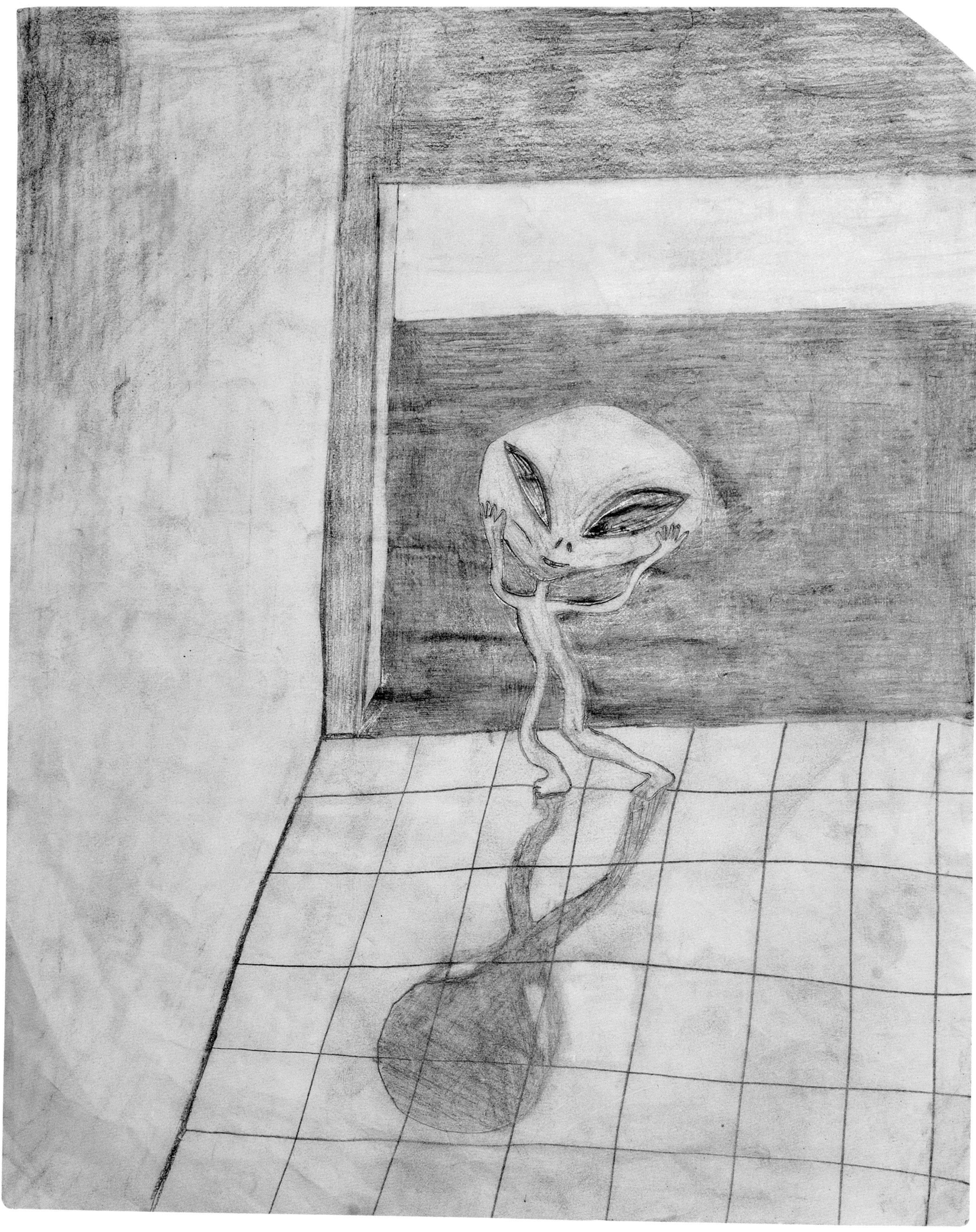

Hello, 2012

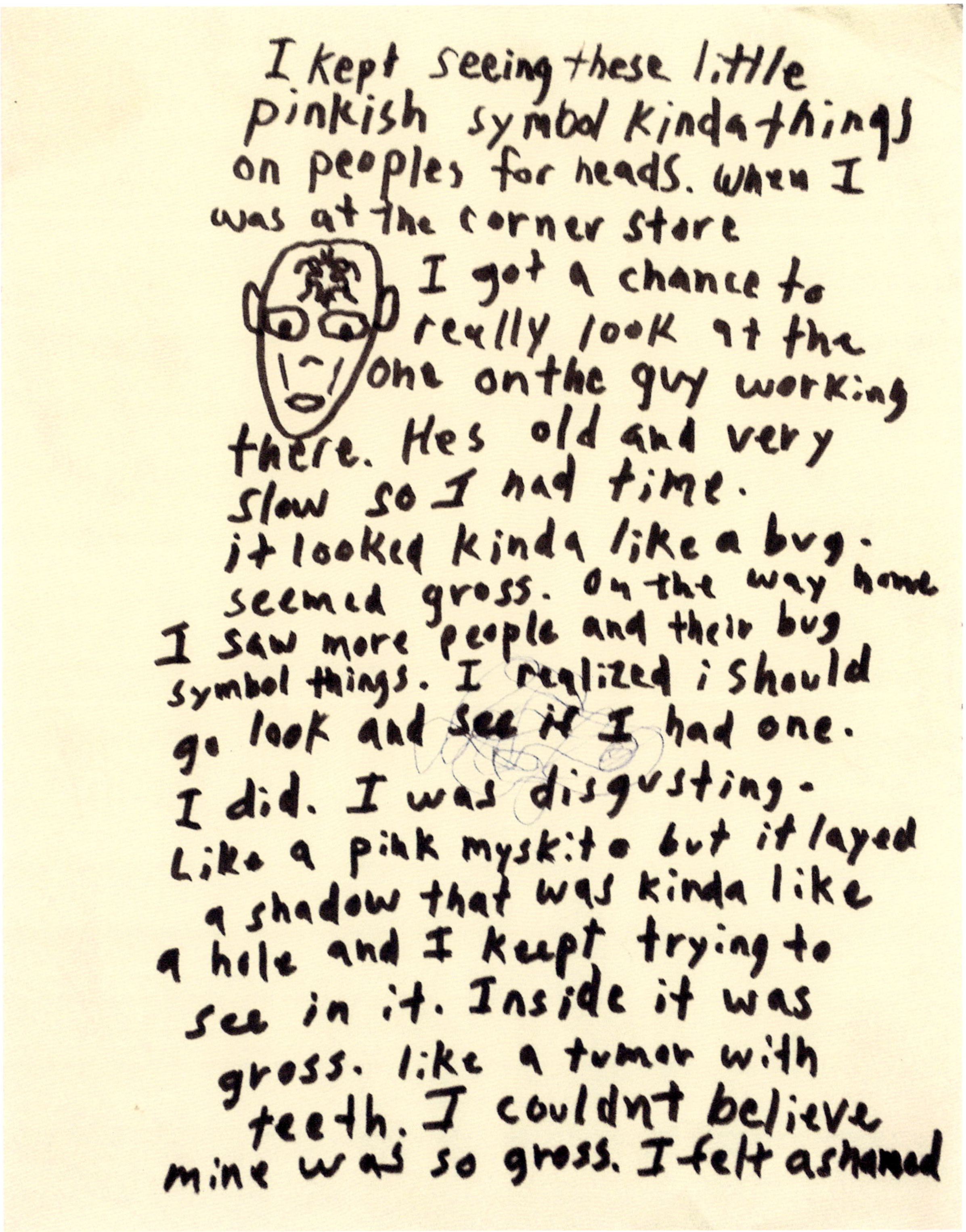

I kept seeing these little
pinkish symbol kinda things
on peoples for heads. When I
was at the corner store
I got a chance to
really look at the
one on the guy working
there. Hes old and very
slow so I had time.
it looked kinda like a bug.
seemed gross. On the way home
I saw more people and their bug
symbol things. I realized i should
go look and see if I had one.
I did. I was disgusting.
Like a pink myskito but it layed
a shadow that was kinda like
a hole and I kept trying to
see in it. Inside it was
gross. like a tumor with
teeth. I couldnt believe
mine was so gross. I felt ashamed

Trip to the Corner Store, 2012

Pages 140–157:
Untitled work, 2012–2014

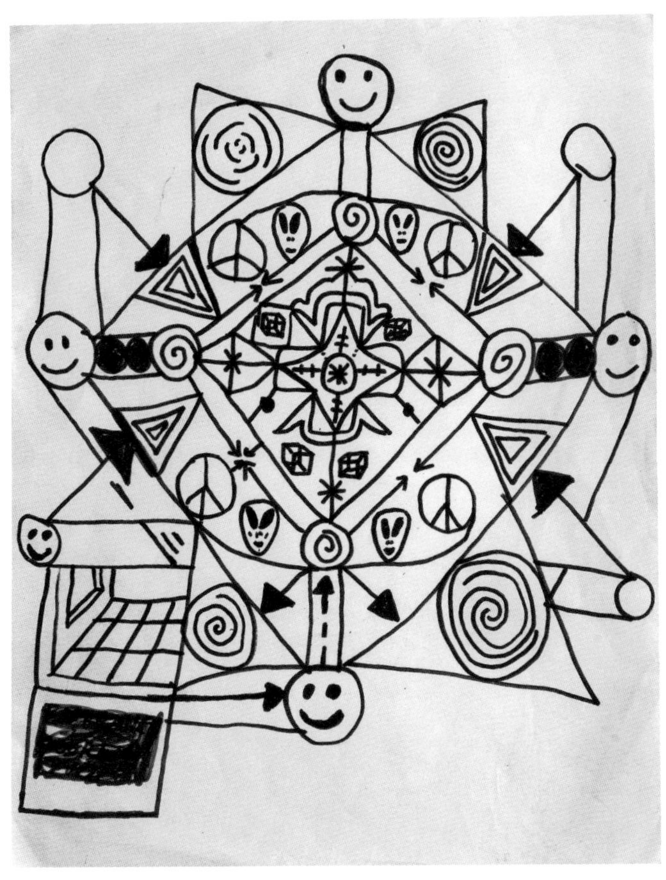

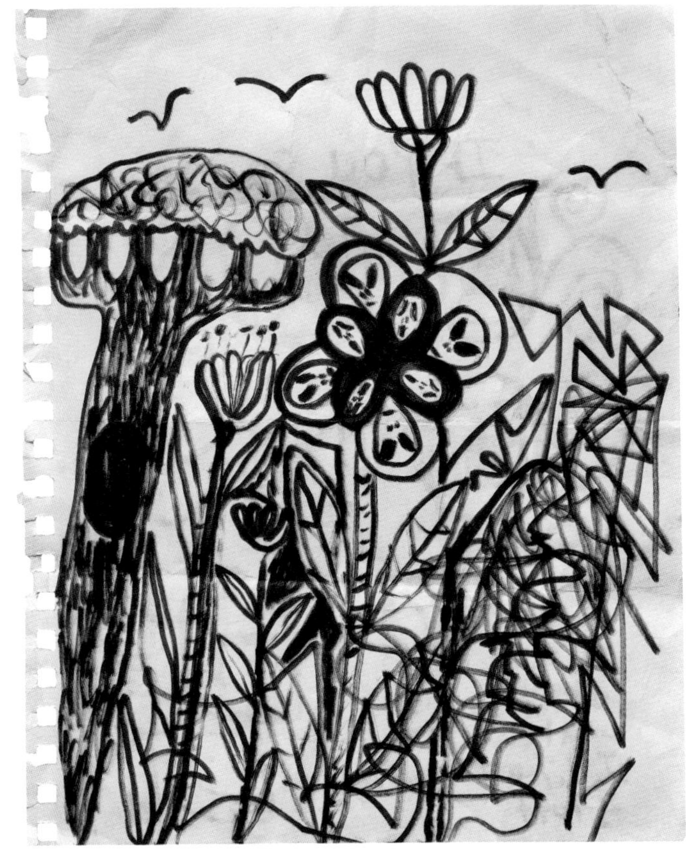

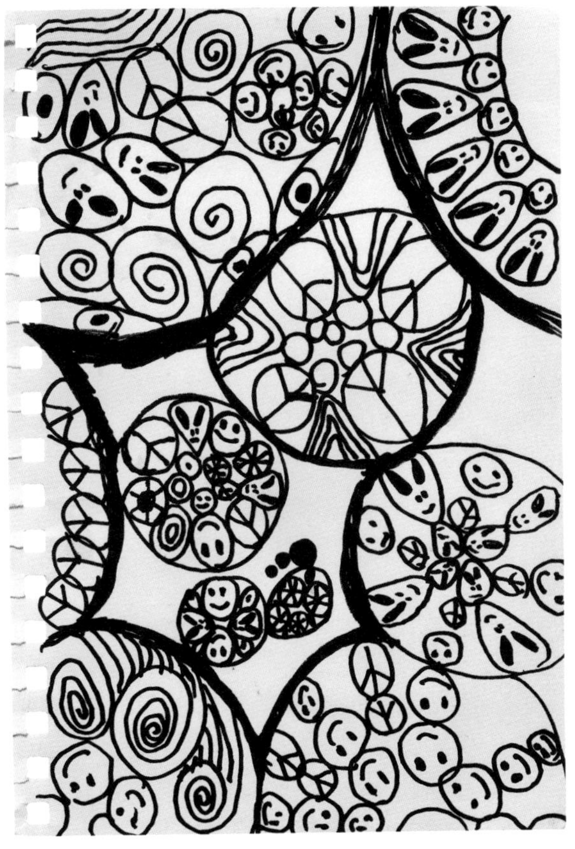

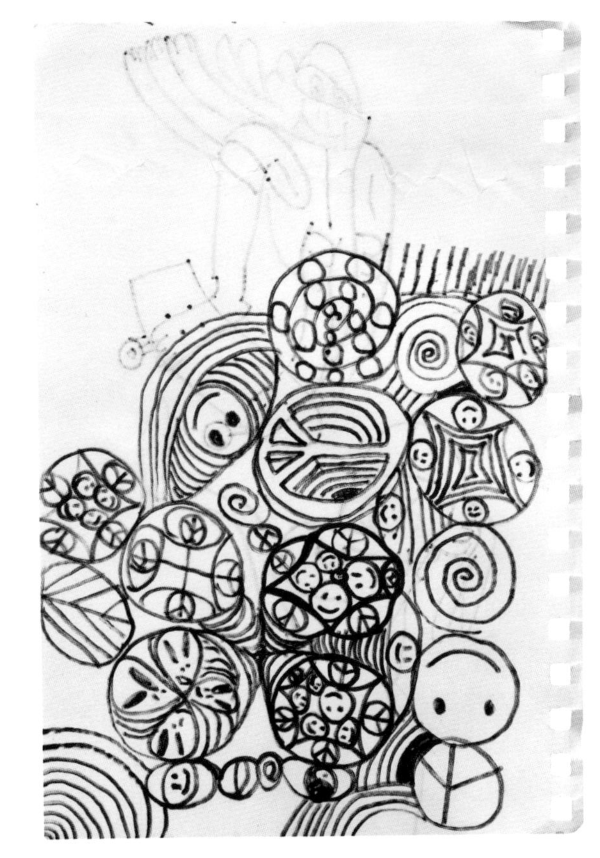

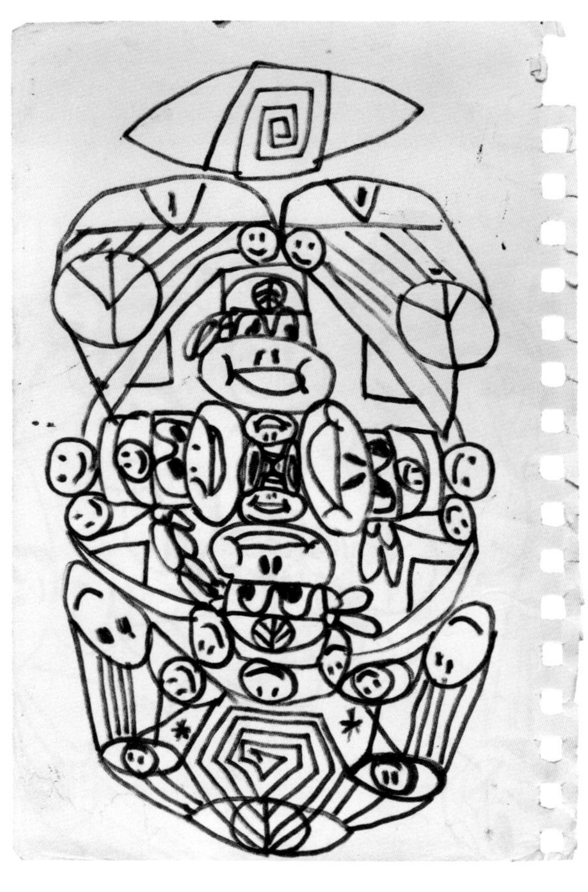

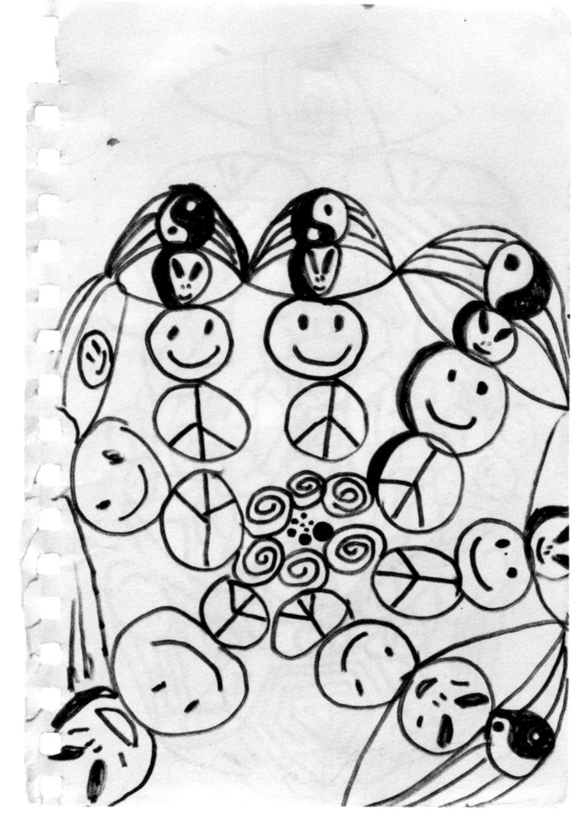

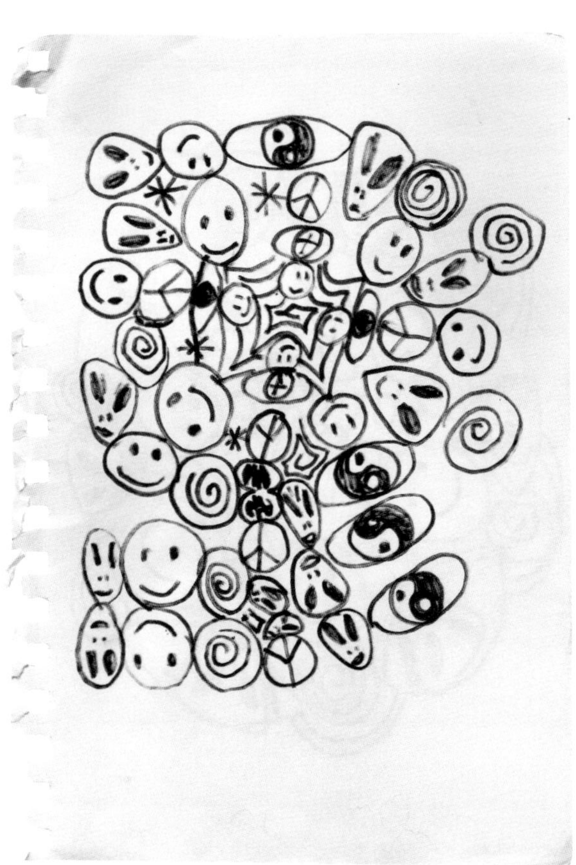

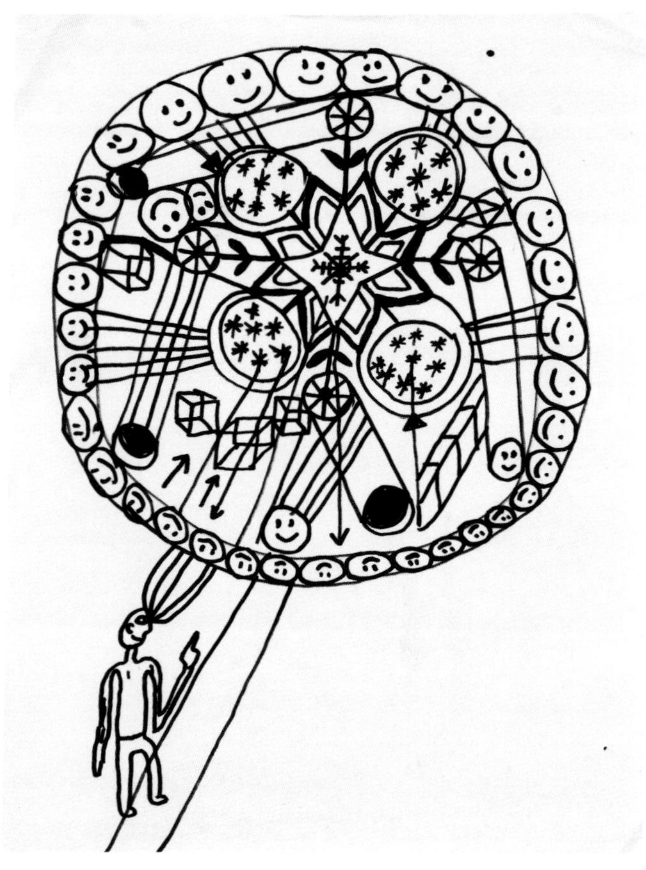

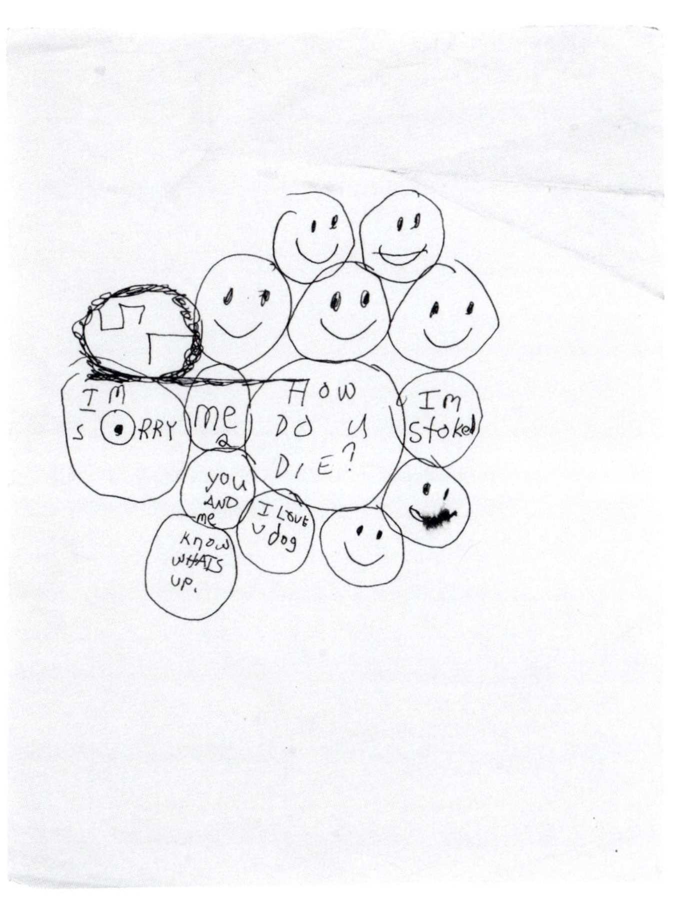

IM SORRY
me
HOW DO U DIE?
IM STOKED
YOU AND ME KNOW WHATS UP.
I LOVE U dog

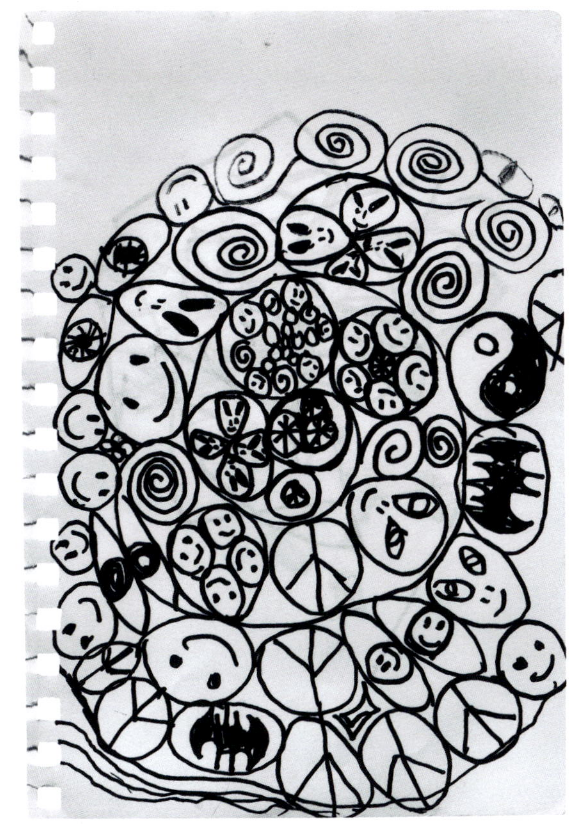

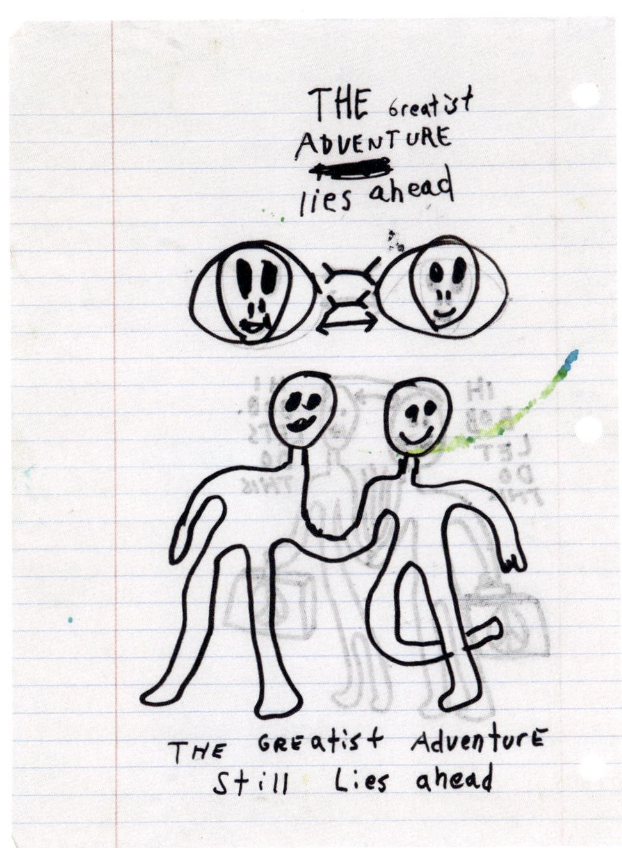

THE greatist ADVENTURE lies ahead
THE GREATIST Adventure STILL Lies ahead

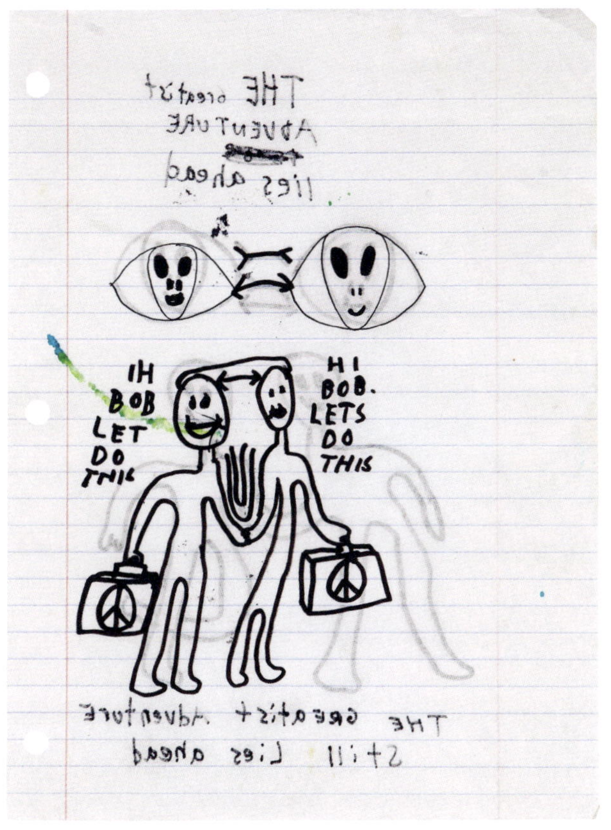

IH BOB LET DO THIS
HI BOB. LETS DO THIS

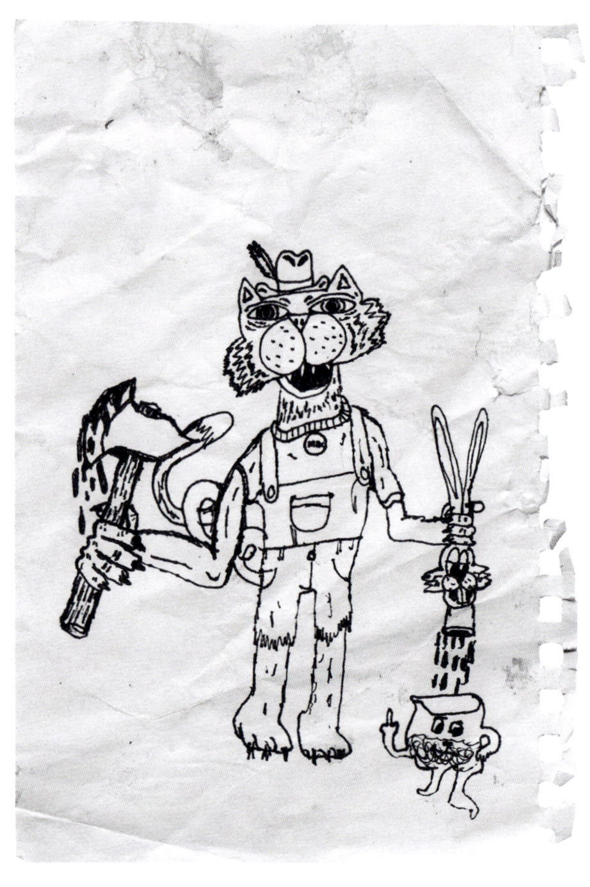
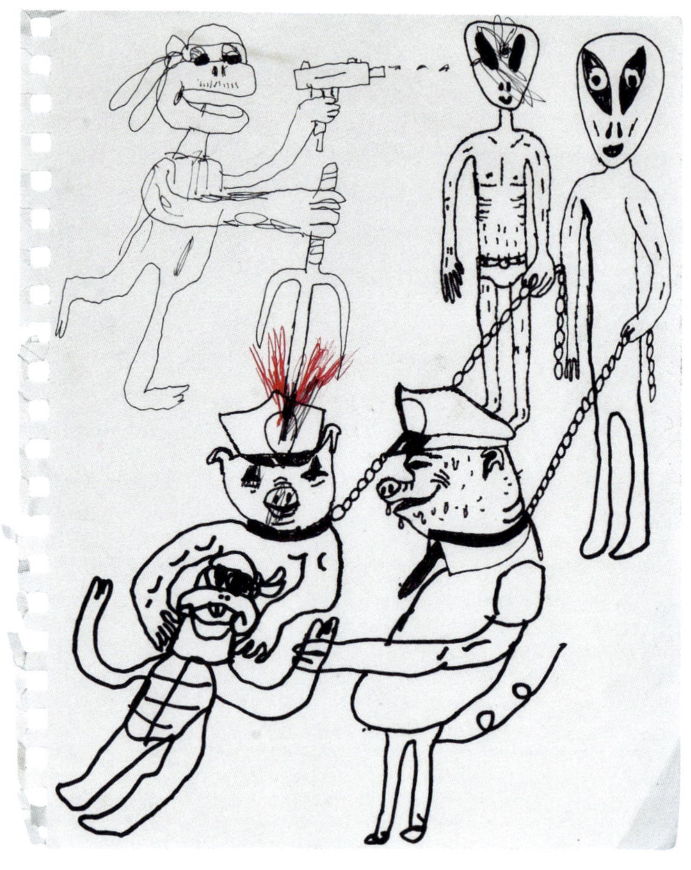
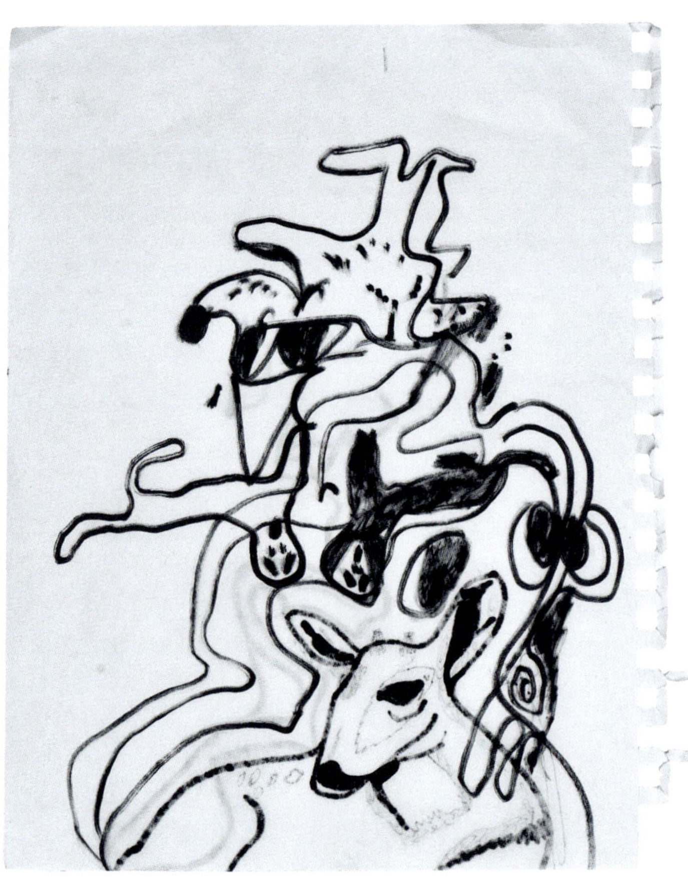
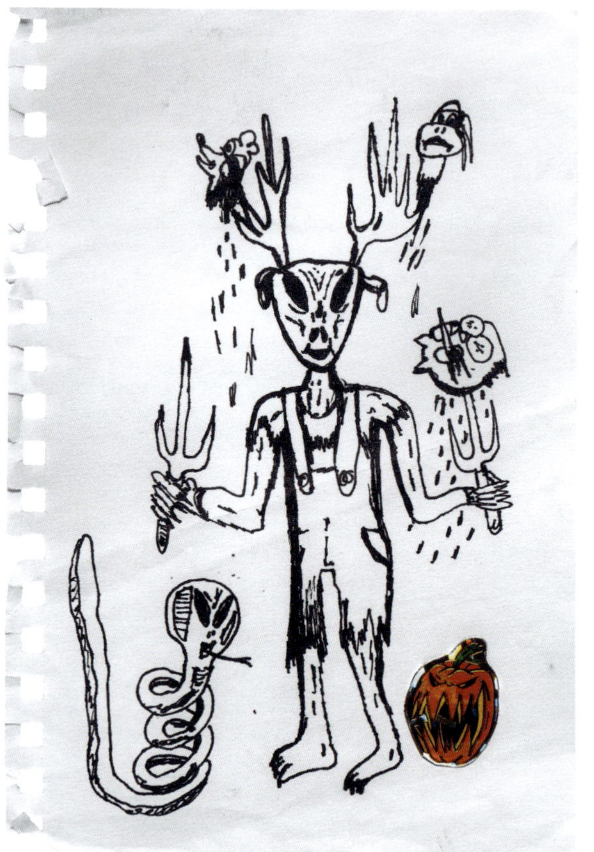

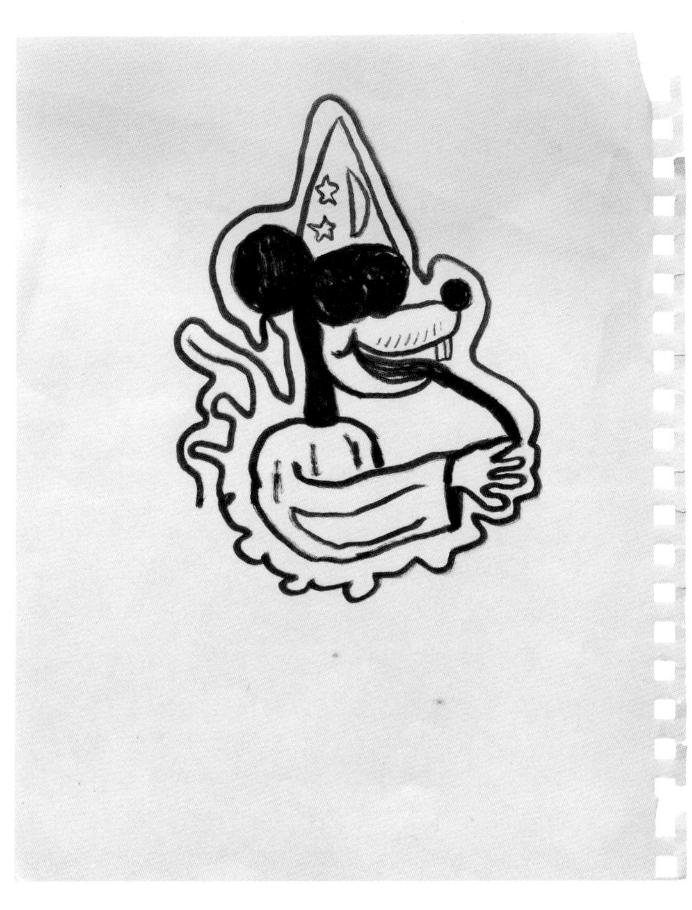

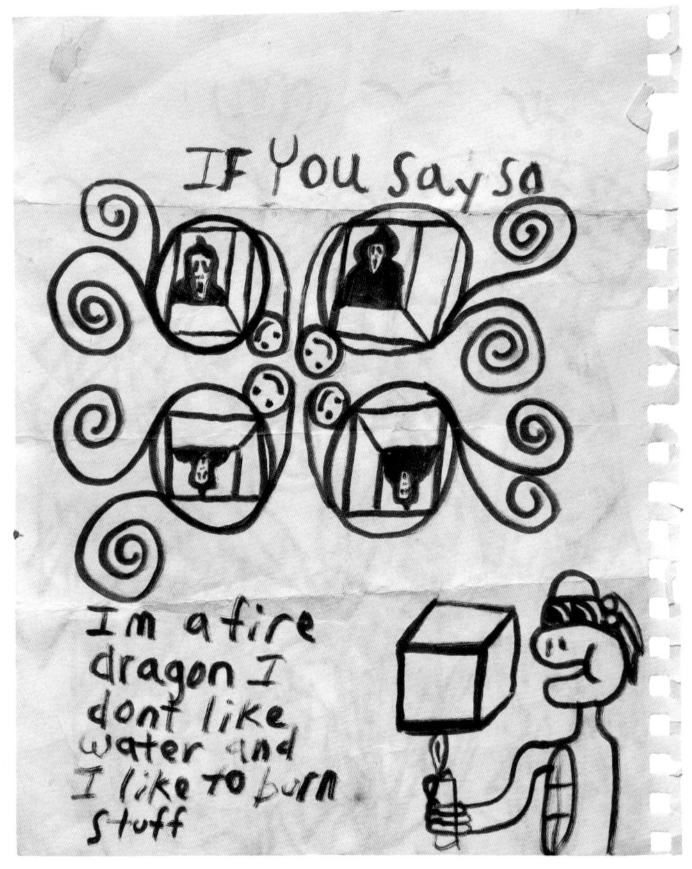

IF You say so
Im a fire
dragon I
dont like
water and
I like to burn
stuff

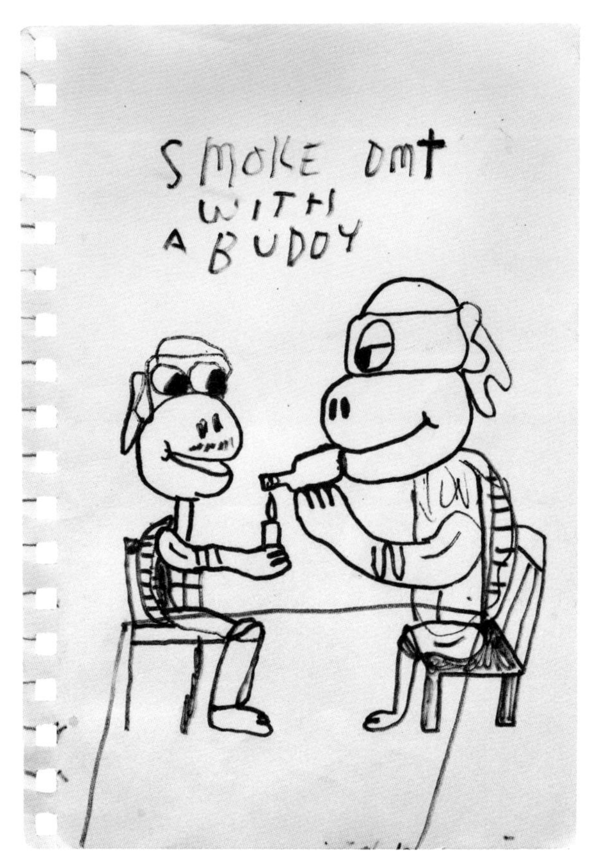

SMOKE ONT
WITH
A BUDDY

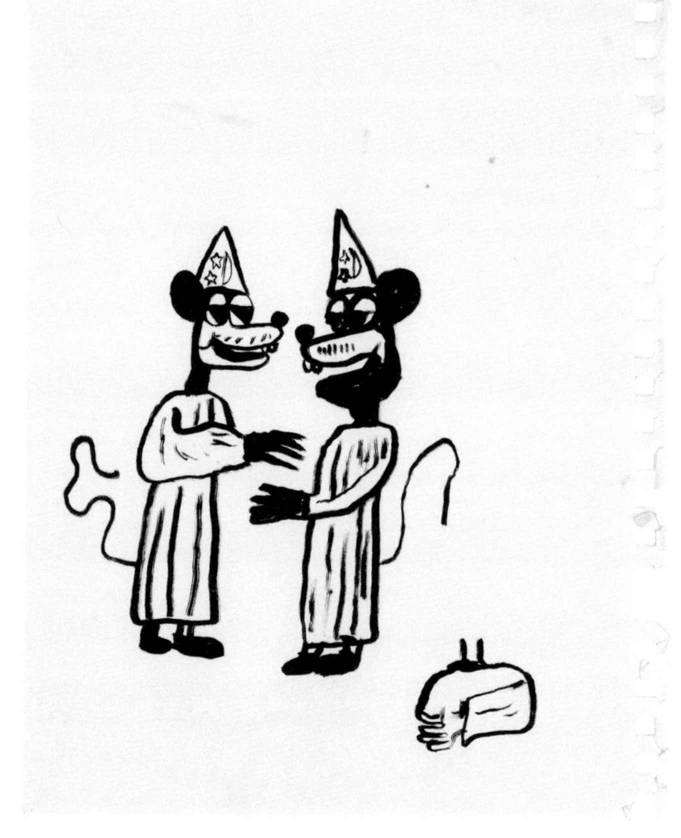

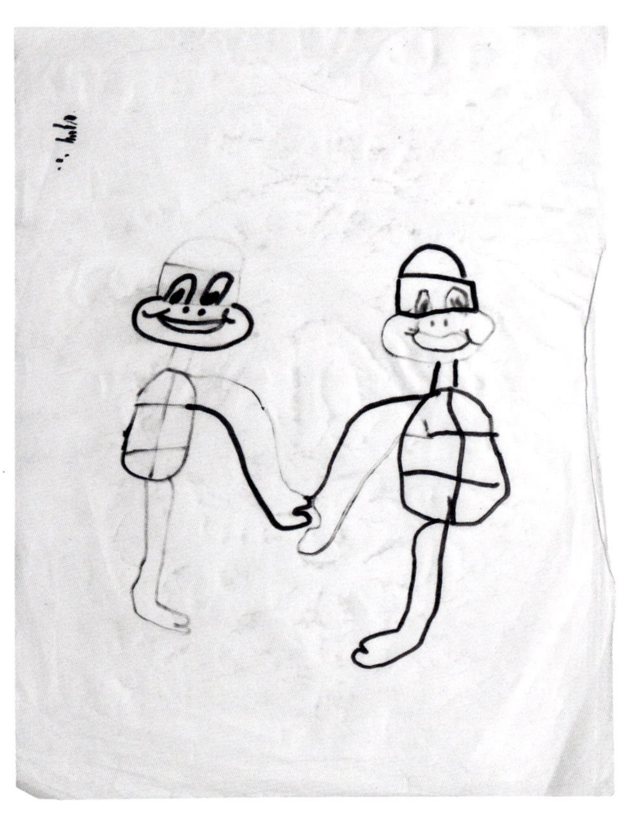

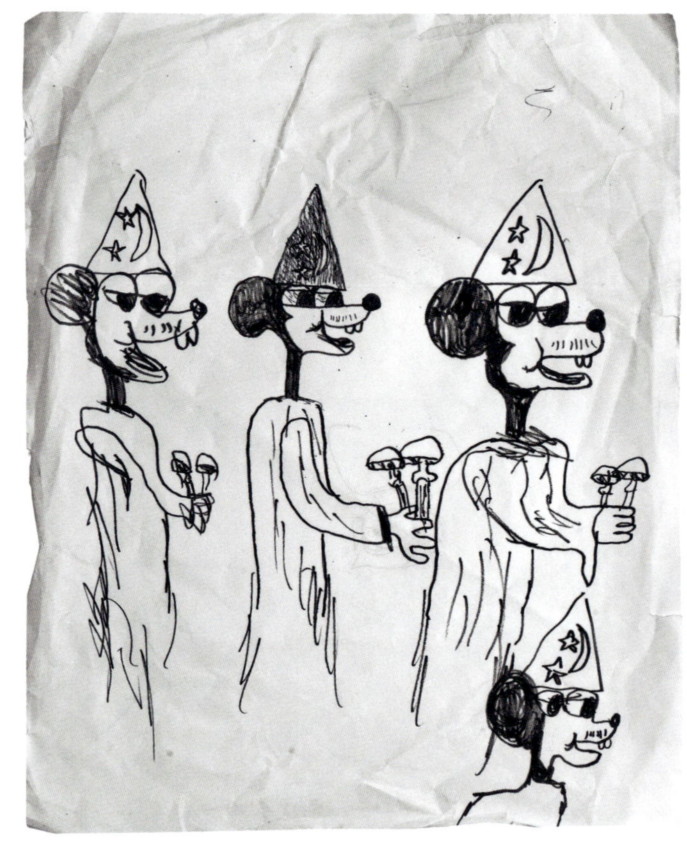

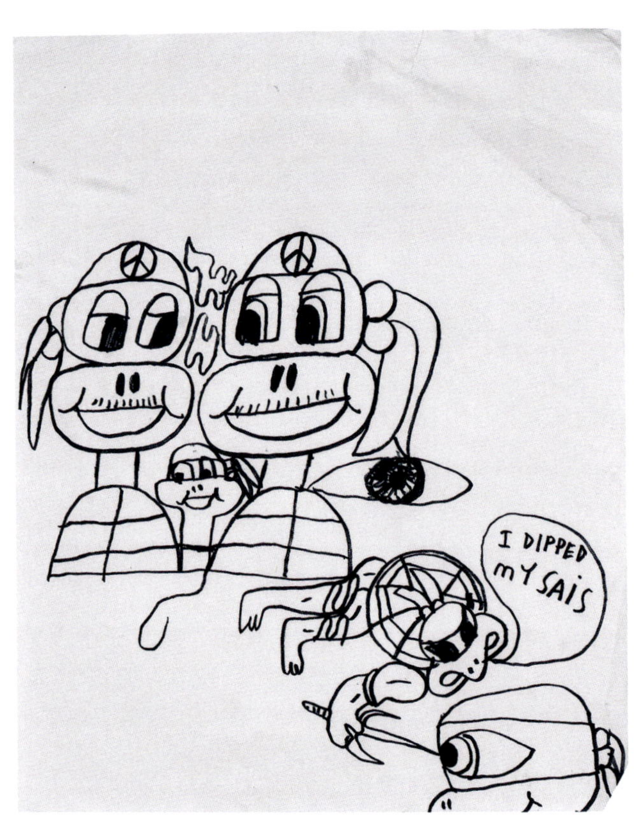
I DIPPED
MY SAIS

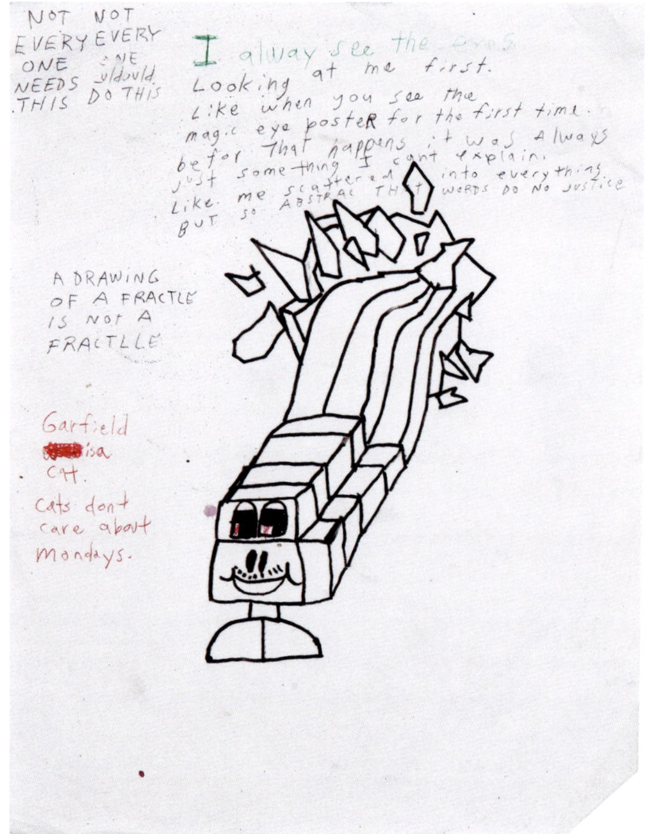
NOT NOT
EVERY EVERY
ONE ONE
NEEDS SHOULD
THIS DO THIS

I alway see the eyes
Looking at me first.
Like when you see the
magic eye poster for the first time.
befor that happens it was always
just something I cant explain.
Like me scattered into everything
BUT so ABSTRAC THAT WORDS DO NO JUSTICE

A DRAWING
OF A FRACTLE
IS NOT A
FRACTLLE

Garfield
isa
cat.
Cats dont
care about
mondays.

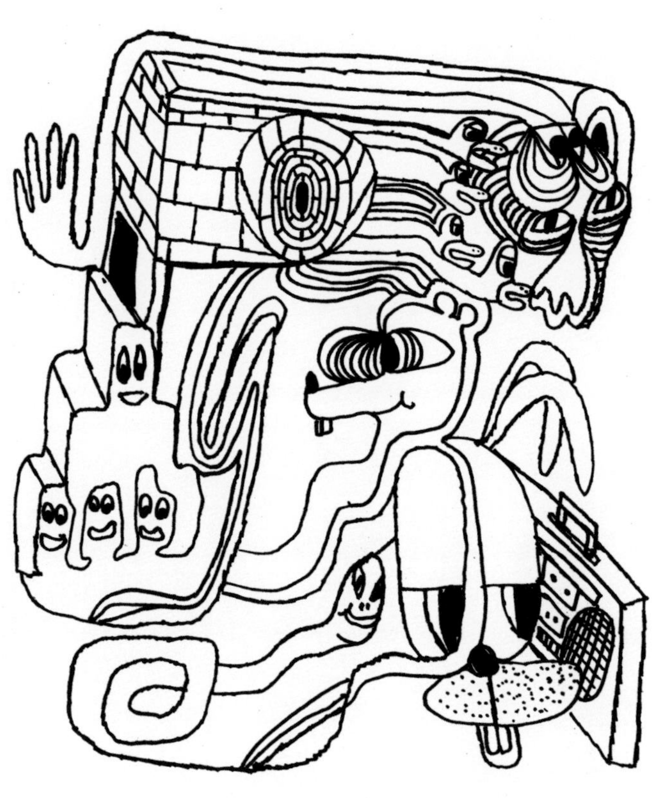

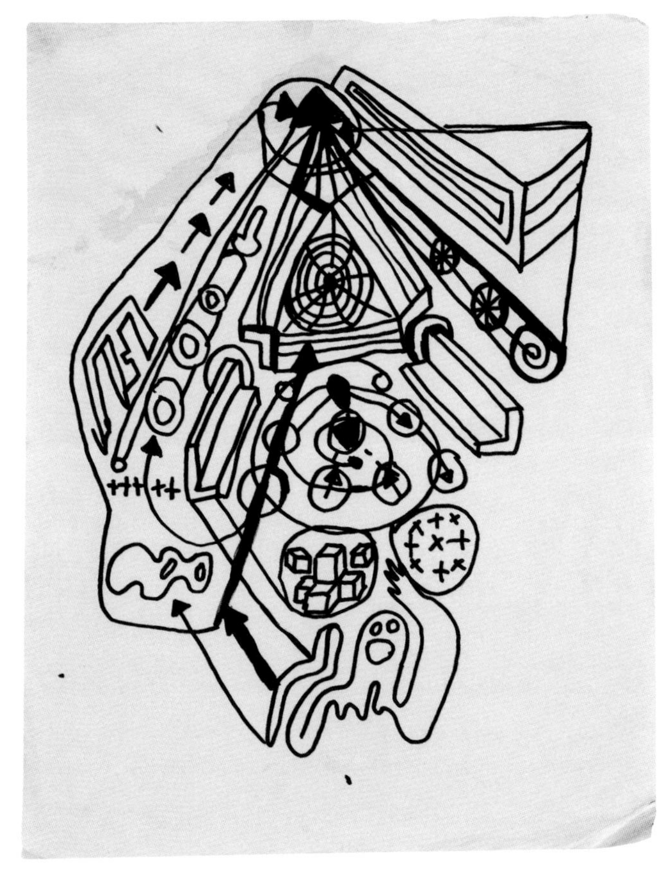

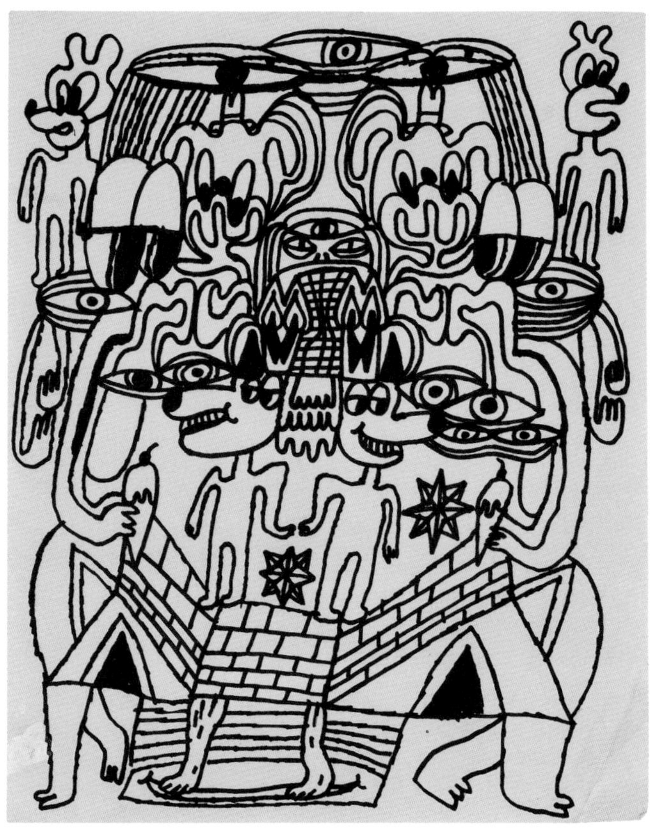

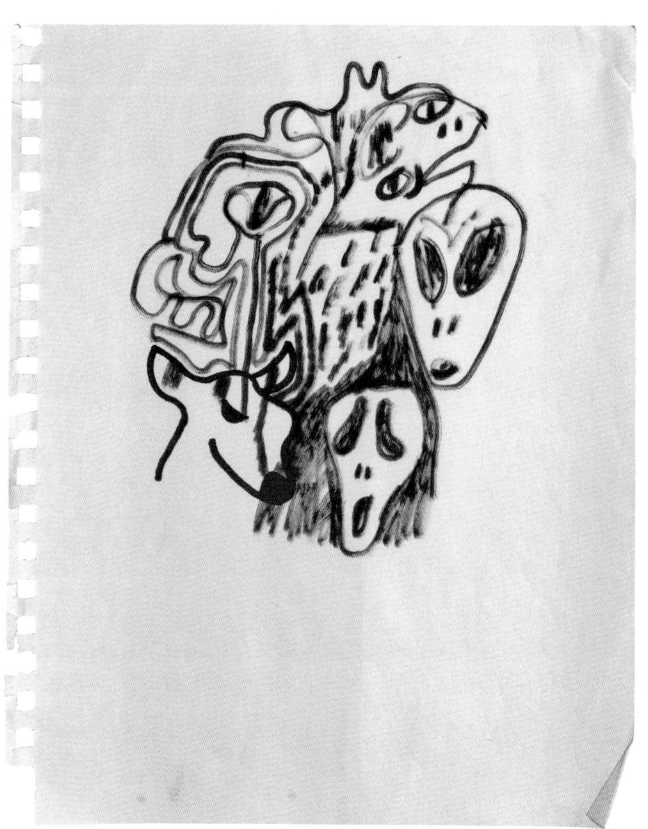

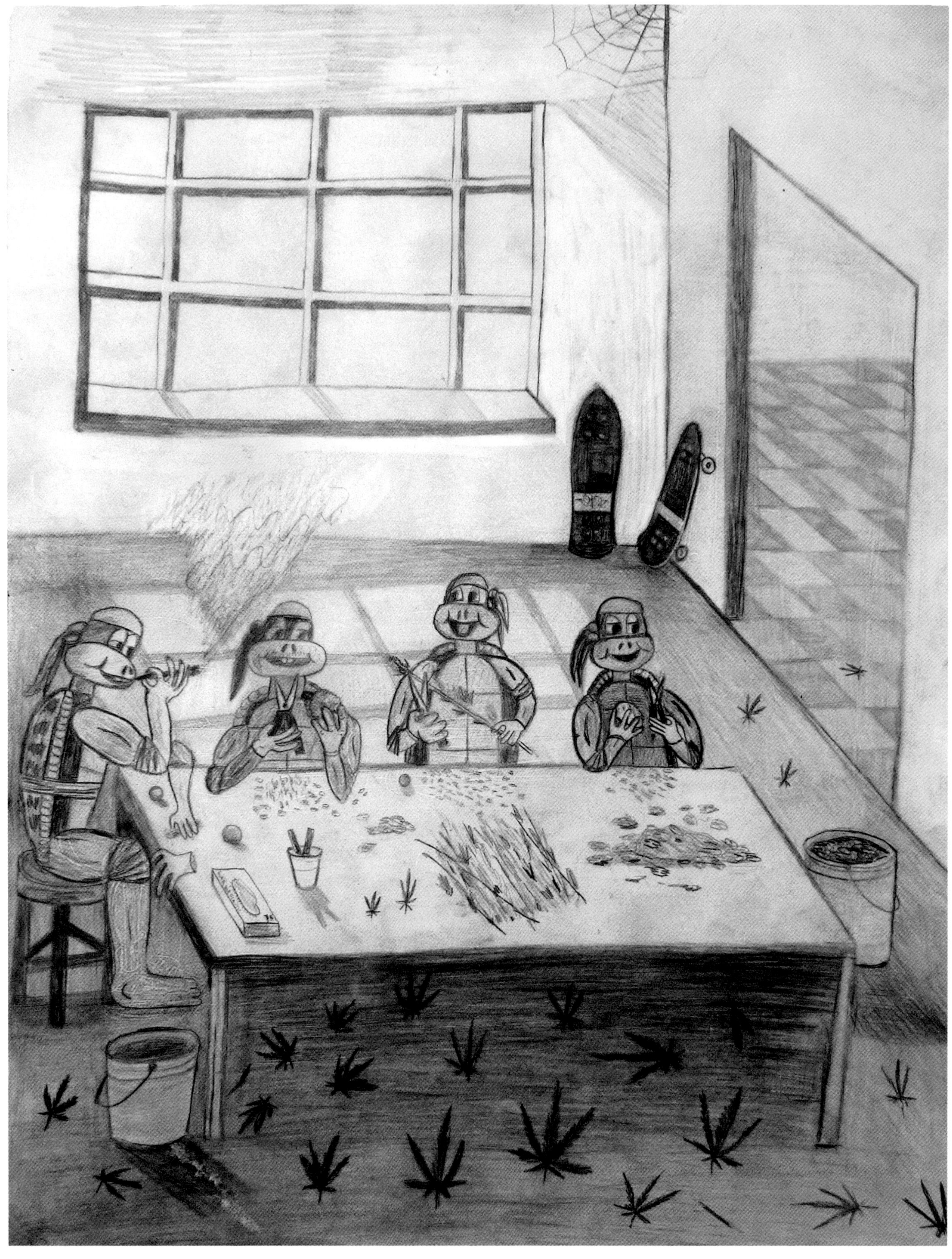

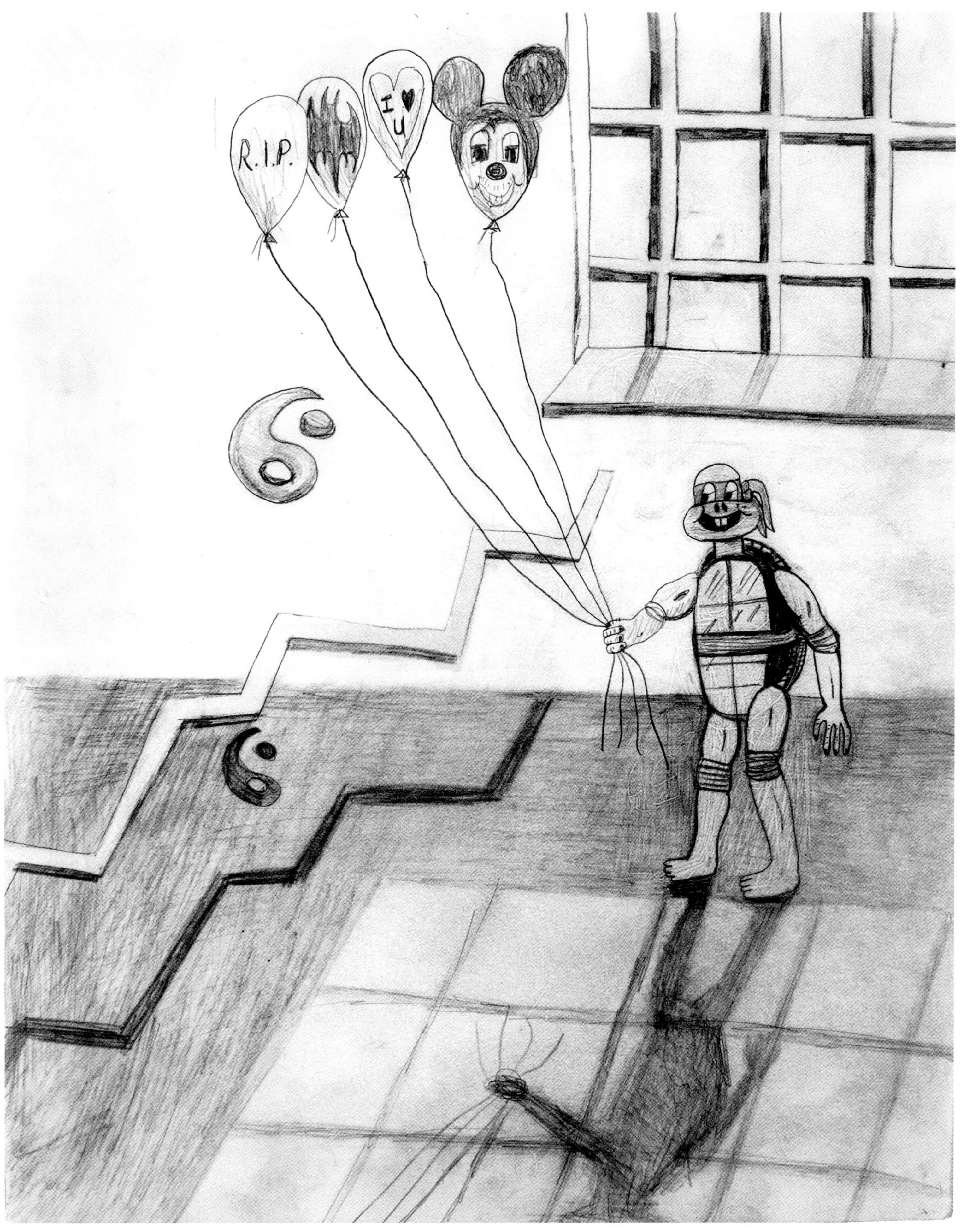

R.I.P.
I ♥ U

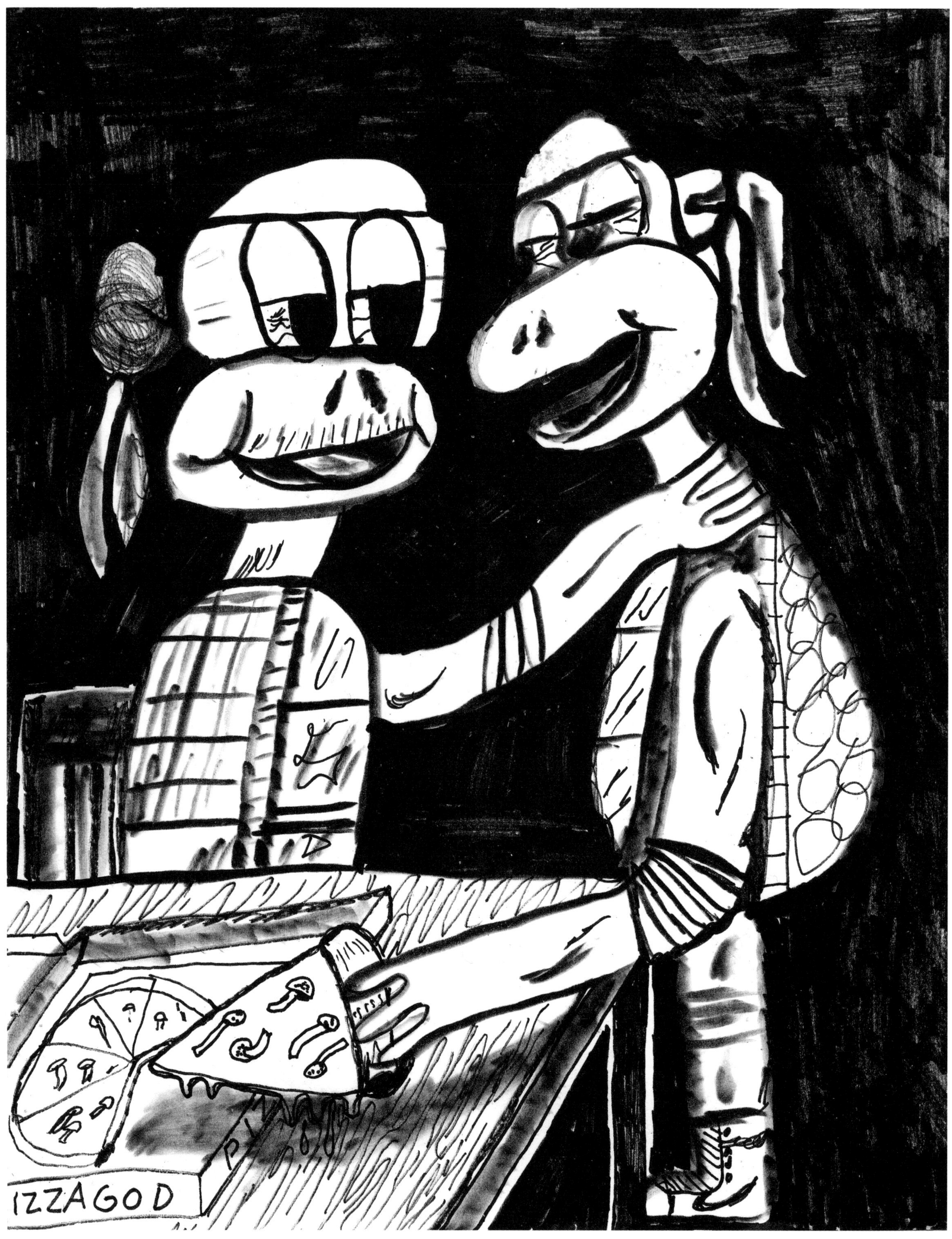
IZZAGOD

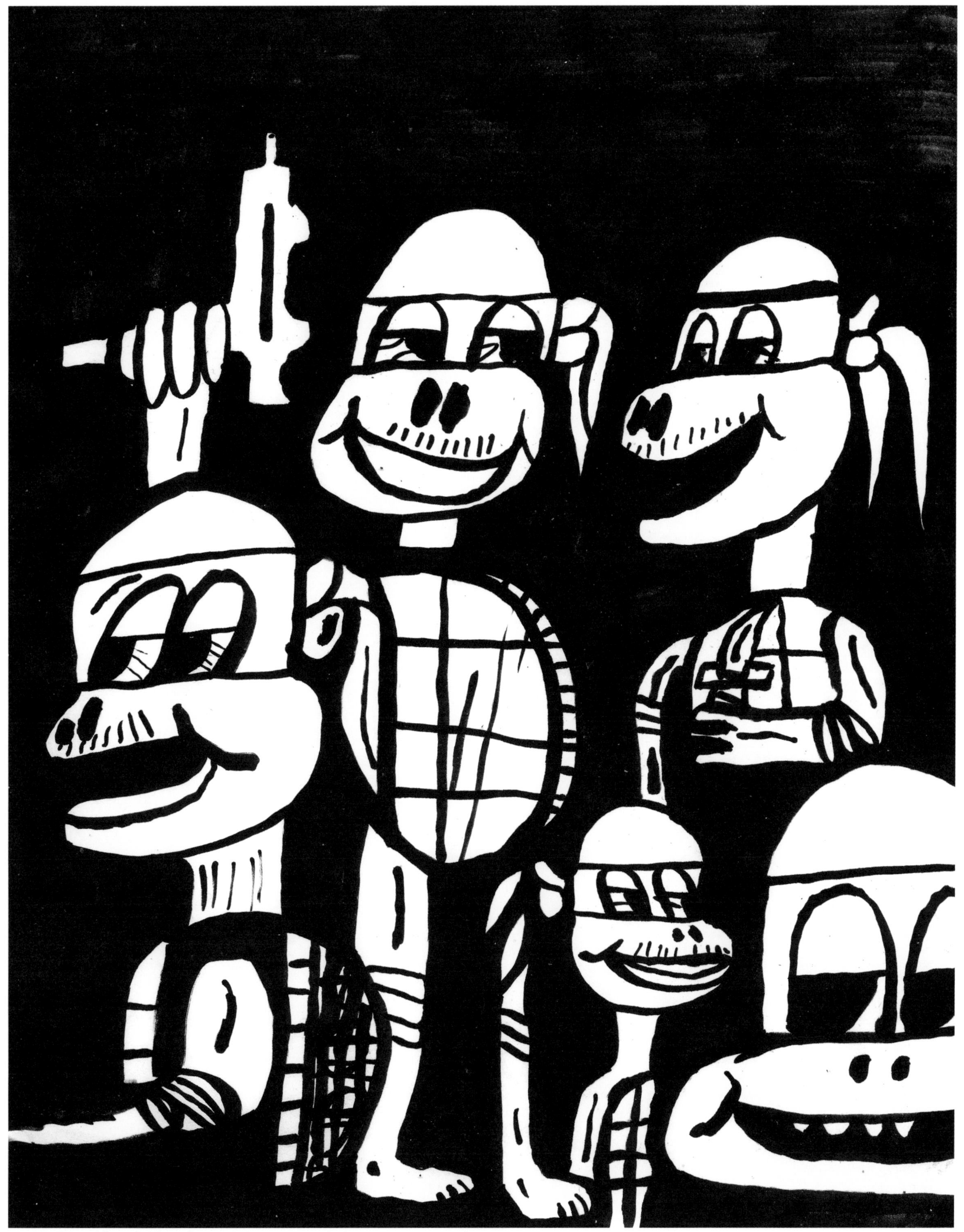

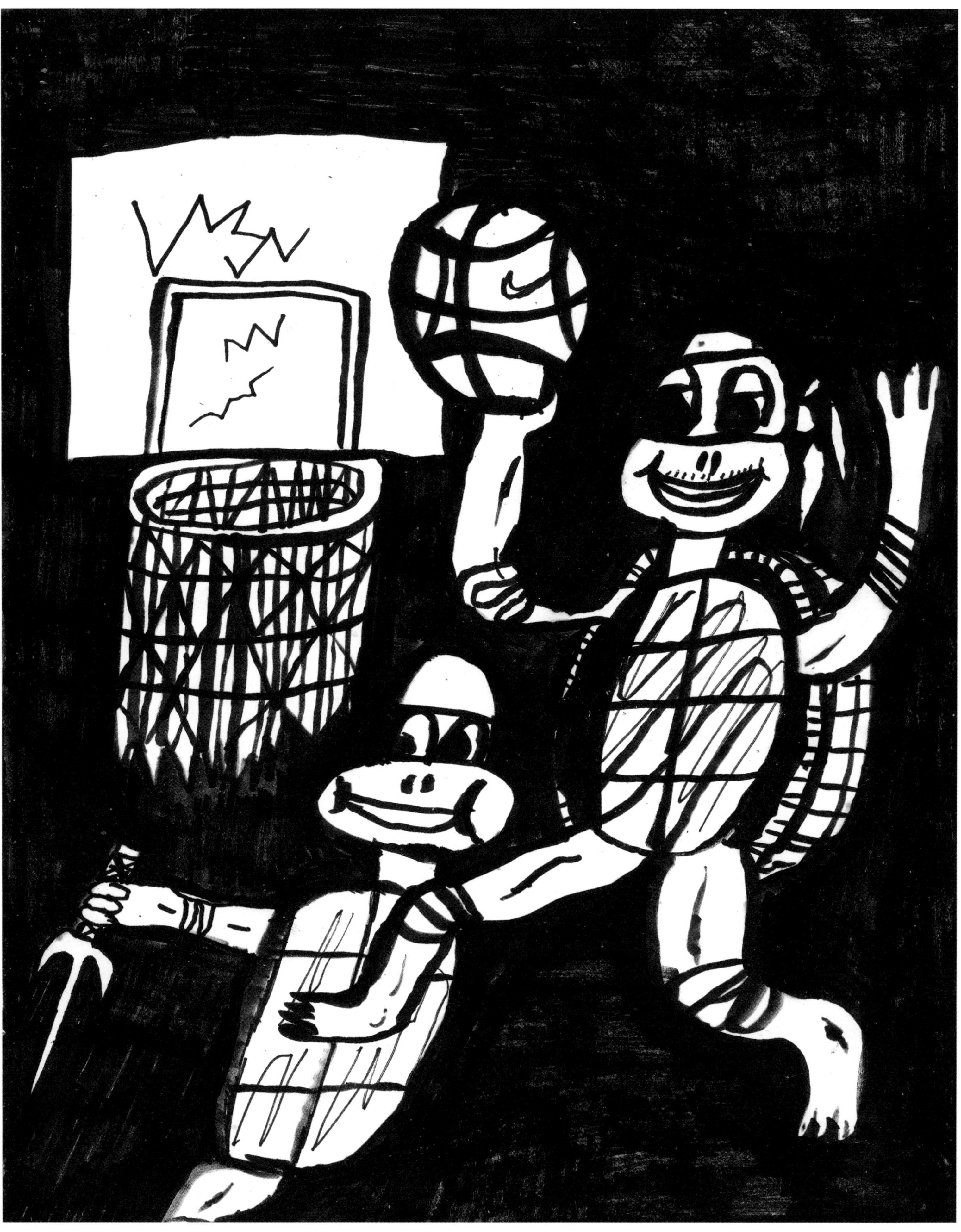

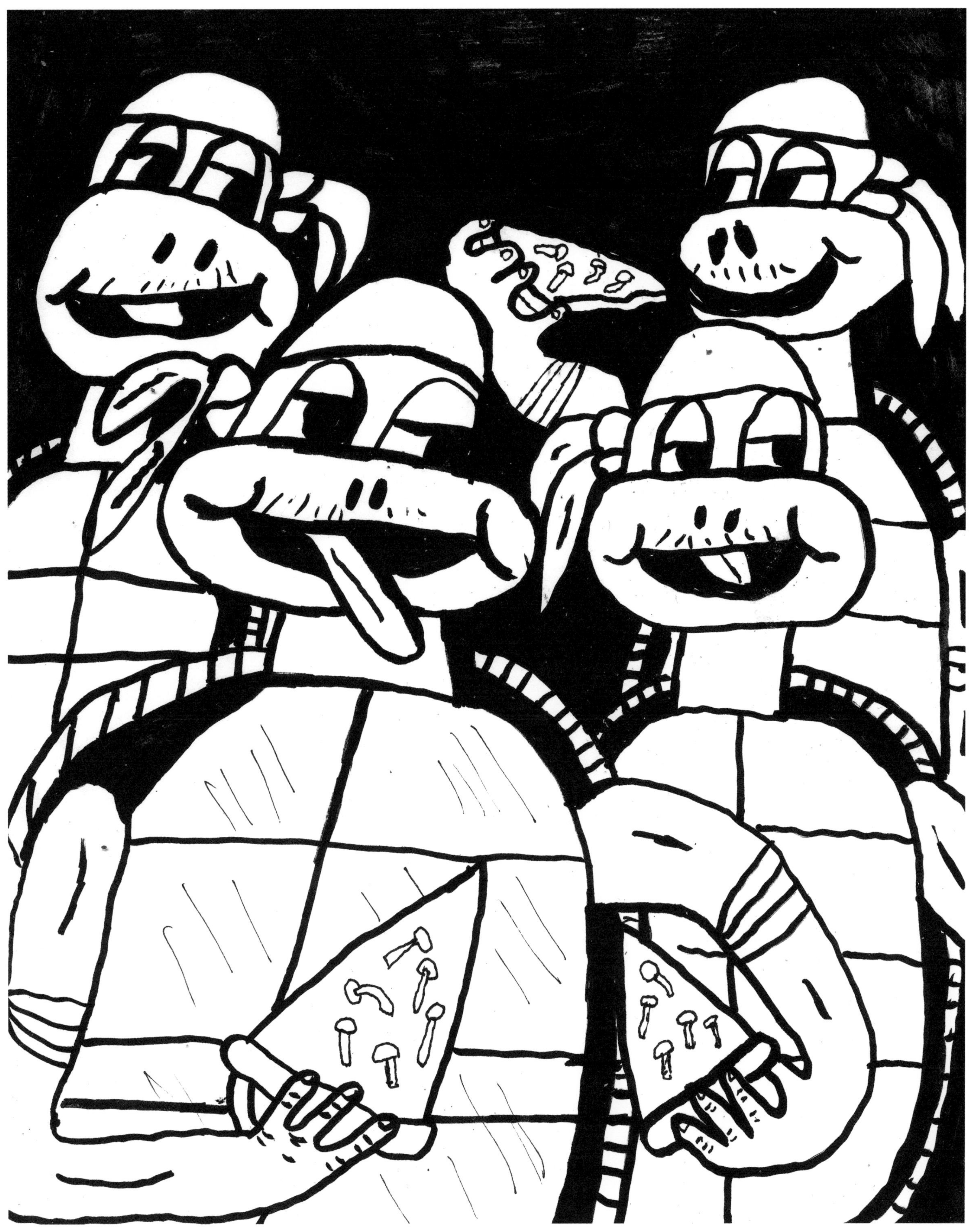

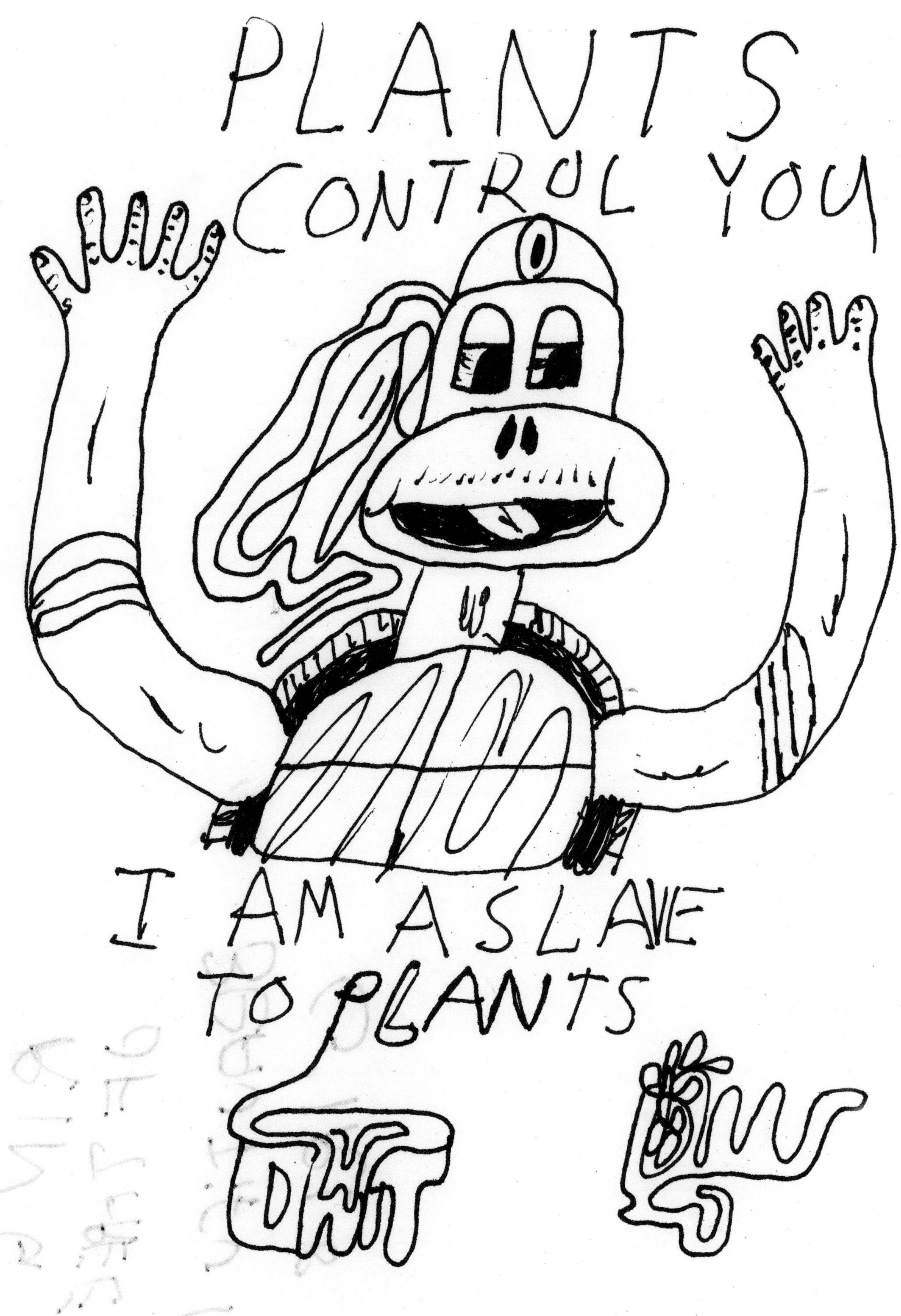

PLANTS
CONTROL YOU
I AM A SLAVE
TO PLANTS

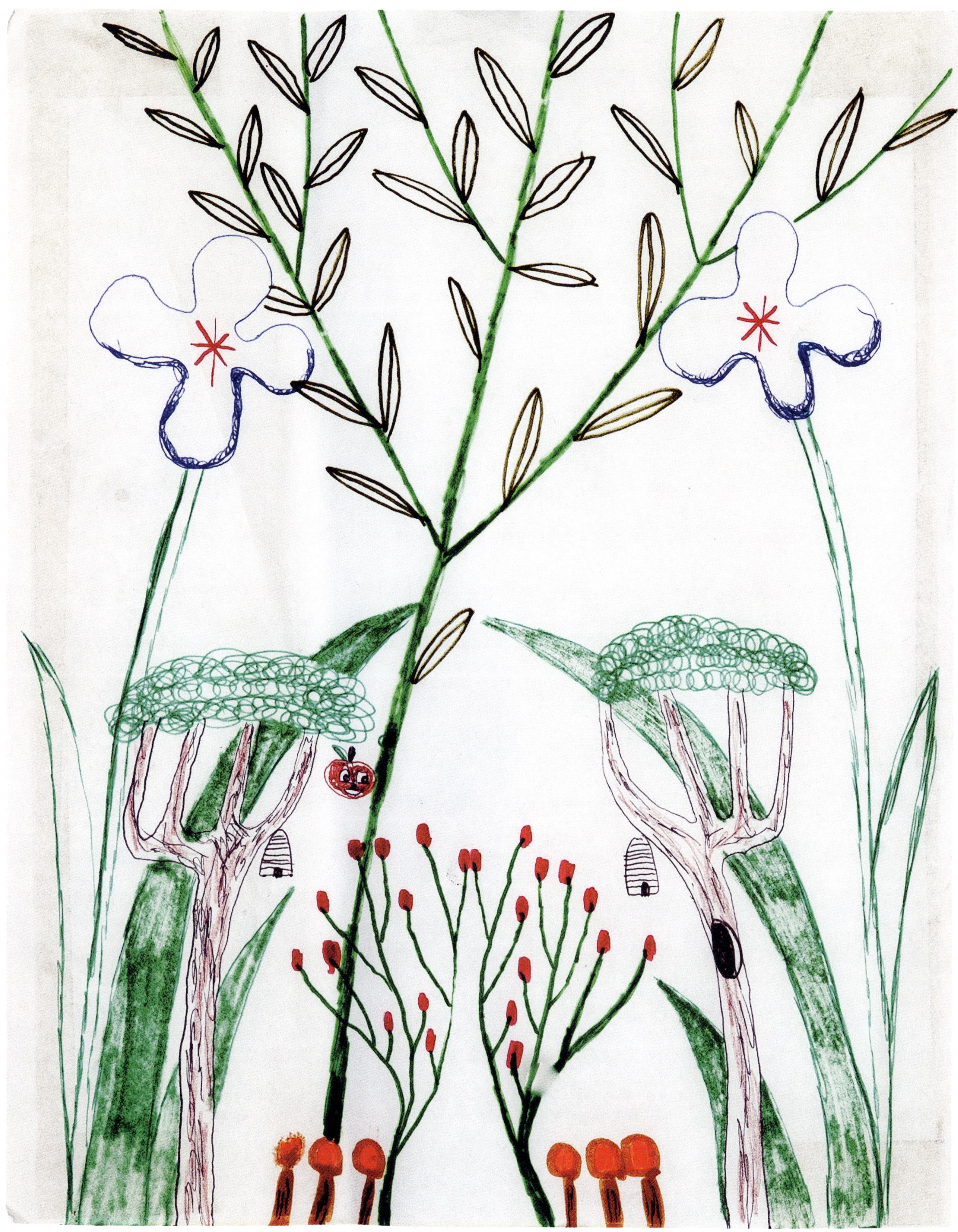

✓ A simple machine to kill yr self
A simple machine to light a 6 ft bong
A simple machine to cut a pizza
A simple machine to make philosophies
✓ A simple machine to put a condom on.
✓ A simple machine to take out tha trash
A simple machine to make yr self feel better
A simple machine to see the futer

* 4 different kinds of happiness *

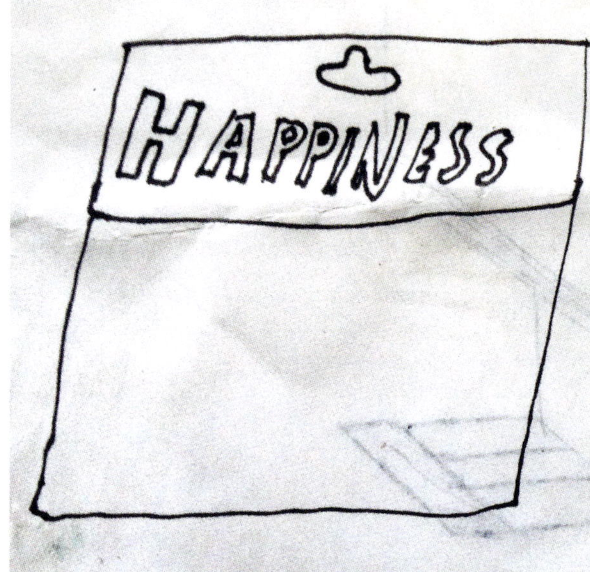

ingredients.
xanex sunshine,
puppies, cool breezes
rap music

XANEX, SUNSHINE
puppies, cool breeze
rap music, pizza

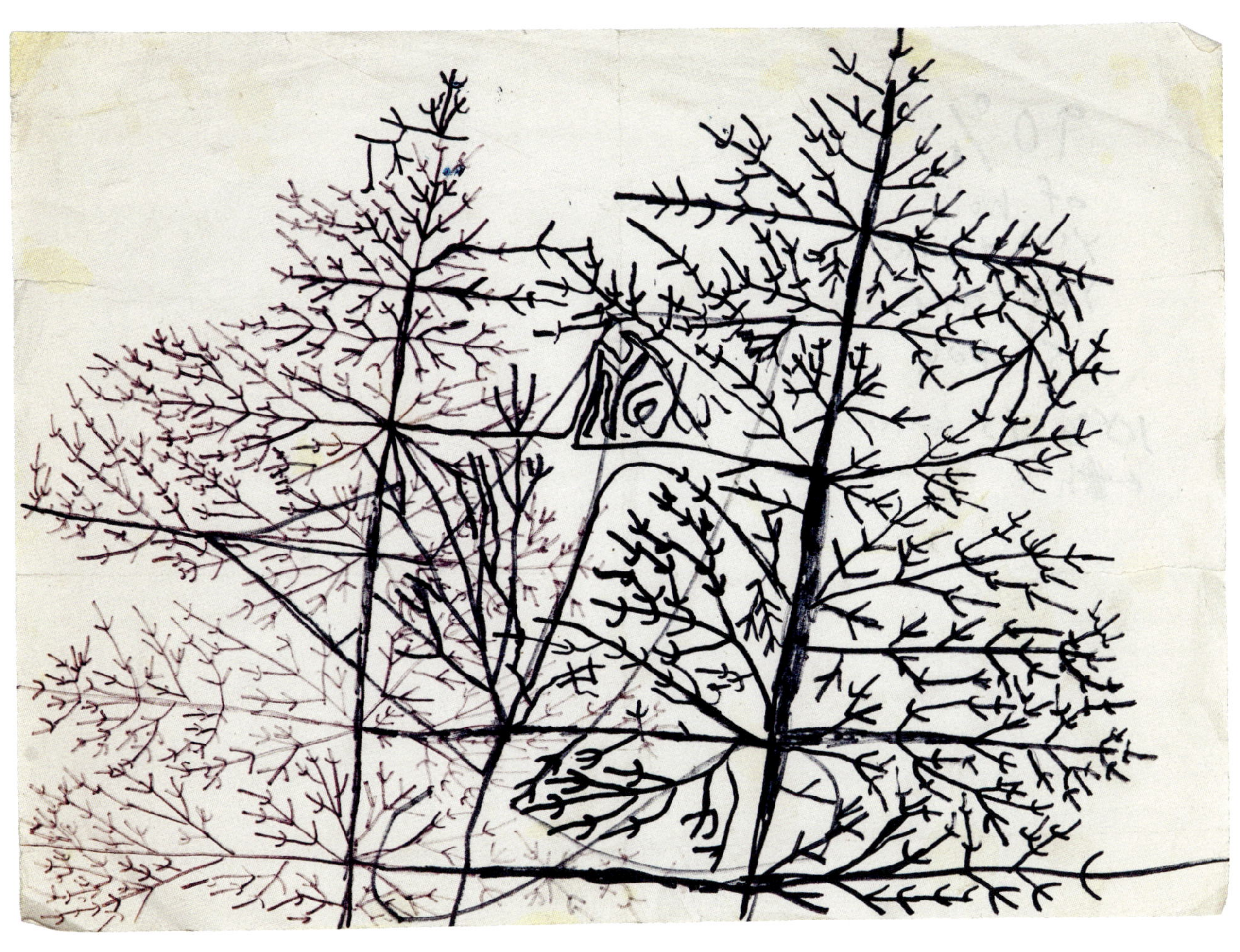

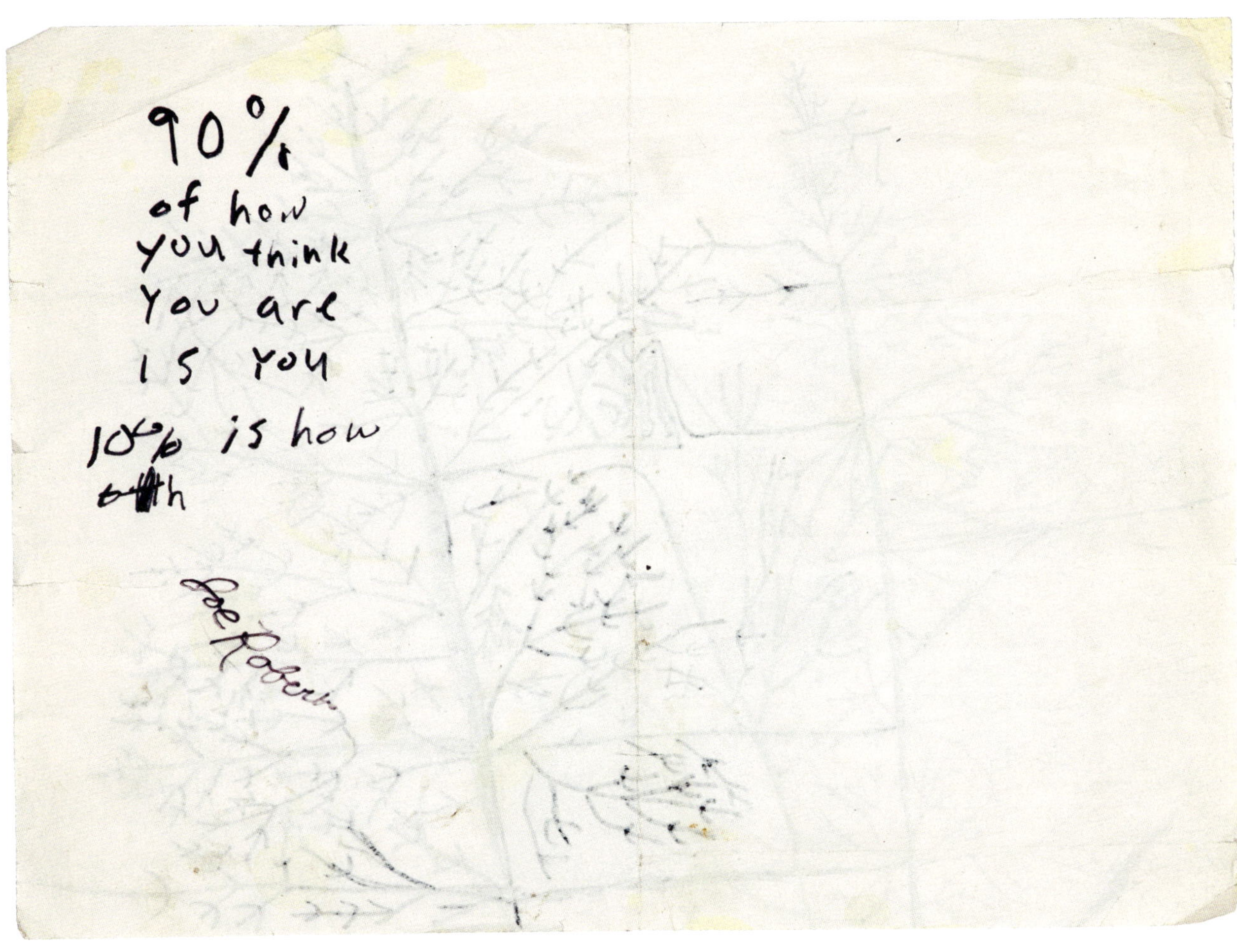
90%
of how
you think
You are
is you

10% is how
oth

Joe Roberts

Acknowledgments:

Matt Alavi, Mikhail Bortnik, Giles Cassels, Blaise Cepis, Tony Cox, Myla Dalbesio, Brian DeGraw, Bryan Derballa, John Dwyer, Josh Ellis, Dave Fallis, Megan Gage, Chris and Courtney Hafner, Dan Johnson, Todd Jordan, Mark Kaiser, Faythe Levine, Blake Lyon, Leah Martin, Dennis McGrath, John McGuire, Nick Neubeck, Mat O'Brien, Kottie Paloma, Nathan Perkel, Aaron Polansky, Greg Rivera, Melinda Roberts, Matthew Ronay, Paul Wackers, Heather Wojner, and Ariel Zambelich.

Originally published in 2014 by Unpiano Books
This edition published by Anthology Editions, 2023

Edited by Jesse Pollock and Joe Roberts
Original design by Mark Kaiser / Omnibus Design
Design by Bryan Cipolla and Jesse Pollock

Printed in China on FSC-certified paper
ISBN: 978-1-944860-54-7
Library of Congress Control Number: 2022941796

anthologyeditions.com
87 Guernsey Street
Brooklyn, NY 11222

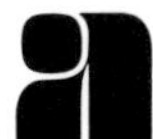

When this book 1st got made it said some thing like:
"Thanks to each and every person I have ever met. C U Later"
so now that it's getting reprinted I'd like to add,
"I see you again book," and I add you and also:
   most importantly god;
   my Dog Kevin;
and then all the dogs my mom ever had starting with Mel,
that dog was cool. and a plant named Clyde.
All my friends dogs : Wizard, kickstand, and even Carl. But mostly
Kevin, thats my DOG.
Some Places I lived in when I made all this:
520 Hampshire for letting me live there when I wasnt supposed to live
there, I thought I was being quiet but looking back I was
   4 sure not, I saw the cameras though so I guess I just didn't care,
   but either way thanks;
1626 and then 520 and then thank you 1314 for giving me
a home for the longest place ever IN my life, in book time
and real time.
THANK You anthology editions for bringing this back 2 life
   and making it better; thank you unpiano for finding this.
THANK You every one that helped make this possible
   tHANKYOU EVERYONE IN tHE FUTURE that reads this.